PENGUIN CANADA

THE HOME TEAM

ROY MACGREGOR has been a journalist for more than thirty years, and for many years has written his immensely popular "This Country" column on page two of *The Globe and Mail,* Canada's national newspaper. He is the author of numerous bestselling and award-winning books, including *Escape, Canoe Lake, A Life in the Bush, The Weekender,* and the popular children's mystery series *The Screech Owls.* MacGregor was named an Officer in the Order of Canada in 2005 and currently resides in Kanata, Ontario.

D1222636

Also by Roy MacGregor

The Dog and I: Confessions of a Best Friend

The Weekender: A Cottage Journal

Escape: In Search of the Natural Soul of Canada

A Loonie for Luck

A Life in the Bush: Lessons from My Father

Canoe Lake

The Last Season

Road Games: A Year in the Life of the NHL

Chief: The Fearless Vision of Billy Diamond

Home Game: Hockey & Life in Canada
(with Ken Dryden)

The Screech Owls Series
(for young readers)

The Home Team

Fathers, Sons and Hockey

ROY
MacGREGOR

PENGUIN
CANADA

PENGUIN CANADA

Published by the Penguin Group

Penguin Group (Canada), 90 Eglinton Avenue East, Suite 700, Toronto, Ontario, Canada M4P 2Y3
   (a division of Pearson Canada Inc.)

Penguin Group (USA) Inc., 375 Hudson Street, New York, New York 10014, U.S.A.
Penguin Books Ltd, 80 Strand, London WC2R 0RL, England
Penguin Ireland, 25 St Stephen's Green, Dublin 2, Ireland (a division of Penguin Books Ltd)
Penguin Group (Australia), 250 Camberwell Road, Camberwell, Victoria 3124, Australia
   (a division of Pearson Australia Group Pty Ltd)
Penguin Books India Pvt Ltd, 11 Community Centre, Panchsheel Park, New Delhi – 110 017, India
Penguin Group (NZ), 67 Apollo Drive, Rosedale, North Shore 0745, Auckland, New Zealand
   (a division of Pearson New Zealand Ltd)
Penguin Books (South Africa) (Pty) Ltd, 24 Sturdee Avenue, Rosebank, Johannesburg 2196, South Africa

Penguin Books Ltd, Registered Offices: 80 Strand, London WC2R 0RL, England

First published in a Viking Canada hardcover by Penguin Group (Canada),
   a division of Pearson Canada Inc., 1995
Published in Penguin Canada paperback by Penguin Group (Canada),
   a division of Pearson Canada Inc., 2002
Published in this edition, 2007

(WEB) 10 9 8 7 6 5 4 3 2 1

Copyright © Roy MacGregor, 1995

All rights reserved. Without limiting the rights under copyright reserved above, no part of this publication may be reproduced, stored in or introduced into a retrieval system, or transmitted in any form or by any means (electronic, mechanical, photocopying, recording or otherwise), without the prior written permission of both the copyright owner and the above publisher of this book.

Manufactured in Canada.

LIBRARY AND ARCHIVES CANADA CATALOGUING IN PUBLICATION

MacGregor, Roy, 1948–
   The home team : fathers, sons & hockey / Roy MacGregor.

First published: Toronto : Viking, 1995.
ISBN 978-0-14-301317-4 (bound).—ISBN 978-0-14-305336-1 (pbk.)

1. Hockey players—Family relationships. 2. Fathers and sons.
3. Hockey players—Biography. I. Title.

GV848.5.A1M29 2002   796.962'092'2   C2002-903265-2

Except in the United States of America, this book is sold subject to the condition that it shall not, by way of trade or otherwise, be lent, re-sold, hired out, or otherwise circulated without the publisher's prior consent in any form of binding or cover other than that in which it is published and without a similar condition including this condition being imposed on the subsequent purchaser.

Visit the Penguin Group (Canada) website at **www.penguin.ca**

Special and corporate bulk purchase rates available; please see **www.penguin.ca/corporatesales**
or call 1-800-810-3104, ext. 477 or 474

For Ann MacGregor:
sister, friend
and lifelong expert on fathers and sons
and the true meaning of family.
With great love and admiration.

Acknowledgments

The author is grateful to the *Ottawa Citizen*, publisher Russ Mills, editor Jim Travers, managing editor Sharon Burnside and sports editor Tom Casey for continuing support and opportunity. He is also indebted forever to editor Barbara Berson, both for the idea and for the patience shown in waiting to see if her notion would stick. The book could not have been completed without the guidance of Barbara Berson, Meg Masters and Cynthia Good, as well as that of Louise Curtis, Lori Ledingham and Shaun Oakey, who carried it into production. Thanks to everyone— players, organizers, executives, oldtimers, authors, poets, politicians, parents—who replied to my letters requesting their thoughts on fathers and sons and hockey. Thanks as well to the great Bruce Bennett, the *Citizen* and Dr Derek Mackesy for photographs, and to my many colleagues— both on the road and with competing newspapers—for hints and suggestions. Thanks to Garey Ris for reading. Thanks, as always, to Ellen for friendship and advice, to Kerry, for coming along on some of the interviews, and to Gordie and all his teammates, who each winter let me into their hockey lives. Thank you to all the fathers and sons who put up with the questions and the annoying hanging around. And thank you especially to Duncan MacGregor who unwittingly supplied me with a lifetime of research. He died, unfortunately, just before this book was published. But he didn't need a bound copy to know how much he meant to its creation.

Roy MacGregor
Kanata
July 15, 1995

Prologue

He is probably the only Canadian who has never been asked where he was that fateful September 28, 1972, when, in the final minute of the final game, Team Canada scored the sixth and winning goal of the greatest hockey series in history. It would be presumed, of course, that Paul Henderson was in heaven at that moment—and in a way he was—and that everything that ever needed to be known about how he felt at the 19:26 mark of the third period was written on his face as he leapt, with both arms and stick raised, into the arms of team-mate Yvan Cournoyer. He *had* to be as ecstatic as the entire country when Foster Hewitt's voice began rising towards hockey's most historical touchstone: "Here's another shot! Right in front! *They score!* Henderson has scored for Canada! Henderson right in front of the net and the fans and the team are going wild! Henderson right in front of the Soviet goal with thirty-four seconds left in the game!" Canadians would be certain that it would *have* to be the happiest moment of his life. But they would be wrong.

"When I scored that goal in Moscow," Henderson remembered in the spring of 1994, "when the puck went over, before there was elation there was a touch of melancholy. I actually thought of my dad. He had died in '68. I remember thinking, 'Geez, if anybody would've loved to see that goal, it would have been him.'"

It may surprise some—and more surprises are coming concerning Paul Henderson and his father—that this country's sports icon would have such thoughts at this moment of triumph. Those who play the great Canadian game of Where Were You When Paul Henderson Scored?

were rarely with their fathers. The game was televised in the afternoon in Canada, so viewers were either in school, at work, in a bar or at home. Families together would have been the exception rather than the rule. Fans did not think immediately of their fathers. Most successful hockey players, however, would understand perfectly. Had they themselves been lucky enough to score the greatest goal in history, their first thoughts might well have been the same—no matter what their personal experience with this relationship that looms so large over hockey.

Sometimes it takes an outsider to notice the unusual in what might seem common to others. When Barbara Berson, the editor of this book, moved from New York to Toronto, she was struck by two very Canadian traits: one, the overwhelming passion for hockey, and two, the number of times during television interviews that players would talk about their fathers and the role they had played in their development as players. There was no sense that mothers were excluded—quite the contrary—but there was also no denying that the relationship between players and their fathers, who were often their coaches, drivers, patrons and friends as well, was somehow different, some-how more powerful than any father-son sports relationship Berson had noticed while growing up and working in the United States.

In the fall of 1993 she approached me with her idea for a book. Being a Canadian, and being the son of a father who once played senior hockey, as well as the father of a son playing minor hockey, it struck me as far too obvious an observation to merit extra study. Why not a book on how *big* Canada is? Or *cold*? Her letter, however, slowly began to haunt me. "National pastime," she had written, "rites of passage, family traditions—hockey is absolutely central and integral to the lives of boys and their dads, and much of what happens between them begins to unfold the very first time a young father leads his little one out onto the ice. Hockey is the vehicle through that complex relationship, and it is also the expression of that relationship. It is background—against which the evolving father-son dynamic is delineated—and foreground, the stuff of that dynamic. It is form and content, both."

I began listening more carefully, and she was right. Perhaps the between-period interviews might be clichéd and shallow, but almost invariably the father was mentioned and, for a moment, the player would take on a different life. Forced to use his own words rather than the standard stock phrases, anxious to talk on rather than just get it over with, a new energy would surface that usually resulted in a player saying "Hi" to his parents, wherever they might be in the country. In a strange way, hockey makes us all family.

I went back to my files. From magazine profiles in the seventies to sports columns in the nineties, the father-son touchstone was consistent. But it had never been explored at length. In just one example, I had written several times about Gordie Howe, a couple of times about Mark Howe and even about Murray Howe, who did not play professional hockey. As well, Colleen Howe had graciously let me quote from a powerful college essay her youngest son had written about his difficulties in coming to terms with not playing the game at which his father and older brothers were starring. Murray Howe had explained to me about how he had eventually resolved his life and gone on to become a doctor. I had barely realized that, in all that talking to and writing about the Howes of hockey, I had really been examining father-son relationships all along.

But a book could not come out of old files alone. While covering the National Hockey League for the *Ottawa Citizen*, I began casually asking players about their fathers. The response amazed me. A player might be sitting at his locker, his head down, the interview apparently a strain to both player and interviewer, but mere mention of what the father had meant to a hockey career would mean a raised head and as much time as you needed. Instead of two minutes in the locker-room, the players would want to sit in the stands and talk more freely. They would give out telephone numbers and invitations to visit as if, ever since they began playing, they had been waiting for someone to ask. The response, to one who has been writing about sports on and off for more than two decades, was both astonishing and admonishing. It has become so simple to grow cynical about sports that sometimes we forget that, in the beginning, there was just a game—and usually someone passing it on.

Every player I spoke with understood Paul Henderson. Even if, as in Henderson's case, the relationship was far from perfect, far from what is usually envisioned in a country where the national pastime can too easily take on a sentimental hue. For Garnett Henderson was no gentle man who would have taken quiet satisfaction in his son's historic achievement.

Paul Henderson's father had been a huge man, tall as his son and nearly half again as heavy, and the son's sharpest memory of the father's earliest instruction in hockey had been "Take your first shot at the goalie's head." He was a demanding, ill-tempered, often intimidating man who also coached his son's minor hockey teams, a coach who once screamed so angrily at one of his son's team-mates for going offside that the youngster refused to come off the ice at the end of his shift, choosing instead to climb into the penalty box and cringe behind the door.

And yet the son loved the father, the player understood the coach who saw everything, even a simple hockey game, as a life-and-death struggle. Garnett Henderson was a victim of his own history, a fine athlete whose youth had been taken by war, a proud, tough man who had survived a mortar attack that killed eight of his fellow soldiers and who returned from war to begin work immediately for the railways in Lucknow, Ontario. He was a man not allowed to chase his own dreams, and when he began again to hope, it was not for himself but for his gifted son. And if sometimes the dream made the father blind, the son could see, and understand, why. If Garnett Henderson was guilty of anything, it was the crime of all parents: he wanted too much for his child.

"I would never have become a hockey player but for my father," Paul says today as he sits high in the empty seats overlooking Maple Leaf Gardens, where he eventually came to play. "He coached the teams I was on. He encouraged me to look at it. He never got a chance to play, and I guess sort of vicariously... I mean, a lot of people told me that he was sort of living through me."

Garnett may, in fact, have made that historic goal possible, for Paul Henderson might never have become a professional hockey player but for the sheer force of his father's personality. "We'd won the Memorial Cup in '62," the son remembers, "and back then they didn't push school that much. I had decided I was going to quit hockey and go to university and concentrate on getting my education.

"Of course, my father almost went ballistic. The thing my father said to me was: 'It will drive you crazy until the day you die wondering if you could have made it.'

"What prophetic words those turned out to be."

Paul Henderson joined the Detroit Red Wings in 1962, the same year that Garnett had his stroke. He was only forty-three years old. Doctors who examined him determined he had had two previous heart attacks but had been too stubborn to admit to the pain. The stroke, however, would not respond to sheer stubbornness. "After that," Paul says, "he was never the same." The doctors told the family he might not live out the year. And yet he lived six more, long enough to see his son become an NHL regular, long enough to see him play three times in the Stanley Cup finals—each time coming up just short—long enough, barely, to see his son become a member of the Toronto Maple Leafs, playing just two hours from Lucknow, but not long enough to see him score the goal.

"My dad would have loved that," the son says wistfully.

Paul Henderson sits, hands folded under his chin, the image of our collective youth now a fifty-three-year-old grandfather. His grandsons live in another country, so far south of winter freeze-up that they do not even play the game that defined the relationship between Garnett Henderson and his son. The man who scored the goal that meant millions of Canadians would never forget where they were on September 28, 1972, with thirty-four seconds to go, who will never forget his own surprising thoughts at that moment, sits in an empty hockey rink, staring silently down at a world where time can be stopped, called, sometimes even added on, where every twenty minutes it all begins again fresh, the outcome unknown.

Beginnings and Endings

They come here like families arriving to celebrate a wedding, also knowing, yet never thinking that it could happen to them, that five or six hours from now some will look like families leaving a funeral. They are—to a player, father, mother, brother, sister, girlfriend—certain, hoping, *praying* that they will not be among the disappointed; today, they believe, will be the realization of the dream that has danced over their homes since that first moment in atom or pee wee or bantam when a shoulder fake, a shot, a sudden acceleration of speed separated the young man from those who have, by the age he is as he heads into Hartford, usually left the game entirely.

The young men who come this day wear new suits in which they do not yet feel right, Italian weave at times clashing with determined acne, pleats and sharp creases drawing attention to walks they have not yet settled on, their step somewhere between adolescence and manhood. Some are beet red, some are sweating, some sit with their young fresh-shaven faces in hands with tortured fingernails. They feel, often correctly, that every eye in the hot, sticky Hartford Civic Center is upon their every movement. They know that their lives are about to be determined by a number over which they have now lost all control. They know some will walk out early as multimillionaires, some will walk out late, in tears.

It will be a long two days. The first two rounds—with rare exception, the only two rounds that count—of the 1994

National Hockey League Entry Draft will begin Tuesday at 6 p.m. The next nine rounds will begin Wednesday morning at ten, and will go on until the last, mostly shattered, partly relieved, eleventh rounder is selected. No one in the building expects to go—or expects a son, brother or boyfriend to go—later than the fourth round. It is what comes of being told they are the best, the very best, for most of their lives: the best in atom, the best in pee wee, bantam, one of the best in midget, good enough in junior, the measuring funnel ever narrowing as the child goes up, suddenly and terrifyingly tightening here at the eighteen-year-old draft in a dramatic two days that will let some go on and choke off the rest.

The only ones even suspecting that it might all go wrong here are the two dozen or so men in fine suits who hover like mother hens over those sections of the stands that have been assigned to them as "rights holders". This is the new name given to agents, who have earned themselves such a bad name in recent years, as NHL salaries have caused ticket prices to soar beyond the reach of those families who count themselves as typical hockey fans. They are still called agents by these particular families, however, and they are seen as gods rather than devils. For it is the agent who will turn all the 6 a.m. practices, all the jumper cables, bad coffee and cold seats, all the hundreds of thousands of kilometres on the odometer, all the money spent on equipment and summer hockey schools and out-of-town motels, all the anguish and jealousies, all the glass-pounding fury and fist-pumping cheering—he will turn all that and more into a career.

Some agents have wisely advised certain of their clients not to come. Any player not ranked by the NHL's Central Scouting Bureau to go in the fourth round or earlier is in risk of not going at all, and those agents who have seen what not being selected at all can do to a family have no wish to see it ever again. They have no stomach for wading into each pocket of sorrow and trying to convince family and player that all the NHL teams and all the NHL scouts were wrong and that their missing name had merely been an oversight that would soon be corrected by free agency or an invitation to camp or a couple of years of playing in the International Hockey League. Remember Marty McSorley, they will say. Never drafted—now an NHL star. But how many Marty McSorleys are there? How many people do you know who have won the big lottery prize? Those who go late, from the fifth round on, have only a slightly better chance of ever reaching the NHL, but even here it is so rare that the luck of Luc Robitaille—a ninth-round choice in 1984, 171st overall—is held up as a talisman for all who must convince themselves that they simply slipped through the cracks.

Two years earlier, in Montreal, NHL teams unexpectedly went on a European frenzy, selecting a Czech first, a Russian second, and eighty-six more before the afternoon was through, leaving more than a hundred young North American players and their families in a state of shock and increasing anger as the day wore on. From the fourth round on, they booed every European name. By the final two rounds, the stands of the Montreal Forum were still filled with furious families surrounding hulking, red-eyed, unchosen sons. No agent wants that ever to happen again.

But then again, only a year ago in Quebec City the pendulum had swung back, a Quebec kid going first, an Ontario kid second, an Ontario kid third. By the end of that day, the first chosen—Alexandre Daigle—had a five-year $12.25-million contract in his pocket. And the "rights holder" who had pulled off that one, Pierre Lacroix, was now sitting at the head of the table with the Quebec Nordiques sign over it. The huge, slow-moving Lacroix had been named general manager of the Nordiques—hockey's equivalent of an Ottawa lobbyist being elected prime minister—and had, the rumours buzzing about the civic centre had it, just pulled off the biggest trade of the year: Quebec's Mats Sundin to Toronto for Wendel Clark. There was not an agent in the place not basking in the new-found glory of Pierre Lacroix, not a "rights holder" in the building that did not think that, by the end of the day, his name too would have new heat, would be part of the buzz.

Some found it difficult to wait. Restless, nervous, anxious players, often accompanied by their fathers, would head out into the mall lobby where they would stand and stare at the Stanley Cup, imagine holding it overhead, imagine their name on a ring, look for old names the father might have once embraced and later passed on. Father and son shouting out names on the Cup both instantly recognize and knew would be there, the shouting out mere confirmation that they are an integral part of the game. "Hockey, as a unique expression of our culture," Bruce Kidd and John Macfarlane had written long before these particular draft choices were even born, "is also a vessel for its values, passing them father-to-son from one generation to the next." Time has not altered this arrangement; the Stanley Cup yearly extends it.

Some head outside into the warm Hartford air and a walk on the appropriately named Asylum Street. Some will check out the brick walk along Pratt Street, where the citizens of Hartford have laid down their names and a donation (unsuccessfully) towards reviving the least-inspiring downtown of all the NHL stops, and where an oddly ironic quote from Hartford's most famous citizen, Samuel Clemens, has been laid for all to consider: "You do not know what beauty is if you have not been here."

Inside, another quote from the man who wrote as Mark Twain is far more appropriate: "I don't see no points about that frog that's any better'n any other frog." The candidates for the NHL's Celebrated Jumping Frog contest look more like an endless string of brothers than a massive gathering of families and their agents. They have, almost to a man, the NHL requirements for size (six feet or over), weight (either over two hundred pounds or with the promise of filling out soon), colour (white) and looks: styled and moussed hair, not too long, sincere eyes, open-mouthed grin, scarred lips, tasselled Boston loafers and, if possible, Hugo Boss suit or a more affordable facsimile.

And yet, in so many other ways, they are not at all the same. They come from Canada, the United States, Sweden, Russia, Finland, the Czech Republic, Germany, the Ukraine and Latvia. And even in a sub-group like the Canadians there are vast differences: the style of playing increasingly grinding as the game travels from east to west. They even have differences far beyond their own control, and that is in the facile labelling that takes place in highly conservative, hidebound North American hockey circles, the sometimes racist generalities still sticking in the 1990s: Russians are selfish and morose but will win for you; Czechs can play but are interested only in money; Swedes can play but not when it counts; Finns are somewhere between Swedes and Canadians; French Canadians are fast but small and afraid; Americans are just beginning to come into their own; western Canadians have heart, and heart is hockey. The clichés grind, but in hockey they stick long past reason, and everyone gathering here this day knows that when it comes to making choices, the generalities of origin will have almost as much to do with it as the specifics of production.

The player who has been tagged number one overall by the NHL's Central Scouting Bureau is from the Czech Republic: Radek Bonk. He sits to the right of the stage from which his name will be called: all the top draft choices are in sections 103 and 104 along the Asylum Street side of the civic centre. He has the prerequisite Czech hair, cropped on top and hanging long and curling down the back of his neck, but has North American size (six-three, 215 pounds) and is said to have a western Canada mean streak. He does not come, as do most of the draft hopefuls, from the Canadian junior leagues, but is most unusual in that he is already a professional hockey player.

At seventeen, Bonk left the Czech Republic to play for the Las Vegas Thunder of the International Hockey League. As a child playing with grown men, many of them former NHLers, many of them equal to fringe NHLers, Bonk scored a remarkable forty-two goals and forty-five assists for eighty-seven points. Even more astonishing—to North American scouts—he had 208 minutes in penalties. Big, mean, with good hands and a great shot. How could he not be chosen first overall?

And yet already, in the narrowest of hockey circles that involves only some NHL general managers and some league officials, there has been an ongoing debate over just who this kid is. One story has him twenty-two years old, having lied about his age. Another story has him from an area of the country known as Bohemia, and the popular interpretation of this is that Bohemians go their own way and have no sense of team. Those who actually run the draft have concluded that the hulking Bonk is, in fact, eighteen years old—but the gossip has already hurt his chances with some clubs.

Bonk's chief rival is a North American kid, Ed Jovanovski of the Windsor Spitfires in the Ontario Major Junior league. Jovanovski turned eighteen on Sunday. At six-two and 225 pounds, he may not even have reached his final height and weight and, as a defenceman at a time when skilled, tough defence are said to be at a premium, Jovanovski's chances have been rising all spring. In only his first year of Junior "A" he scored fifteen goals, had thirty-five assists and 221 penalty minutes. His size, his love of hitting and his potential—he played bantam only two years ago—have made him the insider's choice to go first.

But again, there is innuendo at work here. Scouts soon picked up on Jovanovski's nickname among his Windsor team-mates—Special Ed—and his dismal school record and slow, plodding manner concern some. Others have pointed out that Gordie Howe and Bobby Orr were lousy students. Hockey is hardly brain surgery. And besides, the Canadian value system is such that most of the families gathering here on this sultry day would probably rather tell their friends that their boys are NHLers than neurosurgeons.

The third possibility for going first overall—the ultimate goal of every agent in the building—is a lanky Ukrainian defenceman, Oleg Tverdovsky, who seems oddly out of sorts with his peers here. He is skinny, scholarly-looking. He wears a salmon-coloured jacket and blue pants. The young man from the city of Donetsk—as close to Turkey as it is to Moscow—sits with his father, Fedor, his mother, Alexandra, and his nine-year-old sister Anna, who has stared out at Hartford this June day in 1994 and seen it much as Mark Twain saw the city at the turn of the century. "It's beautiful," she says through an interpreter. Her brother smiles happily, sitting calmly, waiting. Some scouts have said he may be the next Bobby Orr. Tverdovsky has diplomatically said, "After Orr, there was none—and nobody knows who will be the next Bobby Orr." He knows of Orr only through a book he read when he was falling in love with the game. He has never even seen an NHL game.

All three are seated with their families and agents in the close rows of the players' section. The television cameras are already planted, each cameraman with a league-supplied fix on where Bonk, Jovanovski and Tverdovsky are seated. Tverdovsky sits chatting easily with his family. Jovanovski is in turmoil, sweat beading on his forehead like pesky rain on a windshield. Bonk sits with—to quote Twain once again—"the calm confidence of a Christian with four aces."

Kostadin Jovanovski, called Joe by everyone down at the General Motors transmission plant in Windsor, Ontario, has a perfect memory of his first hockey game. It was on the television, and his two boys—Dalibor, known as Deni, and the baby, Edvard, eighteen months younger—were watching this game that made no sense whatsoever to the father: bugs moving on a screen, armoured gladiators chasing something that was so small and moving so fast his eye could not even pick it up. If this was hockey, he had seen enough to know it was not for him. The father walked over to the television and turned it off.

He did this again and again and again until, eventually, he gave up hoping that Deni and little Eddie would take up his game, soccer. Joe had come to Canada half expecting the streets to be paved with gold, but never for a moment had he expected the fields to be covered with ice. Soccer was barely an afterthought here. Hockey was the only thing that seemed to matter and, in the end, the only thing that his sons wanted. He would have to change, not them.

It is part of the father-son ritual to pass on a favourite game. Joe Jovanovski had grown up in Macedonia and had played soccer for twenty-five years, eventually reaching semi-professional status with the Luboten Tefovo team. He had played centre forward and could score goals; in his rookie year he came second in the league in scoring. "I was pretty good," he says. "The people say I was good—I go by the people. I don't want to brag." It was not quite a living. He might get forty dollars a week in today's money, extra for a win, a bit less for a tie, nothing for a loss. His great dream was to make it into the European leagues.

When that dream didn't work out, Kostadin and Liljana Jovanovski began to dream of a better life in Canada. They immigrated, settled in Windsor, and he got work at the machine shop at St Clair College, while Liljana caught on at the Emrick Plastics plant. They soon had two young boys and were settling in to a comfortable home in the Forest Glade section of the city. The father had the boys kicking around a soccer ball from the time they were toddlers until they were old enough to enrol in the city's soccer program. Like him, the father figured, they would play and love the only game that counts.

His sons, however, had other ideas. Soccer did little for them. "It was boring," says Eddie, "not enough action." Deni played, but was far more interested in the game the other neighbourhood kids were playing in their driveways and out on Palm Crescent: street hockey. Their father couldn't stand this ridiculous Canadian game. He discouraged it, dragging them to as many soccer games as he could find.

When Deni was nine, he talked his father into letting

him sign up for hockey. He played house league, and the family came to watch, Joe uninterested and little Eddie too shy to show much interest. The father left it up to the sons: if they wanted hockey, they would have to ask. And when Eddie showed no inclination to follow his brother, Joe Jovanovski thought he might yet have a soccer player in the family. But then, at age eleven, Eddie, too, asked if he could sign up for hockey.

It should already have been too late. So hyper-organized is Canadian minor hockey that the key decisions have long since been made for this age group. At ages seven and eight, those who show any promise at all are moved onto the myriad of competitive teams—the number of them out of all proportion to the house-league teams simply because so many parents are so desperate to claim their child plays "rep" hockey—and those chosen kids begin immediately to receive the extra ice time and superior coaching that makes it all but impossible for a child joining at age ten to catch up. In Russia and Scandinavia, on the other hand, competitive hockey does not even begin until age twelve, when it is felt the essential skills such as skating and passing and shooting are first properly in place. It is the difference, many believe, between European "creative" hockey and North American "survival" hockey.

"If a kid hasn't been recognized at eleven or twelve years of age," admits Murray Costello, president of the Canadian Hockey Association, "he's invited to look elsewhere. In the Canadian system, there's no longer any room for late bloomers."

Eddie Jovanovski was not only a late bloomer, he was a late June baby, on the precipice of another Canadian hockey barrier that both defines the system and defies logic. A dozen years ago, psychologist Paula Barnsley happened to be browsing through a game program for the Lethbridge Broncos of the Western Hockey League and became intrigued that most of the young Broncos had been born in the early months of the year. With her husband, Roger, an educator, the Barnsleys began a long study of minor and professional hockey and eventually came to the inescapable conclusion that "culling" of the stronger and weaker players at such a young age in minor hockey had created a situation where an overwhelming majority of players on élite had been born in the first six months of the year. Bigger than their July-through-December "peers" when the key selections were made, they had been given an advantage few later-born players could overcome. In far too many instances, by ages thirteen to fifteen, when size and maturity tend to even out over the calendar year, those born in later months had already been lost to the game and were either playing house league or had quit altogether. By the time players came of NHL age, there would be roughly four times the number of players born in the first quarter of the year as in the last quarter.

The Barnsleys' research was verified and extended by T. E. Daniel and C. T. L. Janssen of the University of Alberta, all of them reaching the same conclusion: when atom and novice and even pee wee players are divided into skill levels, the January-born are so much larger and more mature than the December-born that those born late in the year tend to be the first players "culled" from the rep teams.

"It could be argued," Roger Barnsley wrote, "that professional hockey players are really drafted when they are nine years old, at the time when they are selected for the top-tier leagues in their age group."

Too much organization leads too easily to too much early competitiveness, and as Dr Benjamin Spock, the

American child-care expert, has been saying in recent years, "excessive competitiveness"—particularly in organized sport for children—"has reached a point in many families where it does more harm than good." Think of American chess player Robert Le Donne, who was able to humiliate chess masters at the age of five, who quit at eight and who, now twenty-five, never plays. Think of Jim Pierce, the father of American tennis pro Mary Pierce, who has a court restraining order to keep him away from tournaments where his daughter is playing. And these are not even the organized *team* sports.

Professor Gai Ingham Berlage of Iona College in New Rochelle, N.Y., surveyed 222 fathers of boys involved in hockey and soccer to try to understand why so many parents seemed willing to let a child's sport dominate family life, often to the detriment of others and other activities, including school. "The reasons are similar to why company men let the corporation interfere with their family life," Berlage concluded. "As social prestige for the father revolves around his work, for the child social prestige at his school and in the community often is a product of his sports participation. As families bask in the reflected status of the corporate husband, parents bask in the reflected status of having an athletic son."

Those perceived rewards—social standing, reflected glory, million-dollar contracts—have distorted playing to the point where organized "play", such as minor hockey, has virtually replaced neighbourhood play. Idle time is distrusted and considered unproductive. The danger, many experts fear, is that North American society is killing creativity. Wayne Gretzky became a great hockey player in his back yard and in his basement, not during a series of fifty-minute practices and games that filled up the kitchen calendar.

But by far the most compelling argument against early decisions in sports was made by a McMaster University professor, Dr Obed Bar-Or, whose studies with Israeli colleague Bareket Falk plead convincingly for common sense and delay. Bar-Or, who is the director of the Children's Exercise and Nutrition Centre at McMaster, says that it is only at puberty that the key decisions on an athlete can be made—four and five years after they have already been made in hockey. It is at puberty when youngsters quickly develop more fast-twitch muscle fibres, the fibres that develop bursts of power. Some sports, such as hockey, require these bursts. Other aerobic activities do not. "This means there is little value in trying to focus children's exercise programs towards developing adult champions before children develop fast-twitch fibres," Bar-Or and Falk reported.

Eddie Jovanovski was not only beginning impossibly late, he was a late-June baby. Statistically, he should not have made it. But Eddie was a huge child, bigger even than those who were born in January of his calendar year, and he was aggressive from the beginning. Even if he could not skate, he attracted the attention of coaches who look for size first, skill second. Joe Jovanovski remembers vividly the first time he took his eleven-year-old out to the first practice. "Eddie didn't know what the blueline was. His feet went out on the side like a new baby." The father cringed along the wall at the back of the rink, convinced the other parents were laughing at him and the coaches were going to send his "baby" back to the dressing-room. But, instead, one of the Windsor travelling coaches came to Joe and asked if he could bring Eddie out to tryouts. The coach had seen something the father had not—size, aggressiveness— and the skating could come later. Right now, the youngster skated exactly as his father said he did: "Like a duck."

In his first game, Eddie admits, he was "gawdawful." But the skills came fast. By the end of that first season the eleven-year-old had moved up into "AA" hockey. "It was unbelievable how fast he developed," says his brother, Deni. The father, however, kept hoping the hockey was merely a phase, and remained convinced it was not working out. "Every time I saw Eddie play I'd say, 'Let's go play soccer,'" remembers Joe Jovanovski. "He'd say, 'No, Dad, I like this game. I'm going to make it.'"

Neither father nor mother ever pushed. "Maybe it would have been different if he had been playing soccer," concedes Joe. "Maybe we never put on pressure because we didn't know the sport. I don't even know how to skate."

Only twice did they ever interfere. The first time was in bantam, when Joe had seen his son play a poor game and tried to tell him, "You made a mistake, Eddie—you should have done it this way," and Eddie, fixing him with a stare the father had never seen, answered, "Dad, I got one coach, I don't need two." "He was right," says Joe. "He was right." The second time was when they decided to push Eddie into going for a college scholarship even though, by Joe's own admission, "he wasn't too crazy for school." In fact, Eddie hated school, wanted out and was sure he could have a career in hockey. "Eddie says, 'I'm going to junior because it's the fastest way to the NHL. I believe I have a future,'" remembers Joe. "We say, 'Okay, we'll support you.'"

Slowly, reluctantly, Joe Jovanovski gave up on talking his son into soccer. The two boys clearly loved another game, but it struck the parents as odd how differently the two youngsters approached this new Canadian sport. Deni was a good player, but not the least involved physically. Eddie, on the other hand, was far more interested in the hitting than the scoring. "We have no idea where that came from," says Joe. "We know when he played street hockey he hated to lose. He was always arguing with the other kids. He hates to lose."

The rate of progress for young Ed Jovanovski might well be unprecedented. It took him a season to find his position, beginning as a forward and eventually moving back to defence. "I couldn't score," he jokes. In the spring of 1992—the year Tampa Bay selected Czech Roman Hamrlick first and Ottawa took Russian Alexei Yashin second—the Windsor youngster was still playing bantam hockey. He was passed over in the junior draft and went on to play Junior "B," which he now sees as the year in which he turned into a real player. He made it to the Spitfires of the Ontario Major Junior league only in the 1993–94 season leading up to the Hartford draft.

"Eddie's a quality kid and the type of kid I want to build this team around," Spitfires general manager Mike Awender told the *Windsor Star* when he selected Jovanovski. "The thing that impresses me most about him is his character. He's such a good, solid kid. He's got physical size and a good mental outlook and he's a good-living kid. He's a quality kid and a very gifted athlete. I've seen good players like Eddie who have messed up later. Ed won't do that."

In the Junior "A" club, his progress was, again, astonishing. In sixty-two games with the Spitfires, Jovanovski played well enough to end his first season with fifty points, but the scouts were far more interested in that other total: 221 minutes in penalties. He was the best bodychecker in junior hockey. "I love collisions," he says. He was mean: a Jovanovski shoulder check on Detroit Junior Red Wings forward Nic Beaudoin broke Beaudoin's jaw, knocked him unconscious and sent him to the hospital. And Jovanovski was still growing. "I thought I'd be an average guy having an average season," he says, "and possibly I might get picked."

At Christmas the NHL's Central Scouting had ranked Ed Jovanovski fourteenth. By early June he was in the top three, with Radek Bonk considered the probable number-one choice and Jovanovski and Oleg Tverdovsky fighting for second. He had an agent, Anton Thun of Richmond Hill, Ontario, and there was talk that Jovanovski would soon be a multimillionaire—perhaps not the $12.25-million bonanza Alexandre Daigle had picked up a year earlier in Quebec City, but not much less.

Jovanovski, like all the young draft choices, was deliberately playing down the prospects of big money. Unlike Eric Lindros in 1991, who had been selected first overall by the Quebec Nordiques but had refused to pull on a Nordiques sweater and had forced Quebec to trade his rights, Jovanovski didn't care where he went, so long as it was an NHL team; and again unlike Lindros, he didn't seem to care how much he was paid, so long as he got to play. Such refreshing enthusiasm was hardly unique: at a reception in New York City earlier in the month, the top draft choices had met with the media and each one had spoken as if the NHL and their "rights holders" had just put the group of them through a course in improved public relations. "It doesn't matter to me whether I make big money or small money," said Radek Bonk. Jeff Friesen, a slick centre from Meadow Lake, Saskatchewan, said he'd go anywhere to play and wasn't even concerned about money. "That's the big thing," he said. "Just to *play*." Ryan Smyth, a winger from Red Deer, Alberta, even said, "I'm not in it for the money—I'm in it for the love of the game." And

Jamie Storr, the highest-rank goaltender, added, "The minute money takes over the game, then hockey's no good for me." Not a single "rights holder" present flinched at any of this talk.

But now that the draft was upon them, everyone was talking money. The number-one pick overall was said to be worth $8 to $10 million, perhaps even more. No matter if Ed Jovanovski went first, second, third or thirteenth, he had it made for life. The pot at the end of the hockey rainbow was as close as centre stage, with NHL commissioner Gary Bettman about to call the initial phase of the 1994 entry draft into session. "I was the one pushing for soccer," a spinning Joe Jovanovski said. "But I'm very glad now he changed."

The father now treasures a home video of the 1990–91 travelling pee wee team, where, one by one, the youngsters skate towards the camera, stop, smile and speak.

"Hi," his curly-haired, determined son says, "I'm Eddie Jovanovski and I'm five-foot-four and 130 pounds. I want to play in the National Hockey League."

The moment was hardly prescient: every other player on the team says almost exactly the same thing on the video. The difference was that only Eddie Jovanovski, now six-two and 225 pounds, was now one of the three possible number-one choices the television cameras were setting up in front of on this late-June day in Hartford.

The relationship between fathers and sons is too complicated for language. Walt Disney once pointed out how few songs were written about fathers and then went back to work at his empire that portrayed fathers as essentially ineffectual, bumbling and usually absent. And British philosopher Bertrand Russell once said, "The fundamental defect of fathers is that they want their children to be a credit to them." Fathers can't help themselves, particularly when it comes to sports, even more particularly when it comes to *their* sport. "To show a child what has once delighted you," the British writer J. B. Priestley wrote, "to find the child's delight added to your own, so that there is now a double delight seen in the glow of trust and affection. This is happiness."

What makes the parent-child relationship special in hockey is necessity as much as anything else. The circumstances are simply different from those associated with most other North American sports. Ken Rappoport has covered all sports for the Associated Press out of New York City for more than three decades. He has also written nearly twenty books on sports, all of them aimed at a young audience, each of them concerned with team values and family values and personal values. An American, Rappoport long ago came to the conclusion that he liked the Canadian game best. Not so much because of the way it is played—though that, too, matters a great deal to him— but because of those who play it: their politeness, their manner, the values they carry. Ken Rappoport's theory is that it all has to do with family—usually Canadian families, so often small-town or rural families—and that hockey players have a need of family that is unmatched in any other team sport.

"They've got to make those 5 a.m. practices," says Rappoport. "Someone's got to make those drives. If there's no family support, they won't have the right equipment and they won't be able to afford to play the game. There has to be that family environment or they don't become hockey players."

Part of the story is, unfortunately, economic. The great

players of the past—Maurice Richard, Gordie Howe, Bobby Orr, Guy Lafleur, even Wayne Gretzky—all came out of the working class where a happy combination of idle time and few other distractions produced the best and most creative players for generations. For some time now, hockey has been a sport that would, in all likelihood, be out of reach today for a Gordie Howe, if he were today growing up in Saskatoon in near poverty. The family of modern hockey too often means two parents, two cars, money for registration, money for equipment, money for ice time, tournaments, jackets, parties and snack bars.

And yet, in an odd way, perhaps it is precisely this deepening involvement that makes it even more a *family* sport in the 1990s than it was in the 1940s, when Gordie Howe was first enraptured by the game and stuck to it despite a father who had precious little involvement and thought his son "clumsy and backward and bashful."

It would be an impossible task to spend much time around the National Hockey League and not be aware that there exists something very special between sons who play this game for a living and their parents. Sports fans who move to Canada from other countries, the United States included, are often taken aback by the corny "Hockey Night in Canada" player interviews where the scarred, stitched-up, gap-toothed player seems to be forever asking, or being asked, if he could say hello to his folks back home in Kamloops or Moose Jaw or Sudbury or Trois-Rivières. Each relationship is, obviously, entirely its own, but there are so many parallels in hockey that it is undeniable that there is something about fathers and sons and hockey worthy of examination.

Rarely has the father-son link been better described than in a diary goaltender John Tanner kept for journalist

Robert Olver, who in 1989–90 was working on his book on junior hockey, *The Making of Champions*. Tanner recorded what he felt at the moment his team reached the Memorial Cup: "The feeling's great. You look up in the stands and Dad was there. I held up the trophy and just looked at him. That's the culmination of everything I've ever done, winning that trophy. And he's a part of it, just because he was there. I couldn't have been more happy. My uncle was there, friends were there, but I didn't see anyone in the stands except him."

If the young players gathered here today in the Hartford Civic Center were asked to identify their best friend, a surprising number would name the older man sitting beside them or directly behind them—their father. The total would be entirely out of proportion to any other gathering of eighteen-year-old males. Take an established NHL player aside and ask him about his goal scoring, his slump, his injuries, his team, and the answers will be short, polite but sometimes impatient, the ground being covered so familiar it is regarded as a slightly irritating detour between the dressing-room and the bus and the afternoon nap before the evening game. Ask an NHLer about his dad—even if those relationships were far removed from the sentimental—and the conversation might go on for days. The link between fathers and sons and hockey is so established, so significant among players, that at times it can take on absurd, even pathetic, tones. Members of the Montreal Canadiens of the mid-1980s still shake their heads over the insecure player who gave out cigars and bragged about his wife giving birth to their first son, when in fact it was a second daughter.

Such desperation is rare in hockey. Robert Bly, the American poet and author of *Iron John*, and the renowned advocate of such New Age notions as "male mothers" and the necessity of forced male bonding, would find little empathy in hockey circles. When Bly says, "One could say that the father now loses his son five minutes after birth," he does not speak to those men standing around the boards with their styrofoam cups of coffee at six o'clock in the morning. When he talks of the need for "ritual spaces" he does not know the hockey dressing-room. When he tells of group sessions where grown men gather to chant the words "Dad," "Father" and "Daddy" until they begin to cry, he should know that when Marty McSorley, the NHL's toughest player, arrived late to join Wayne Gretzky's 1994 European tour, he greeted his father, Bill, with a kiss.

Olga Silverstein and Beth Rashbaum wrote in their 1994 book, *The Courage to Raise Good Men*, that there exists in America a "cult of father hunger" and cited as proof such movies as *Field of Dreams*, *Star Wars*, *Indiana Jones* and *Hook*; they would find some, but surprisingly little, such hunger in hockey. Most élite hockey players, having been raised in a team-and-coach atmosphere since ages seven or eight and often having to leave home at fifteen or sixteen to play junior hockey, never did go through the traditional rebellion-separation-reconciliation that is the substance of the prototype father-son relation.

Perhaps it is because so many of them learned the game from their fathers. Perhaps because it was the father got them up, got them dressed, drove them to the rink, waited through the practices, argued with them, fought with them, comforted them, rationalized with them, believed in them or didn't believe in them, perhaps for these reasons the father-son relationship in hockey tends to have a different intensity than that of the player and his mother. Mothers tend generally to be worshipped by hockey players—and surely, are worthy of their own study. So often they have given undying support no matter what—no matter if the husband was challenging the very core of their child with his criticisms and with his own personal frustrations. It is, generally speaking, how "the home team" operates in hockey, and obviously in other endeavours in this huge and cold country. It is significant to note that a 1994 survey of twenty-two thousand thirteen- and sixteen-year-olds determined that Canadian teens idolize their parents far more than traditional sports and media heroes.

Hockey is a highly conservative sport, not given to change, not open to challenge. The traditions in hockey often lag behind the realities of society by decades. When most players talk of their mothers, it is of someone who was usually at home, waiting, always positive, supportive, quick with meals and comfort and applause. The image of 1950s television. Mothers might drive them, but fathers usually *drove* them—in as many different ways as there are sons playing this game. Sometimes, as in Brett Hull's case, the father didn't even need to be there to have the most pro-found effect on his son's career. To all this mothers have been witnesses, spectators, sometimes participants, but they know better than any that there are matters that come into play between a man, his boy and this game that is as much environment as it is invention.

Rappoport's observations are well founded. What other sport would dedicate a section of its Hall of Fame to the family living-room, a national shrine on a cold winter's Saturday night? Furniture and fashion may change—the 1950s black-and-white TV may now be a full-colour giant-screen home entertainment centre—but the experience and values have a stronger link than that of tube to transistor.

The Hockey Hall of Fame's Household Family Zone is as legitimate a display as Howie Morenz's skates.

The patriarchal lines run even among the team tables assembled here for the 1994 NHL entry draft. Dick Patrick, sitting at the Washington Capitals table, the team of which he is president, is first cousin to Craig Patrick, the general manager sitting over at the table belonging to the Pittsburgh Penguins. This coming season will mark the seventieth year in which a Patrick has been involved in some capacity—player, coach, general manager, president—in the NHL, yet the family roots in this game are as long as the roots of the game itself.

Joseph Patrick was an early Canadian lumberman, involved in cutting massive stands of white pine along the Ottawa River and shipping that lumber through the St Lawrence. His sons, Lester, born in Drummondville in 1883, and Frank, born two years later in Ottawa, learned the game on the frozen Point St Charles waters of the St Lawrence near Montreal, using tree branches they cut on Nuns' Island and a block of wood for a puck. They were phenomenal players at a time when the game was only beginning to find its form, the sweep of change perfectly illustrated in the fact that another brother, Ted, was considered a fine defenceman despite his having lost a leg in a sleigh accident and playing on a wooden peg that he jabbed into the ice surface and pivoted around on a single skate. Lester was one of the greatest players in the history of the game, scoring the winning goal when the Montreal Wanderers defeated the Ottawa Silver Seven in the 1906 Stanley Cup, a match that has long been called the greatest game in hockey history.

In 1908, with the white pine of the Ottawa Valley too thinned out for profitable harvesting, Joseph Patrick moved his large family to new timber rights near Nelson, British Columbia, where the Patricks, particularly Frank, would later be credited with bringing the game to the West Coast. Lester, however, stayed behind, though his father had advised him to forget about hockey and get down to the lumber business. The player who would come to be known as the Silver Fox chose hockey instead, signing with the Renfrew Millionaires for an astounding $3,000 a year, and began a new Patrick dynasty in a new family business.

Their contribution is described in full in Eric Whitehead's *The Patricks: Hockey's Royal Family*. It was Frank Patrick on the West Coast who built the first rinks in that part of the country and who refined the revolutionary method of keeping ice frozen indoors. It was Frank Patrick who gave hockey post-schedule playoffs and the Stanley Cup final, Frank Patrick who invented the penalty shot, the forward pass, assists, bluelines and who fought, successfully, to have goaltenders go down if wished. Lester became coach and general manager of the New York Rangers and led the team to three Stanley Cups. Lester's sons, Lynn and Muzz, starred for New York in the 1930s and 1940s and later became coaches and general managers of the Rangers, the Boston Bruins and the early St Louis Blues. Lynn's son, Craig, played for four NHL teams before turning to coaching and managing, and was the architect of the Pittsburgh Penguins' Stanley Cup–winning teams of 1991 and 1992.

Given such lineage, it only seems appropriate that in the eighth round, the Washington Capitals will select eighteen-year-old Chris Patrick of Kent School in Connecticut. Heading for Princeton on a scholarship, Chris Patrick would seem to have an outside chance, at best, of ever reaching the NHL—so few eighth rounders ever do. But almost everyone in the building will recognize the name:

the Silver Fox's great-grandson, Muzz Patrick's grandson, Dick Patrick's son, Craig Patrick's nephew.

"The boy becomes a man," Ken Dryden wrote in his renowned hockey book, *The Game*, "the player becomes a coach, a manager, a scout, a father, a game is passed on like tribal history, one voice, one mind. There is no bigger picture."

No matter who you ask in a gathering such as this, they are keen to describe their own picture. "My father was a decent player," "Hockey Night in Canada" analyst Harry Neale remembers. "He played junior hockey in Toronto. I can also remember as a kid the Leafs, Foster Hewitt on the radio coming on at nine o'clock. In order to listen to games on my radio—a portable, you could plug it in or use about a three-hundred-pound battery—my parents used to make me go to bed at seven. This is when I was six, seven and eight years old. And they would wake me up at nine so I could listen to the game.

"Hockey meant a lot to me. And I can remember more than one Sunday morning waking up and just be pissed off at my mom and dad—they didn't wake me up. But my dad said he had me up walking around and then when I lay back down to listen to the game I guess I really hadn't awakened.

"In Sarnia I was really lucky. I could listen to the Leaf games and we could get the Detroit games. But I was a Leaf fan. And when we moved to Toronto I can remember telling my dad, 'Is there any chance of getting a house right beside Maple Leaf Gardens?' Not having any idea where that was. He took me to the games. Not a lot of games because we didn't have a lot of money, but he did take me to the game in '51 when Bill Barilko scored in overtime. I remember that.

"Like most kids I knew I was going to be in the National League. I knew all the players in the six-team league. I used to love *The Hockey News* because they gave you the game summaries. I'm sure my father more or less created the interest, like most fathers who've played, and as I've more or less done, too, at home. He used to tell me that the only reason I had to worry about not playing hockey was if I didn't do well at school. That was kind of the one thing he held over my head. He was an easygoing guy, but he loved the game, too, and I often wondered if my marks were on the edge whether or not he really would have not allowed me to play. But I was afraid to try him, so I passed everything.

"I played junior hockey with the Marlboros with some pretty good teams and some pretty good players. Toronto wanted to sign me and I was halfway through university. And my father told me, 'You should finish university and then do it.' But by the time you're twenty years old, your father can only suggest.

"So, I found out when I went to the Leaf camp that I wasn't good enough to play for the Leafs that year. But I could have played for Rochester because they were sponsored by Montreal at that time. I went to the Rochester camp in Montreal. I sat beside Freddie Shero—this is 1956 or 1957—and Freddie was a quiet old guy, and he says, 'Where'd you play last year?' 'Marlboros.' 'Well,' he said, 'did you go to school?' 'Oh, yeah,' I said, 'I'm finished two years of my three-year B.A. at the University of Toronto.' He dropped a skate and he looked at me and he said, 'You're at this training camp when you have one year of university to go?' 'Yeah.' He said, 'Get the hell out of here and get back to school. None of us here have that option. You're crazy!'... And so I went home the day before I had to re-enrol at the University of Toronto or I couldn't get in. And that was the end of my pro hockey."

Dave King, sitting near the head of the table of the Calgary Flames, has similar memories, if a different location. His father worked with the minor hockey program in North Battleford, Saskatchewan. "There was a bunch of equipment stored in the basement. That was the first time I had ever seen ice hockey equipment when I was little. I can remember being two or three years old and going down into the basement, and I used to try the sweaters and equipment on and wear it around. That's basically where I started thinking about hockey. I don't remember my first actual playing, but I do remember my mom and dad having a chair on the ice and pushing it around. That was the way I learned how to skate. I can remember my dad being out and being very patient. And falling down and crying a lot—that was all part of it."

All part of it; all part of the lore—sentimental, simplistic—that forms the early chapters in virtually every story from those about to be drafted this day to those they once held up as their idols. Lanny McDonald growing up in the Hand Hills heartland of Alberta, his feet stuffed into a pair of hand-me-down skates two sizes too large, skating over a rough creek to get to school where his mother taught and where the fathers had built a real rink and where, each day, the game would already be under way when he arrived. Guy Lafleur sneaking in through the broken boards of the old Thurso rink, the arena manager turning a blind eye to the youngster he could not keep off the ice. Wendel Clark's father teaching his boys how to give and take a bodycheck in the kitchen. Marty McSorley's father taking the farm tractor down onto the creek to clear it off after every snowfall and building an equipment box down by the shore that he stuffed with second-hand equipment, first-come, first-served. Mike Modano's father—and sometimes his mother—wearing a baseball catcher's mask and holding up a garbage can lid in their Detroit-area basement so the youngster could practise his slapshot.

This moment, the annual NHL entry draft, has been building since that first moment it became obvious—to others, as well as the parents—that the child is something special. Usually, that initial difference becomes so common in his playing group that his own specialness vanishes, yet there are some for whom the difference merely increases as time passes; and the anticipation builds towards this moment.

The pressure is enormous. When Eric Lindros, now seen as one of the toughest and best players in the NHL, was sixteen and about to be drafted into the junior leagues, he began having spontaneous nosebleeds in the two weeks leading up to the big moment and spent the morning of the draft alone in his room, crying because he knew the Sault Ste Marie Greyhounds were going to select him and he did not want to play there. Two years later, when the Quebec Nordiques were going to take him in the NHL draft and he again did not want to play for that particular team, he described the pressures of the day as being "like a playoff hockey game." He took his younger brother, Brett, with him everywhere for security.

Now, three years later in Hartford, it was eighteen-year-old Brett Lindros's turn. He was expected to go in the top twenty, but the name alone might move him into the top ten, especially among the American teams, where his potential as a name-drawing card would overcome his drawbacks as a skater.

The big names—Jovanovski, Bonk, Tverdovsky,

Lindros, Jeff O'Neill, Jason Bonsignore, goaltender Jamie Storr, Ryan Smith, Jeff Friesen—all sit in carefully designated areas to the right of the podium. The lesser names, the ones who pray their names will be called in the second, third, fourth or fifth rounds, sixth, seventh, eighth, ninth, tenth and eleventh if necessary, who cannot even imagine the humiliation and disappointment and despair of not being called at all, sit off to the left and high in the orange seats.

Andrew and Jason Boudrias of Val d'Or in northern Quebec sit up in section 114, waiting for the lottery to begin. The father, Andrew, is so nervous that he cannot sit with his son, but stays one, sometimes two rows behind, watching his son fidget, Jason's right knee pumping frantically as the day gets under way. This is the fourth amateur draft for the father—he previously went to two in Montreal and one in Quebec City—but practice has done nothing for him. "It's not the same thing," he says.

Jason Boudrias is an Algonquin Indian who plays for the Laval Titan of the Quebec Major Junior league, a six-foot, two-hundred-pound centre whose skills and development have been a matter of concern to team, to player and to family for some time now. He scored only seventeen goals with the Titan in 1993–94 and had only two assists in the Memorial Cup that Laval hosted in the spring. "He didn't have a great year," says Andrew. "People said he'd have to have a better year." He didn't.

Because of the native connection, father and son had sought out Hartford assistant coach Ted Nolan—himself an Ojibway from a northern Ontario reserve—and Nolan had talked to them about high expectations and reality. "He said being drafted was the easy part," says Andrew. "Making the team is a lot harder." But it has not ever been easy for Jason Boudrias. His older brother, Stephane, had far more skills but not Jason's drive to succeed. Stephane Boudrias had played for St Jean and Trois-Rivières, but as his father said, "he didn't have the discipline." Stephane's coming up just short, he felt, had in fact served the younger brother well: "I think Jason got a good scare to know it's not going to be easy."

Driven to find better and better competition, Jason had crossed over into Ontario when he had a chance to play for the Gloucester Rangers in the lesser junior leagues, and to allow this to happen his father and mother, Hélène, "doctored it" to make his dream possible. The father laughs. "We had him adopted." Working with a lawyer and an agreeable family, they signed the legal papers and Jason Boudrias became someone else's child for as long as he played in Ontario. When Laval drafted him in 1992, Andrew says, "we had the deal reversed." Jason was "adopted" by his blood mother and father. The Boudrias family all moved down to Montreal to be closer to their son and his new team.

Jason Boudrias believed he would go in the fourth round, fifth at the latest. His father believed so, too, but in the back of his mind he was already working on what he might say to his son if their worst nightmare came true and his son did not get chosen this day. Hockey had been selected as a "career", not an "option", and there was no room at this point for failure. "I don't know what I'd say," the father kept saying. "I just don't know."

For more than a decade this dream had been the driving force behind the Boudrias family. "Any parent who puts a kid through minor hockey," Andrew says, "you have to like it. It has to become your pastime." And now the pastime had become the "job", with applications being decided as they sat waiting. Jason's agent, Larry Kelly of Ottawa, had told a number of his charges not to come to Hartford in case this did indeed happen, and he knew that Jason Boudrias was on dangerous ground. But like everyone else, he hoped it worked out. The fourth round, the fifth, sixth, seventh...

Lower down in the seats sits Winnipeg's Jason Botterill, a tall (six-three), solid left winger from the University of Michigan Wolverines who is certain to go in the first round, but only after the big names are gone. Wearing a light brown suit, Botterill sits with his family, his father, Cal, tall and gangly and nervous, by his side. Cal Botterill is a sports psychologist at the University of Manitoba and has had a long history as team psychologist for various NHL teams. His latest work has been with the New York Rangers and, less than two weeks earlier, he had been a small but significant part of the organization that brought New York its first Stanley Cup since 1940. The elder Botterill's many friends around the league have found him a little "spacey" this week in Hartford. All are amused. "This is the guy who's paid to preach cool, calm and collected to Mark Messier," jokes Ottawa Senators assistant coach E.J. McGuire, who also holds a Ph.D. in psychology.

In a 1993 news special on CBC, "The Spirit of the Game," Cal Botterill seemed one of the more sane minds in the game when it came to perspective on minor hockey. As he told CBC reporter Mark Lee: "When parents start feeling that their worth as a person is on the line every time their kid skates up the ice—it's insane." Years earlier, Botterill and fellow sports psychologist Terry Orlick, now with the University of Ottawa, had studied youngsters who were dropping out of sports in the province of Alberta. Their research, Orlick says, demonstrated "how many kids were not having a good time in sport. They felt left out. I talked to kids, some as young as seven and eight, who had already dropped out. And if I asked them, 'If you were better, would you want to play the game?' they'd say, 'Yes.' They all said, in their own little words, that they didn't like the emphasis on winning."

Botterill and Orlick had found that mothers generally were supportive, while fathers essentially wanted their children "to perform." Often, children were being yelled at from the stands, yelled at by the coach and then yelled at all the way home in the car. Canadian minor hockey, Orlick decided, is far worse than other parent-child situations revolving around sport for the alarming reason that, too often, "the outcome of the game becomes more important than the outcome of the child."

A decade after the original work by Botterill and Orlick, Orlick published follow-up research that showed some progress in the organization of children's sports, but little in parent-child relationships. Children, he wrote, "learn that they are always being judged, must always do their best or suffer the consequences of being 'a failure'." Now Jason Botterill, Cal's son, was about to be judged by the National Hockey League. And the father, having done the research, knowing all the right things to say, was still a nervous wreck.

He should not have been concerned. Derek Mackesy, who has served as team doctor for numerous Team Canada ventures as well as a number of Canada Cups, says that Jason has all the characteristics necessary to make it as a professional hockey player: size and skill, obviously, but also "a maturity beyond his years—as well as excellent blood lines." Cal Botterill had been a superb player himself as an amateur, and Jason's mother, Doreen, went to two

Olympics as a Canadian speed skater.

In an odd reversal of form, Jason had left his Winnipeg home at age fourteen to play in the United States. His father had then been working with Mike Keenan, then head coach of the Chicago Blackhawks, and the team's star centre, Jeremy Roenick, himself an American, had suggested to young Jason that he consider the prep school route, as Roenick had. Instead of being an American kid headed for the junior leagues for better competition, as often happens, Botterill became a Canadian kid headed south for scholarship and, he hoped, good competition.

He attended St Paul's in New Hampshire and, at one point, went on tour with the Canadian Olympic team, serving as the team's equipment helper and water boy. It was this short tour of American colleges that convinced him that this was a viable alternative route to the NHL. It became, his father said, "his mission". Keenan, by now the coach of the New York Rangers, had taken a liking to the youngster and recommended him to Red Berenson, the coach at the University of Michigan. Berenson scouted Botterill, and a scholarship was soon offered.

As a freshman winger with the Wolverines, Jason helped Michigan to the number-one American college ranking. Strong along the boards and sharp in front of the net, he scored twenty goals and nineteen assists in thirty-six games. Berenson declared him "physically and mentally mature" enough to be headed for the NHL, but others still had doubts as the Hartford draft loomed. Jason's skating remained highly suspect, and was certain to work against him until he demonstrated that he could be a quick big man as well as a strong big man in hockey.

Doug Johnston sat dead centre in section 115 with his son, B.J., and knew that size was a consideration with B.J.

as well. The boy was six-three but skinny at 177 pounds. He knew that some scouts had declared his son too "timid". He had good speed and an excellent shot, but would it be enough?

The Johnstons had come to Hartford from the small southwestern Ontario town of Blenheim, where Doug teaches mathematics and physical education at the high school. They had come up through minor hockey together, Doug always coaching, B.J. always the star—but, as the son says, "Dad never treated me any different than any of the other players." Doug Johnston had already been through it all with B.J.'s older brother, Ryan, now attending the University of Ohio on a full hockey scholarship, and he had long since formed strong ideas on what coaching should be and what a youngster should be able to take with him when he left the Doug Johnstons of minor hockey for the more competitive junior leagues and college.

"I want them to be good people when they come out," Doug says. "A better person. I want them to know what it means not to be selfish, to play on a team as part of that team. You think there's a lot of pressure when you have to play a big game or you think you might get drafted? You don't know what pressure is until you have to worry about your job and your family and whether or not you're going to be able to put food on the table for them." What he saw in hockey was opportunity, the opportunity for a short happy experience before getting on with life, the opportunity to make friends and contacts to last a lifetime.

He encouraged his younger son to take just such an opportunity when B.J. was only fourteen. The Blenheim bantams had gone to Chicago to play in a friendship tournament and, while there, B.J. had been invited to come back and play high-school hockey if he liked. His father thought it a terrific idea. "I was glad I went," B.J. says now. "It was a great experience."

He returned to Ontario at sixteen to play Junior "B" in Orillia and then, the next year, moved on to the Oshawa Generals in Major Junior "A" hockey. By the time he turned eighteen, he was coming off a vastly improved second season with the Generals in which he had scored twenty goals and twenty-four assists in sixty-six games. The Johnstons believed from the bottom of their hearts that B.J. had a good chance. The January rankings of the NHL Central Scouting Bureau had him ranked forty-seventh overall among North Americans who would be eligible for the draft. That would be second round if only North Americans were available, so even if you matched North Americans and Europeans one-for-one—and few would be so generous to the Europeans—it meant B.J. Johnston should be going somewhere around the end of the fourth round. How could he miss?

B.J.'s agent, Don Reynolds, had said they may as well go to Hartford. He didn't seem worried. The father and son had been watching the Stanley Cup playoffs on CBC the night Don Cherry used his "Coach's Corner" spot to advise all prospective draft players not to go to Hartford "unless you're in the top three rounds," and they'd talked it over. Doug had questioned the advisability of going, and B.J. had replied, "I don't want to be a no-show." Two friends who had also been highly ranked—Peterborough Petes big forward Matt Johnson and talented Owen Sound Platers centre Wayne Primeau—were flying down and wanted B.J. to come with them. He talked it over with his father and decided to go; Doug Johnston would drive down later.

"He says to me, 'Well, Dad, are you going to come?'" Doug Johnston remembers. "I said, 'Well, B.J., you won't need me there if you do get drafted. But if you don't get drafted, you're going to need me.

"If you don't make it, there'll be only one guy sitting there with you—and it'll be me."

Radek Bonk's father, Jaroslav, did not make it to the Hartford draft. He remained at his home in Koprivnice in the Czech Republic with his wife, Anna, their daughter, Andrea, a year older than Radek, and Andrea's two little boys. Instead, Bonk went to Hartford with one of his agents, Jiri Crha, a fellow Czech who, fifteen years ago, played a couple of seasons in goal for the Toronto Maple Leafs. They made an odd couple around the Hartford Civic Center: the studious-looking Crha, with his long, greying hair, half-glasses and constant briefcase, the big, splay-kneed Bonk bouncing through the corridors with his long, flowing rocker's hair and sad eyes that remind his peers of Jason Priestley, their parents of James Dean.

Wherever Bonk went, a camera or two would usually be following close behind, the networks gathering footage on the one certain to go first or second. There were rumours of a $20-million contract demand from the Bonk camp even before there was a team to deliver it to. If Alexandre Daigle was worth $12.25 million only a year earlier, then the sky, surely, would be the limit for the phenomenal Bonk. As Crha put it: "I don't know how many goals Alexandre Daigle scored when he was seventeen playing in the IHL."

Daigle, though, had never been a seventeen-year-old professional playing in the International Hockey League. But then, no one had until Bonk came along. He was the first seventeen-year-old professional hockey player since Wayne Gretzky and Mark Messier jumped early to the old

World Hockey Association and, like Gretzky, Bonk had established immediate credentials: eighty-seven points with the Las Vegas Thunder, named to the IHL all-star game and voted rookie of the year. Bonk was a happy mix, it was being said, between the elegant Jaromir Jagr and the ferocious Eric Lindros. Bonk had been so certain of going first overall in the June NHL draft that he had taken to wearing a Florida Panthers cap around Las Vegas. By dint of a coin flip at the 1993 entry draft, Florida would have the first selection in 1994. He figured he was well on his way to Miami.

That Bonk had ended up in Las Vegas was both a stroke of genius and a stroke of luck. The Thunder became a new franchise in the IHL in 1993, and the team's new general manager, Bob Strumm, knew that he would have to compete in a city where even the Rolling Stones can have difficulty selling out a show. Nowhere in North America, New York City included, is the competition for the entertainment dollar so intense. "When I got the job," says Strumm, "I knew I needed an attraction."

Strumm contacted Wayne Gretzky's agent, Mike Barnett of the International Management Group, based in Los Angeles, and it happened that IMG already had an agreement with the young phenomenon out of Koprivnice. Barnett had engaged Crha to prowl the European leagues for IMG, and Crha had been pushing this huge teenager who had played in the Czech élite league at sixteen and seemed absolutely determined to come to North America and the NHL. It was presumed that Bonk would select the route favoured by some Europeans and come to play junior hockey in Canada, and to that end the Owen Sound Platers of Ontario Hockey League had drafted him and currently held his rights.

On Crha's recommendation, Bonk had gone to Minnesota in the summer of 1993 to attend a hockey school. He had been told to work on his skating, which was partially true, but it was also an advantageous spot for Barnett to showcase Bonk. Strumm headed off for Minnesota, liked what he saw, and a deal was struck for approximately $100,000 (U.S.). Instead of heading off to Owen Sound, a sleepy little city on Georgian Bay that had peaked in the steamship era, Bonk was off to a city where, twice daily, a pitched high-seas battle is waged along the main drag, where every fifteen minutes a volcano erupts, where the hotels pump a rose smell, Odorant 1, through the vents because they believe it will up the take on the slot machines by 45 percent, and where the hookers stand along The Strip handing out their glossy, revealing business cards, MasterCard and Visa accepted.

His first night in Las Vegas, Radek Bonk could not sleep. He went to the window of his hotel room and stared out over the lights that are never turned off—the lasers rising from the pyramid of the Luxor, the brilliant cartoon pastels of Excalibur, the shining eyes of the black sphinx in front of the MGM Grand—and the seventeen-year-old swallowed hard, doubting he could survive.

Like Ed Jovanovski growing up in Windsor, Radek Bonk's introduction to sports had been through his father's game, soccer. Jaroslav Bonk had never played hockey but, unlike Kostadin Jovanovski, he did not dislike it. He simply preferred other games—soccer foremost, but also tennis. Jaroslav's only son, Radek, was huge for his age from the beginning, and the father had high hopes for his son excelling in Europe's chosen game. At the age of five, Radek had been enrolled in the local Koprivnice program, had learned the fundamentals and was just beginning to attempt playing the game when his father took a day off from the vegetable depot where he worked to come and see the boy's early progress. What Jaroslav saw disgusted him: the coaches ignoring the youngsters, standing along the sidelines smoking cigarettes and joking with each other when they should have been teaching. A furious Jaroslav Bonk stormed onto the field and yanked his son off in the middle of play.

"We have to find something else," the father said.

They found a hockey rink.

It is difficult to explain why some games fit some youngsters and some youngsters fit certain games. From the moment he first went out on the ice with skates and a stick, Radek Bonk was demonstrably different from all the other youngsters. Different in ability, decidedly different in size. He could do things no one else at his level could, and they began moving him higher and higher to find competition. Even though he was soon three years ahead of his age group, he was still so big and so good that, whenever he scored, the other kids would all shout, "He's too old! He's too old!" These doubts about his age would hound him right up to the NHL draft.

By the age of seven, Radek Bonk was imagining himself in the NHL. He dreamed he was playing with the Edmonton Oilers, the team that was just beginning to dominate with Gretzky and Messier and Coffey and Kurri. He saw himself, not Gretzky, passing to Kurri, who had become his idol. He soon believed that he was going number one in the NHL draft. He was not yet ten years of age.

It is not unusual for a child to have such ambition, but this dream was shared completely by the father and mother, who began to count on Radek one day reaching the NHL. Jaroslav, who had no experience in the game, had become his son's hockey coach, almost a personal coach, and drove his son as hard as he dared. Even when Radek had won rookie of the year in the IHL, Jaroslav would still acknowledge only that he was "a little" proud of his son. "Radek must still learn," he said.

Even so, they were so certain of him reaching his hockey goal that education had been let slide. He had finished the Czech equivalent of grade eight and had taken some courses in hotel management, but the family was convinced that all Radek would need to know about hotels in the future was in which room the team meal would be held.

Bob Strumm knew he was taking a risk in bringing such a youngster to a city like Las Vegas. A youngster from a small industrial city that, not so long ago, was also protected by the Iron Curtain. A youngster who barely spoke a few words of English. A youngster not yet old enough to drink beer, making $100,000 a year in a city strategically designed to burn holes in pockets. But Strumm was certain he would be able to connect with his new young star. He had had the sense to talk to Bonk about his likes and dislikes as well as hockey when he had signed him in Minnesota. Strumm picked up his young star at the airport, threw his luggage in the back, jammed Def Leppard's latest into the tape deck, turned the volume up full and headed into the city. He never said a word during the drive.

The Thunder brought Bonk's parents over to join him. Jaroslav left his job at the vegetable depot, Anna stopped working at the Koprivnice car plant. They took an apartment where Anna could cook her son's favourite goulash with omacka sauce. Radek got his North American driver's licence and the hockey player's chosen vehicle of the 1990s—a Jimmy four-by-four—and the season got under way with Arnold Schwarzenegger and Andre Agassi in the stands. Team tough guy Lyndon Byers took it upon himself to teach the youngster his first English: "Me Radek—you babe."

Bonk played well from the first, but he established himself on the night of November 12, 1993, when, in a game against Peoria, he scored four goals in overcoming a 6–3 deficit going into the third period, his fourth goal on an extraordinary effort with only five-tenths of a second left in the game. The raves began immediately and continued throughout his remarkable rookie season.

Las Vegas fell in love with Radek Bonk, and Radek Bonk with Las Vegas. His parents liked it. He had new friends—in particular, a seventeen-year-old high-school senior named Janell—and everyone seemed to know him and like him. He could play tennis, drive his four-by-four, listen to Metallica and Guns n' Roses and Def Leppard. He could drive The Strip, drive out into the desert, sun all day and play at night. "Nowhere in the world is a place like Las Vegas," he was soon saying. "I love it here. I belong here."

"Radek Bonk is a winner," said Thunder associate coach Chris McSorley, NHL defenceman Marty McSorley's younger brother. "He's extremely competitive. He doesn't shy away. He considers it his fault if we win, his fault if we lose."

McSorley even went so far as to predict that Bonk would one day be consistently in the top fifteen of NHL scorers. "He's the complete package," he said.

Not everyone, however, was quite so convinced. From the beginning Bonk suffered the criticism that has plagued all big forwards from Frank Mahovlich in the 1960s to Keith Primeau in the 1990s: a sense that they lack intensity, a feeling that, unless awakened, they drift through games like a Tall Ship looking for a calm harbour to set anchor in.

When then general manager Bob Clarke, the man who would be making the selection for the Florida Panthers, learned that the projected number-one selection would be playing professional hockey at age seventeen, he seemed unimpressed. "He should be playing junior hockey," Clarke said. "It's stupid for him to be playing here. He's playing against men. They're bigger, stronger, better players than he is."

Bonk threw away his Florida Panthers cap.

"My child has this nearly obsessive attachment to hockey," author M. T. Kelly wrote in a 1994 essay on minor hockey for *This Magazine*. "He loves it. After his first few games, watching the kids come on in waves in their brilliant uniforms, I loved it too. Very quickly, I got caught up in the syndrome of nearly every parent whose son gets really involved in competitive hockey: I lived and died by his ice time.

"A year later, I heard the phenomenon explained to me this way: 'It's narcissism. You put so much into the kid, your own feelings, things that aren't right with your life, that you feel if he doesn't perform well, your own ego will die.'"

Such observations were even more intriguing in that Kelly was experiencing something as the father of a child that was absolutely alien to anything he had known as a child of a father. Kelly grew up in the poorer sections of Toronto in the late fifties and early sixties and hockey struck him as "a metaphor about being left out." Hockey was for him a myth. "I had no father, so no father could help me with my shot; the main sport of the men I knew was drinking. There were no outdoor ponds (in fact, no kind of 'ice time') where you could dream of greatness.

There was certainly no money for equipment. Anyone who played hockey with any skill, who could even skate, came from places with names like Leaside and Rosedale. They all seemed to have two parents, money, and not to live in apartments."

A generation later, with young Jonah Kelly taking to the game with enthusiasm and skill, a child who had once resented the game became a father as caught up as his own son in the game—in fact, at times more so than his son. Kelly found himself screaming at games, wound up at times beyond reason, but he could not help himself. The day he realized he was finally coming to terms with both his son's chosen game and the surprising emotions he felt watching was the day "he told me that I'm 'not a hockey father any more.'"

But, of course, he was, and remains, one. And they are all around us, identifiable not by external markings but by an internal weakness of the heart: sometimes painful, sometimes sentimental, sometimes soaring. Hockey fathers in Canada can relate to what American writer John Updike felt as he watched his young son play soccer: "When the boy scores a goal, he runs into the arms of his team-mates with upraised arms and his face, alight as if blinded by triumph. They lift him from the earth in a union of muddy hugs. What spirit! What valour! What skill! His father, watching from the sidelines, inwardly registers only one complaint: he feels the boy, with his talent, should be more aggressive."

When Senator Alasdair Graham rose in the Canadian Senate in May 1994 to offer debate on Bill C-212, an act to recognize hockey and lacrosse as the two national sports of Canada, he made reference to the first true hockey father—Governor-General Lord Stanley—and how the pleasures this British lord got out of watching his two young sons play for the Rideau Rebels led to his paying for a Cup that would bear his name—and one day be the most recognizable sports trophy in the world. Graham spoke of what the game has meant to his country: "The sound of the first slapshot, the first puck hitting the boards, was and is the first shock of psychic electricity that unites hearts and minds in this country. All that irrespective of regions, time zones or ethnic backgrounds, because if there ever was a visible, passionate and inspirational spirit of our magnificent multiculturalism it was, and is, hockey."

Graham talked of a family ritual that takes place each Boxing Day in Sydney, Nova Scotia, when the annual Graham–Joseph hockey game is held, with the skill level running from a puffing Canadian senator to Fabian Joseph, captain of the silver-medal-winning 1994 Olympic hockey team. He talked of grandchildren who play in Ottawa, one a boy, one a girl, each in the same minor program. He spoke as hockey player, father and grandfather—bragging, and proud of it.

There is nothing absolute about the draft. It guarantees neither money nor success, though it is most assuredly perceived as capable of doing both. Hockey history proudly recalls the 1971 draft, when Guy Lafleur went first and Marcel Dionne second; the 1979 draft, considered the deepest ever in talent; the 1984 draft, when Mario Lemieux was available; and the 1991 draft, when Quebec's selection of Eric Lindros ultimately changed the fate of not one but two teams, the Nordiques and the Philadelphia Flyers. No one ever mentions the very first entry draft, 1969, when the St Louis Blues took ten players, none of whom were ever heard of again.

First-rounders, however, are supposed to make it. Most are supposed to star in the NHL. It doesn't matter that the NHL entry draft has gone from twelve teams in 1969 to twenty-six teams by 1993; the myth of the sure first-rounder persists. More players were made available by first the baby boom, then the Scandinavians and, most recently, the fall of the Iron Curtain. But, in fact, first-rounders fail often and regularly: Don Tannahill and Frank Spring went third and fourth respectively in 1969; Barry Dean and Ralph Klassen went second and third in 1975; even number-one overall picks Greg Joly (Washington, 1974), Doug Wickenheiser (Montreal, 1980) and Brian Lawton (Minnesota, 1983) had middling NHL careers, at best.

No matter. The consensus is that those taken first, second or third overall had better star—or else the scouts who tagged them and the general manager who selected them are in real danger of losing their jobs over what is considered the single most important decision a low-level team will make each year. In hockey mythology, smart drafting brought the New York Islanders four straight Stanley Cups. Poor drafting has been blamed for the shortcomings of teams such as the St Louis Blues, the Washington Capitals and, more recently, the Montreal Canadiens. If any team gets a top-three pick and blows it, that team has made a serious error in judgment.

By the time NHL commissioner Gary Bettman called the Hartford Civic Center to order for the first round of the 1994 draft, it was widely expected that the Florida Panthers, selecting first, would be going for Ed Jovanovski. General manager Bob Clarke had already expressed some disenchantment with Radek Bonk and was said to be luke-warm about European players in general. Florida president Bill Torrey had been the architect of the drafting prototype, the New York Islanders, and the Islanders had been built around Denis Potvin, the number-one overall selection of the 1973 entry draft. Jovanovski—big, strong, still developing—was a perfect fit, and to no one's surprise, with the possible exception of Jiri Crha and Radek Bonk, the Panthers chose him.

With a half dozen television cameras following, with his parents kissing and weeping in the near stands, the big Windsor Spitfires defenceman made his way to the podium, yanked on a Panthers sweater and cap and stood there sweating profusely as the still cameras moved in on the top story of the day as he dwarfed a smiling Bettman and Clarke. Ed Jovanovski was, at that moment, the luckiest kid in Canada. In the minds of those watching live in Hartford or by television across the country, he had it made. For ever and ever and ever.

The real surprise of the 1994 entry draft was yet to come. The Ottawa Senators, drafting third, had presumed they would be getting Oleg Tverdovsky. It had been Senators director of player personnel John Ferguson who had compared the young Russian defenceman to Bobby Orr, a tag that the media had loved and Tverdovsky had tried, unsuccessfully, to shrug off for fear of irrational expectations.

The Senators would have preferred Jovanovski, but Tverdovsky was considered a fine consolation. The team already had two promising young centres in Alexei Yashin and Alexandre Daigle, and it was time to start work on the blueline. So when the Mighty Ducks of Anaheim rose and chose Tverdovsky second, it sent shock waves around the civic centre and stunned the Senators. In a panic, Ottawa general manager Randy Sexton grabbed for the telephone at the end of the desk. He was already on the record the day before as saying, "You have to take the best player available." What general manager hadn't mouthed this familiar hockey bromide in the past twenty-four hours?

Yet the last thing in the world the Ottawa Senators needed was another young centre, Bonk, when they had no wingers, no defence and no future goaltending. They had now to choose between the draft wild card—goaltender Jamie Storr—and hockey's rule of thumb when drafting: always, *always* take the best player available. Sexton had even done research that had convinced him, as late as the day before, that "traditionally, you don't need to take a goalie in the first round—83 percent of the great goaltenders tend to come from the third round or later." But clearly, he hadn't expected this. Ottawa would certainly soon have need of good young goaltending, but he had never really seriously considered not getting either Jovanovski or Tverdovsky. "It's a question, really, of having the balls to take a goalie that high," he said. It was unlikely anyone in the top three, or even top ten, would have those "balls".

The Ottawa table huddled, and Sexton hurried up the steps onto the stage to announce that the player everyone had always believed would go first overall, Radek Bonk, was going to Ottawa. Bonk himself didn't even have a clue where Ottawa was. When he'd asked, he'd been told it had "clean air". For a youngster who'd revelled in Las Vegas and who'd visited Miami and Los Angeles to see for himself how he might like the sun and sand and glitter of the Panthers and the Mighty Ducks, the notion of heading for another country, another currency and a city that makes winter in Prague look like a February thaw was a shock indeed.

Crha tried to downplay the surprise. Ottawa, he said in

a quick press gathering, was "a possibility we discussed." But from the look on the blinking Bonk's face, the possibility had never come up in his mind. Butch Goring, the former Islander who was then Bonk's coach in Las Vegas, was both flabbergasted and angry.

"What more did he have to do to be number one?" Goring wanted to know. "Borderline NHL players don't come down to our level and score forty goals. How do you bypass this guy? He's one step closer to the NHL than any other player."

But both the Florida Panthers and the Mighty Ducks of Anaheim had made their decisions. Perhaps it had to do with wanting to build around young defencemen. Perhaps they had decided that Bonk's lumbering skating style was too much of a risk. Perhaps, too, their choices were reflections of the changing style of NHL hockey as the realities of five new expansion teams settled in. Thinning talent had led weak teams like the Panthers and the Mighty Ducks to embrace an old trick, the neutral-zone trap, and when it was coupled with open interference, hooking and holding that was rarely called by the officials, then victories became possible for teams that otherwise had no hope of success. The league's desperate desire to succeed in the American Sun Belt had led to a disintegration of officiating, with interference allowed to rise to—by the NHL's own official admission—"an art form", and soon briar-patch, taffy-pull boring hockey was the flavour of the decade. Strong defencemen became a priority for all teams, and if not strong enough to bull through—as an Ed Jovanovski might one day be—then mobile and quick enough to fire those perfect lead passes that can defeat a neutral-zone trap. Passes such as Oleg Tverdovsky was capable of making. They could worry about play-making centres later.

"There was nothing I could do," Bonk said. He conceded that "everyone wants to be number one," but it was out of his hands. The dream of a $20-million—even of a $10-million, perhaps of a $5-million—contract had evaporated in the amount of time it takes three men in suits to mount a stage, walk to a microphone and call out three names. Jiri Crha bravely said it shouldn't affect his client's marketability, but no one was convinced. Radek Bonk had just been delivered the first massive setback of his charmed life.

Interest in the draft began dwindling in direct proportion to the rising numbers. The rumoured Toronto–Quebec Sundin-Clark trade was now official, and as the drafting continued people began talking about Wendel Clark in a Nordiques uniform. Edmonton took Niagara Falls forward Jason Bonsignore fourth; Hartford took Guelph's Jeff O'Neill fifth; Edmonton, drafting again, took Moose Jaw winger Ryan Smith sixth; and Jamie Storr, the goaltender, went seventh, to Los Angeles. Brett Lindros went ninth to the New York Islanders. Jason Botterill went twentieth to the Dallas Stars, his stressed father wiping his face when the announcement was finally made. The family and friends hugged and kissed, took photographs, deep breaths, and Cal Botterill went back to being the calm, collected team psychologist, a renowned expert on dealing with sports stress and pressures.

The following morning the draft began again with the third round, the new "stars" all gone now and the hopeful prepared to wait as long as it took. Up in section 114, not far from where the Botterills had been sitting, Jason Boudrias and his father, Andrew, settled down to wait, expecting it would soon be over for them. The third round passed. The fourth round passed. Jason had expected to be gone already, but Andrew was not so sure. He figured fifth, maybe even sixth. When the seventh round came and went, Andrew began working out in his head what he would say to his son, who by now was so nervous no one would dare speak to him or look at him.

At one o'clock, having eaten nothing for lunch, Jason had his hands over his face, his right leg pumping frantically. The eighth round began—Florida with the first choice—and soon "Jason Boudrias!" was pounding through the civic centre. He was sitting between his mother, Hélène, and his girlfriend, Natalie, but he turned around and first hugged his father, who could say nothing but only laugh. He was laughing because, he said, "Now I won't have to have that talk."

Round nine came and went, round ten, and late in the afternoon the final round began. The draft boards had been long since filled. NHL commissioner Gary Bettman had long since moved on, the finishing up of the 1994 entry draft left to lesser officials. Some teams were not even sending their general managers up to the podium for the announcements. The teams had long since come to the conclusion that even ten rounds is far too many and were hoping to cut down to a maximum of eight rounds—no one ever makes it that late anyway, they argued, and if there are any exceptions they will find another way—but the NHL Players Association, keen to create as many job opportunities as possible, had so far refused to consider cutting back.

The crowd had thinned. No one remained in the key lower sections where once the certain draft picks had sat. They sat in spots higher up now, sat where their "rights holders" had assigned them seats and where their agents, and perhaps the odd local paper, could quickly find them once their names were called out. By the eleventh round there were only a couple of hundred people left, and most of them family or friends or the curious, staring at those who, by this point, could no longer bear being stared at. It was hot, but it was even more uncomfortable.

Doug and B.J. Johnston were still sitting dead centre in the middle of section 115. Neither could believe what had happened. B.J. had been thinking about his older team-mate with the Generals, B.J. MacPherson, who had been the second-last player taken—283rd overall—in the 1992 draft. That, at the time, had seemed like the worst fate possible. Now it seemed like a great stroke of luck.

By the seventh round the Johnstons had started to get quite apprehensive. B.J. took his jacket off and sat sweating through his white shirt. By the tenth they could both feel a sense of dread. A car sliding on ice, the impact knowable long before it happens. They could feel it coming. Doug Johnston felt angry and helpless. Absolutely helpless.

The eleventh round began and seemed to go too fast. And too often it seemed that teams were taking flyers on players about whom they knew precious little. Florida took a Swede, Chicago took an American high-school kid, Edmonton took a Czech, more Russians, Scandinavians, high schoolers, lots of goalies. The New York Rangers had the very last pick of the 1994 entry draft—286th overall—and they took Kim Johnsson of Malmö, Sweden.

It was over. It was over and the Hartford Civic Center was almost instantly emptied, most who had come celebrating and relieved, a rare few shattered. Doug and B.J. Johnston sat for thirty minutes after it was over, two figures sitting silently in section 115, exactly in the middle of row L, both weeping openly, the father not knowing what to say, able only to hang a big arm over his boy's shoulders and wait until there was nothing to do but go home and try to come to terms with their shared shattered dream.

"I wanted to accept the pain he was going through," Doug remembers. "And I couldn't. I couldn't do anything."

"I felt crushed," B.J. said of this moment many months later, when he could finally discuss it without feeling anger, or shame. "My dream was crushed. Everything I'd ever given for hockey was suddenly for nothing. It was the worst I have ever felt in my life."

They sat alone with their tears and their thoughts. B.J. wondered how he could ever have been so stupid as to come. The two friends he had flown down with had gone high—Wayne Primeau taken seventeenth overall by Buffalo in the first round, Matt Johnson going in the second round to Los Angeles, thirty-third overall—and they had long since bounded up onto the NHL platform with the civic centre crowd cheering their names. They had pulled on the jerseys and the caps and posed for photographs with the commissioner and their new general managers and coaches, and B.J. Johnston had sat their applauding along with everyone else, wondering which jersey and cap he would be wearing, wondering which general manager would say the words he had been dreaming about for years: his own name, followed by applause. "I'll never go to another draft," he told himself. Never.

Doug Johnston was mad at the system. He had been to other drafts and he had felt the disappointment in the air in Montreal in 1992 when all those good North American kids were snubbed by teams suddenly desperate for Europeans. "You can't rate what's inside," he liked to say. And he knew his own son's heart was as big as any he had ever seen in hockey. "Was Central Scouting wrong?" he asked himself. "How could you be listed in the second to seventh round and then not even be considered? Does it not mean anything? And if it doesn't, it shouldn't even be in the papers making all these people think something was certain to happen that wasn't going to happen at all."

They sat and waited, and finally Doug Johnston suggested to B.J. that they go back to the hotel. They lay down, B.J. cried a bit to himself, and then they both fell asleep. When they woke up Doug suggested they just go out for pizza. They stayed away from the hotels and the bars and the restaurants where everyone else seemed to be celebrating. They ate their pizza and went back to the hotel and to bed. Doug got up at four in the morning to begin the drive back, alone. B.J. had a return air ticket and he'd be going back with his buddies, one a Buffalo Sabre, the other an L.A. King.

Doug Johnston stared at his sleeping son before he turned off the hotel-room light, the father standing at the bedroom door as he had a thousand times before, for the first time dreading the future.

A year after the 1994 NHL entry draft, matters were not quite so clear as they were during those two days that ran from Ed Jovanovski's triumph to B.J. Johnston's tears. The first of the top three choices to sign a professional contract was Oleg Tverdovsky, who signed for $5.9 million over three years with the Mighty Ducks of Anaheim. It was, at the time, looked upon by the others as a rather hasty decision.

Ed Jovanovski and his agent, Anton Thun, were still measuring up against Alexandre Daigle's 1993 deal for $12.25 million over five years, but the Florida Panthers would not even discuss such a figure. Radek Bonk and his agents, Michael Barnett and Jiri Crha, were still hoping to reach Daigle's mark as well, but their arguments about his proven performance in the IHL did not carry with the Ottawa Senators. The Senators were prepared to offer around $7 million over five years.

The rest of the summer was taken up with Jovanovski and Bonk and their agents submitting counter-proposals and waiting for what they believed would be the inevitable. But the contract of note went not to them but to Brett Lindros, who signed a five-year deal with the Islanders for $10.5 million, a figure that astonished the hockey world, given the large doubts about Lindros's abilities compared with his brother. What the Islanders liked, though, was the similarity of name, and they believed "Lindros" on the back of an Islanders sweater could fill some of the empty seats at the Nassau Coliseum. Brett Lindros was now considered the luckiest draft pick of 1994.

B.J. Johnston had a tough summer. His grandmother, Doug's mother, died. The threat of an NHL lockout meant that most teams were passing on inviting free agents to training camp, and so he lost the opportunity he had hoped might prove to some team how wrong they had been. In the end, he headed off to the Oshawa Generals fall camp determined to give junior hockey one more chance, and he would see what happened.

Ed Jovanovski went off to the Florida Panthers training camp at Peterborough and performed erratically, some-times with great promise, sometimes demonstrating just how far this still-developing youngster has to go. He was being compared to New Jersey Devils captain Scott Stevens, which only made the contract possibilities seem all the greater. Stevens, after all, had a new deal that was going to pay him more than $8 million *a year*. The agents and the Panthers talked contract, but they were $6 million apart on a four-year deal and the Panthers did not seem in much of a hurry to hire. They seemed content to wait until they moved into a new, larger arena before raising the payroll significantly. They talked incessantly about the need for the youngster to develop in a proper setting—which most took to mean going back to junior hockey.

Bob Clarke was no longer the general manager, having left the Panthers for the team he had once played for, the Philadelphia Flyers. The new general manager was Bryan Murray, formerly GM with the Detroit Red Wings, and was being extremely cautious. "I think Ed has enough presence to be considered," Murray told the press who came to the Panthers camp. "We just have to decide whether it's the right direction for him and the team. What we have to be concerned about is the proper development." There was talk of all the ice time Jovanovski would receive if he returned to the Windsor Spitfires. There was mention of the upcoming World Junior Championships, which would be held in Red Deer, Alberta, and how he would benefit from the international experience. "Eddie is like the rest of us," his father, Joe, told the *Windsor Star.* "He doesn't want to get ahead of himself. I have already told him, you can make $100 million but don't change up here." He pointed to his head.

But everything was changing, and everywhere. At the end of the NHL training camps, the lockout began. The NHL owners not only blocked the season for the next 103 days, the league decreed that there could be no contract negotiations during the work stoppage. Jovanovski had got nowhere with the Panthers and headed back to the Spitfires. The Ottawa Senators, still reeling from an ugly summer renegotiation battle with their 1992 top draft choice, Alexei Yashin, had been trying to sign Bonk to a deal that would be backloaded so as not to offend Yashin, meaning Bonk would not start out immediately making more than the team's one genuine star. Barnett and Crha had turned it down. The Senators put the word out that the deal might have been struck but for the intervention of Bonk's father, Jaroslav. The suggestion infuriated the younger Bonk. "That's stupid!" he said from Las Vegas, where he had returned to play with the Thunder of the IHL.

But Bonk, who had dreamed so long of one day reaching the NHL, could not simply pick up with the Thunder where he had left off. The IHL rookie of the year in 1993–94 was soon being talked of as the bust of the year for 1994–95. He appeared listless, uninterested on the ice. The team's manager, Bob Strumm, had also taken on the coaching duties and soon lost patience with Bonk and began to bench him. In a bizarre twist of irony, Alexei Yashin struck a deal with the Thunder and became the first NHL name to switch North American professional leagues during the lockout. Yashin soon had Bonk's ice time on the power play, and eventually the Thunder headed out on road trips with Bonk. His production collapsed, his value fell.

Even more worrisome for Bonk and his agents, when the lockout finally did end in January, was that the new NHL collective bargaining agreement set a salary cap of $1.1 million for rookies. Those drafted in 1994 would be temporarily exempt, but the pressure was on to sign. Having talked about $20 million in June, in January Radek Bonk and the Ottawa Senators finally agreed to a five-year deal worth $6.125 million. Bonk played no better for the Senators than he did for the Thunder, ending the season with an unimpressive three goals and eight assists and the disenchantment of a great number of Ottawa fans. Oleg

Tverdovsky also began slowly, playing in thirty-six games for the Mighty Ducks of Anaheim and scoring three goals and nine assists, but the Ducks proclaimed they were perfectly satisfied with the young defenceman's first season. Neither young man was even a remote consideration for rookie-of-the-year honours.

Compared to Ed Jovanovski, however, both Bonk and Tverdovsky were having banner seasons. Jovanovski returned to the Windsor Spitfires and did play for the Canadian juniors in Red Deer—returning with a gold medal—but negotiations with the Panthers went poorly through the winter. He fired his agent, Anton Thun, and signed on with Don Meehan, who promised to "get a deal done."

In late February, Jovanovski and two team-mates were charged with sexual assault of a young woman. All three proclaimed their innocence and chose trial by jury. In June, Meehan finally struck a deal with Florida—$7.8 million over four years—but there was little celebration with so much uncertainty surrounding the young man's hockey career. Regardless of the outcome—the charges were dropped in August when testimony at the preliminary hearing proved inconclusive—Jovanovski's life had already been affected. The young man's lawyer, David Tait, said at the time that, no matter what happened after the charges were laid, the No. 1 draft choice of 1994 would be living "under a cloud." When prosecutors sought to blow away that cloud by dropping the charges, Jovanovski could only say, "It really hurt me."

B.J. Johnston was slowly getting over what had happened to him in the Hartford Civic Center on June 29, 1994. He had initially felt he had somehow failed his father, failed his family, failed himself. He went back to hockey largely because he didn't know what else to do with himself. He worked out and he began filling out, eventually reaching 190 pounds. The Generals, however, no longer seemed the place he should be. The Oshawa team had a new coach who kept telling the players and media that the Generals were "rebuilding". More and more, he was going with younger players and rookies, and veterans like B.J. were either sitting on the bench or not even dressing.

By November he had made a decision. He was going to demand a trade. He had only four goals, but he knew he had to get out. He set up a meeting, drove to it, but was kept waiting until they called him in and told him he was part of a package deal of players going off to the Sarnia Sting, a new team in the Ontario Hockey League that was, by far, the worst. One coach had already been fired and the new one was supposedly already in trouble. But it was close to Blenheim, close to home, and it was a way out of Oshawa.

It turned out to be the best thing to happen to B.J. Johnston that year. He went from a team that was passing on him to one that was passing to him and expecting him to score. He scored twenty-five goals for the Sting and, along with the team-mates who came from Oshawa and a third new coach, Mark Hunter, they picked up the rocky franchise and took it to third place in the standings. He ended up with sixty-nine points on twenty-nine goals and forty assists, and his line was the Sting's top-scoring unit. His five-goal performance in one game against the Belleville Bulls was only one short of the league record, and in an end-of-season poll of league coaches he was said to have one of the best shots in the league. By spring there was talk of an invitation "to go to a pro camp" in the fall of 1995.

The 1994 draft was a quickly fading memory. "I'm not moping around about it any more," B.J. said. "I don't even much care any more. There are so many teams in pro hockey now and by being a free agent I can pretty much go anywhere that wants me. I'd rather be in the position I'm in than have gone to the New York Rangers in the fourteenth round or something.

"Maybe I'll even play in Europe. Who knows?"

His father, Doug, felt better as well. His son was back home, Blenheim an easy drive to Sarnia, and he could go to all the games and once again enjoy seeing his son play on a team that needed him and appreciated him. His son even came out one night and joined Doug's old-timers team, and the two got to play on the same line, B.J. setting Doug up for four goals that kept the dressing-room humming with insults for nearly an hour when the evening was over. B.J. was back in the game and everything was going better than they had imagined that day back in Hartford when the father had turned off the hotel lights and quietly closed the door on a red-eyed son. Ryan, the older of the two Johnston boys, had even made first team all-American at Ohio and first team in scholarship as well. He would be going back to play again, and to work on an M.B.A. in finance.

What all this meant came home to Doug Johnston on a cold day in late February 1995 when he raced for the paper to read about B.J.'s five-goal game against Belleville. He opened it and found the story in the sports section, the kid who wasn't good enough in June the new star of February.

Tour of Memory

He can throw his mind back more than a thousand years and it all makes perfect sense to him. He has come, on a grey, drizzling day, out onto the Bigdøy peninsula on the edge of Oslo. At the Norsk Folkesmuseum, he has walked by Thor Heyerdahl's Kon-Tiki raft and seen how the first explorers from the other side of the Pacific Ocean may have reached North and South America. He has stood on the observation platforms of the nearby Vikingskipshuset and has stared at the Viking ships and agreed that the first explorers to head across the Atlantic would have set sail from here and somehow, even without compasses, must have landed at L'Anse aux Meadows in Newfoundland. He has seen the Norse funeral boats that, more than eleven centuries later, have been raised from the preserving muck of Gokstad, Oseberg and Tune, and he has pointed to the charred oak and known that here was where the dead were laid out with their weapons and finery and even their favourite horses, all committed to the gods by those who once believed you could sail on forever.

He has talked about his love of history and the previous visits he has made to historic landmarks from Gettysburg to Auschwitz. He has talked about the family link that his wife, Phyllis, can trace all the way back to Sir Isaac Brock and the Battle of Queenston Heights. He has talked about the letter his eldest son owns that they believe proves Alexander Graham Bell did indeed invent the telephone in their hometown of Brantford, Ontario. He has even talked about the Monday afternoon on May 7, 1945, when World War II finally came to an end, and how the teacher told them they could all go on home early to be with their families, and how, at seven years of age, he had raced out into that bright, promising Canadian afternoon and felt that he could run on forever.

Walter Gretzky is fifty-six now. He is the most famous father in his country, a man who is recognized and whose autograph is sought simply because his son Wayne figures largest in the game that matters most to the people of that country. The story of his son is better known by Canadian schoolchildren than is that of the one who did most to put the country together, Sir John A. Macdonald, or the one who almost tore it apart, Louis Riel. Wayne Gretzky—as this tour of Europe during the 1994–95 lockout will underline—is now the most famous Canadian in the world, largely on account of one extraordinary decade, the 1980s, when he dominated hockey as no one before had ever managed. Four Stanley Cups with the Edmonton Oilers, sixty-one NHL records, including most goals, most assists and most points. Nine times the league's most valuable player. Ten times the scoring champion. Wayne Gretzky, forever young in his blue Edmonton Oilers uniform, "99" on the back, "C" for captain over his heart, the Stanley Cup held high over his head, is a dominant Canadian icon—a glorious hockey image branded forever in the memory of every Canadian. Except one.

Wayne Gretzky's father, Walter, a man who worships history, cannot remember a single one of his son's trips around the ice with the Stanley Cup. He cannot remember the ninety-two goals in 1981–82, the 163 assists in 1985–86. He cannot remember the forty-seven points in the 1985 playoffs, the four goals in one period during the

1983 All-Star Game. He cannot remember the stunning play his son made that led to Mario Lemieux's emotional goal in the 1987 Canada Cup, nor does he have any recollection of the most famous trade in hockey history, August 9, 1988, the day Wayne Gretzky, Canada's hero, became a Los Angeles King.

There is a period back in the 1970s, before his son turned professional, when every moment suddenly comes alive again for Walter Gretzky and stands out in that same crystal brightness that he felt that Monday afternoon back in 1945 when the war ended and school let out early. And there is a period upon him now when he can remember again, perfectly, what happened last night, last week, last month. But in between it is gone, erased by an aneurysm that almost killed him in the fall of 1991. His speech gradually came back, his old memory and his ability to read, and he has been told that, with time, it is possible for the brain to reprogram itself. He has felt the fog lift from certain areas: family, old friends, new experiences. He likes to think that, one day, his brain will come across that closed door that holds his son's extraordinary accomplishments.

Walter Gretzky shrugs as he talks about the lost years. There is nothing he can do about them. He has considered watching tapes of the Edmonton Stanley Cup victories, but he would remember watching the tapes, not the events themselves, and it would not be the same. The facts he can get out of a book. The *feeling* lies locked somewhere in a brain that is slowly rediscovering itself.

"It's like I was asleep for ten years," he says as he stands marvelling at a display of eating utensils from the ninth century.

"It's all kind of like a dream."

Wayne Gretzky had a dream in the fall of 1994. He was going on thirty-four. Having been all but written off with a damaged back in early 1993, he had somehow come back to the point where he had just won his tenth NHL scoring championship. He had a new three-year contract that this year would pay him more than $9 million, making him the highest-paid athlete in professional team sports. This new season, with Gretzky back in form, with his new contract signed, was supposed to be the year in which he made what might be one last try at bringing a Stanley Cup to California while he was still near enough the top of his game. But then came October 1 and the owners' lockout. October became November, with the sides growing further apart rather than, as he had expected, closer together through common sense alone, and an idea came upon him that he might now do something that had been nudging inside his head since 1989 when he had first suggested it to the NHL hierarchy and been turned down flat.

He would undertake a goodwill tour of Europe. He would take a team—back in 1989 he had envisioned an all-star team, but why not now a team of friends?—and he would take the North American game barnstorming through Sweden and Finland and perhaps even Russia and France. It would be good for the game. It would be good for the players, who were growing rusty and bored. And it would be a chance to repay some old debts.

He made his first call to his old friend and assistant captain from Edmonton, Mark Messier, who had succeeded Gretzky as captain in Edmonton and led them to one more Stanley Cup, and who then had gone to the Rangers where, in June that year, he had brought the Stanley Cup to New York after a fifty-four-year absence. Messier was also thirty-three, also bored and anxious to play and, like Gretzky, increasingly pessimistic that there would be any settlement to the NHL labour situation before the New Year. They talked about the players they could bring—old Oilers like Paul Coffey, Marty McSorley, Charlie Huddy, Pat Conacher, Grant Fuhr; new friends like Brett Hull, Steve Yzerman, Sergei Fedorov, Steve Larmer, Kirk Muller—and the teams they could play. If they played in Helsinki, they could have another old Oiler, Jari Kurri, join them. Perhaps Doug Gilmour, the Maple Leafs captain who had already left Toronto to spend the lockout playing in Switzerland, could come up for a game or two. They could make it a bit of a social event as well. Some of the players would want to bring their wives to Europe; they might even include a shopping stop in Paris or Milan or London. Each player could bring one person: a wife, a girlfriend, a friend.

"Let's take our dads," Gretzky suggested.

He was sure Walter would be up to it. The progress, the doctors said, had been remarkable. As Dr Derek Mackesy, the long-time Team Canada doctor who joined the tour just before it left Detroit, put it, "Walter's ninety-nine per-cent back—which is a pretty lucky number in that family." No longer was it necessary to have constant care. The full-time therapist was no longer needed. Old family friend Charlie Henry of Hull, Quebec, was happy to come along and room with Walter. He would be all right.

Messier thought it an excellent idea. His own father, Doug, was also waiting out the lockout. As his son's agent, Doug Messier could do nothing about the $18-million contract his son was looking for from the Rangers—all contract negotiations were put on hold by the league dur-ing the labour dispute—and he, too, was looking for some-thing besides golf to fill his days at the Messier family's new home in Hilton Head Island, South Carolina.

"We'll make them assistant coaches," Gretzky said.

When Mark Messier asked his father, Doug Messier didn't know what to think. Slightly older than Walter Gretzky, Messier was still at the peak of health, a granite-faced man with thick, silver hair and enormous pride. He had no intention of being made a fool of; he thought perhaps it was "some kind of an honorary thing" they were talking about. He had the qualifications—years of playing in the minor leagues, then coaching junior hockey, as well as in the American Hockey League and then in Germany—but he hadn't been on skates in years. His job would be to help former Chicago Blackhawk and former San Jose Shark Doug Wilson, who would be the real coach; he doubted he would have anything significant to do. But when he arrived in Detroit for a small "mini-camp", he found that Wilson fully expected him to work the bench. At the first practice, Wilson even handed him a list of drills they were going to go through. "You do that if you like," Messier told Wilson. "I just want to concentrate on standing up."

Gretzky called Marty McSorley, his friend and on-ice protector both in Edmonton and now in Los Angeles. McSorley, like Wilson, was one of the key figures in the NHL Players Association that was attempting to put an end to the lockout. In his heart—though he would not dare say so publicly—McSorley was convinced the season would begin only at the end of January, if at all, but he had no idea at first if he could go or if he *should* go. Gretzky pushed: he had chartered a plane that would be on stand-by twenty-four hours a day in Europe; the first flicker of a possible settlement and they would be back in less than half a day; Marty could play that night and be at the bargaining table in the morning if he wanted. It was tempting.

"Wayne said, 'Bring your dad,'" McSorley says. "I

thought great, but I wasn't sure I'd be able to go. I didn't want to put Dad in an uncomfortable position. I remember saying to my little brother that I might not be there for him, but then I started thinking. Paul Coffey was there. Charlie Huddy was there. The whole essence of this trip is friends. He'd be looked after even if I didn't make it."

Farmer Bill McSorley had figured on spending the week calculating how much his four hundred acres of soybeans had brought in and how much it had cost him to grow the crop. He agreed to leave his farm in Cayuga, Ontario, and go down to Detroit to see the exhibition game against the Vipers of the International Hockey League on the eve of the NHLers' departure for Europe, but he would only do so if someone would drive him down. A neighbour happily offered, and Bill McSorley had packed a couple of extra shirts into his bag. He also remembered to put his passport into his overcoat pocket—why not? he was going to another country—but there was no way on earth he was going across an ocean on an airplane. No way on earth.

Bill McSorley had gone down to Detroit and out to the Palace at Auburn Hills, where he had seen the pesky Vipers—a full-formed, well-conditioned team well into their season—score three magnificent goals in a row to take a 5–4 overtime victory over the makeshift team of NHLers that still hadn't decided whether to call themselves Wayne Gretzky & Friends or the Ninety-nine All-Stars. His son Marty hadn't made it to play: negotiations were still under way in Chicago. He wouldn't be flying to Europe with the Gretzky team, but he might try to catch up later. It was all too uncertain for a quiet farmer from Cayuga.

All Bill McSorley meant to do was go down to the back of the arena and stand behind the autograph seekers to see the team off. He stood—a big man with hair like new-fallen snow—his hands in his pockets, watching, when suddenly the bus that had been backing out for the race to the airport came to a dead halt. The doors opened and a skinny man in jeans, jean jacket and a baseball cap ran up to Bill and began pulling on his arm. The big farmer kept shaking his head, but no matter how many times he said it, Wayne Gretzky would not take no for an answer.

Six hours later, Bill McSorley was in Keflavik, Iceland, walking around the terminal while the plane was being refuelled. He stood, for the longest moment, in front of a pay telephone, his arms folded, hand on chin, big head shaking gently back and forth in astonishment as he tried to connect the instructions written in Icelandic and Danish and German to those of English at the bottom. He still couldn't believe it had happened. Wayne Gretzky, tugging at his arm—"You come," Gretzky had said to him. "We'll take good care of you"—the bus waiting, the waiting players staring from the windows, Bill McSorley giving a bit and then losing any control he might have hoped to employ. Wayne Gretzky pulling him towards the bus, the neighbour who had driven him down handing him the suitcase, his topcoat over his arm and the passport tucked safely inside. The bus, the airport, the air, the ocean—and now the first foreign country and foreign language of a lifetime.

He stood twisting the big ring on his left hand, wondering if Marty would still make it, wondering how on earth he would ever catch up to them in the middle of the ocean. The ring was from Marty's second Stanley Cup with the Edmonton Oilers, in 1988, a big diamond-studded ring that sometimes made Bill laugh when he looked down and saw it on his thick farmer's fingers that, in more than half a century, had never worn a ring of any sort, let alone a flashy one like this. But what the hell, he thought: "I guess I could put it in a safety-deposit box or something, but I figure I may as well let people see what one looks like." The ring might bring him good luck, and good luck would be the son who had given him the ring. It would all work out.

The telephone in Iceland was but the beginning of this adventure of a lifetime. He was starting to feel glad that Wayne Gretzky had refused to take no for an answer. "This is something, boy," he said as he boarded the plane for the continuation of the flight to Helsinki, "let me tell you."

It was a fly-by-the-seat-of-your-pants operation. Gretzky and his agent, Los Angeles-based Michael Barnett, had contacted various European teams and the International Ice Hockey Federation. The IIHF, with reluctance, agreed to help—"What can you do?" asked IIHF president René Fasel. "He is so famous"—and, to speed things up, they left the arrangements in each city up to the host teams. They would play twice in Finland, once in Norway and three times in Sweden. Russia didn't seem possible on such short notice and with such uncertainty in the country. If there was time, perhaps they'd tack on a trip to France, or Switzerland, or maybe Germany.

They did not even know for certain which hotels they would be staying in at each stop. They had, thanks to Charlie Henry and a contact in Prime Minister Jean Chrétien's office, managed to arrange three emergency passport renewals—including Gretzky's own—and a quick visa for Sergei Fedorov, whose last passport had been issued by the Soviet Union and had been abandoned in Seattle four years earlier when Fedorov had defected during the Goodwill Games. "We're kind of winging it," an exasperated

Gretzky had said the day of the Vipers game. "This is going to be my first and *last* tour."

They landed in Finland in the late afternoon, eighteen hours after leaving once the seven-hour time difference was added. They played the next night against Jari Kurri's and Teemu Selanne's team, Jokerit—Selanne staying with his old team, Kurri dressing for the team now known as the Ninety-nine All-Stars. Jokerit, playing their fourth game in six days, exhausted from a match the previous night to settle first place in the Finnish élite league, put up little resistance. With Grant Fuhr brilliant in goal, Team Gretzky won easily, 7–1.

In the morning they boarded the bus for Tampere, Bill McSorley, overcoat over his arm, sitting in his now-accepted seat towards the front of the bus. He was tired and had his head down when some of the players at the back stirred as they noticed a big man with curly blond hair fly through the lobby and stop for a moment to sign some autographs for the Finnish kids who had staked out the Hesperia Hotel. It was Marty McSorley, exhausted from an all-night flight, but anxious to play. Marty McSorley, "Gretzky's Bodyguard", feature attraction on Don Cherry's endless series of "Rock 'Em Sock 'Em" videos, quite possibly the toughest, often meanest player in the entire National Hockey League.

Bill McSorley did not see his son coming. Marty, having already been informed by Gretzky that his father was here, bounded up the steps and into the aisle and turned so quickly he caught his father off guard, just lifting his head to see what all the sudden commotion was about.

And Marty McSorley, six-one, 235 pounds, with more than fifty hours—3,012 minutes—in penalties, leaned down and kissed the startled, white-haired man full on the lips.

Walter Gretzky sizzles with nervous energy. At times he will stick one foot out in front of the other and pump back and forth like an early rock 'n' roll guitarist, the effect made more striking by his black pompadour hairstyle and skinny, chiselled features. He will rub the inside of his left thumb with his right thumb and right index finger, his head slightly bobbing and weaving as he waits, an over-active nervous system with synapses going off like a string of small firecrackers. And yet he has calmed considerably since before 1991, before the aneurysm. There was a time when Walter Gretzky could barely sit in a car, a time when he simply could not sit in an airplane.

"Well, Walt," said Jack Coffey, Paul's father, who caught up to the team in Norway, "that's one good thing that's come of it then, isn't it?"

"What's that?"

"You can fly now."

"I can, yes. No trouble."

So much has changed since the aneurysm. The erased years have caused time to collapse on Walter, and the effect is sometimes startling, sometimes oddly beneficial. It took him a long time, he says, to get used to seeing his sister, Ellen, again. Ellen Gretzky, who has Down's syndrome and lives with Walter and Phyllis, had been kept on a long-term diet by Phyllis Gretzky during the past ten years and had slimmed down to approximately half her earlier weight. Walter's memory is locked into the heavier Ellen, and when he sees her today it is as if she lost the weight walking from one room of his mind to the next.

This bizarre effect, however, turned out to be beneficial when, earlier in the fall, he felt well enough to return to his first love, coaching hockey. He began helping out with a minor atom team, and though he had worried about it, having been away from coaching so long, he found the return so easy it was laughable. "I remember Wayne and Brent and Keith at that age perfectly," he says. "So there's been no transition for me. I can see the difference like it was yesterday and today." One small difference is that today's kids call him Wally. Their parents call him Mr Gretzky. He tells the kids not to call him any different. "I love it," he says. "I absolutely love it."

There is impairment—he is afraid to be alone for fear of getting lost; too much activity sometimes confuses him—but each day he draws closer to becoming again the Walter Gretzky whom Wayne wrote about in his 1990 autobiography, *Gretzky*: "My hero as a kid was a man with constant headaches, ulcers and ringing in his ears. He's a funny little guy who stays up drinking coffee every night until 3:00 in the morning even though he's got to be at work at 8:00 the next day. He doesn't have to work if he doesn't want to, yet he never misses a day…. He was my hockey instructor. He was also my lacrosse, baseball, basketball and cross-country coach, not to mention my trainer and chauffeur. He's still my coach, but he's also my agent, manager, amateur lawyer, business partner and best friend. He doesn't have a college degree, but he's probably the smartest guy I know. He's taught some other good players, too. He has kind of a funny, pointed nose and a crinkly smile and his hair sticks up sometimes. He can't go anywhere in Canada without people saying hello to him. His name is Walter, but I always call him Wally. Or Dad. I'm crazy about his wife, Phyllis, too. I've sometimes said that everything I have I owe to hockey, but I guess that's not true. Everything I have I owe to them."

It is from Walter that Wayne Gretzky's remarkable politeness comes, and from Walter his patience, even though Walter's patience seems hardly in keeping with a body that hums with chemical energy. Walter Gretzky's voice, however, is soft and slow and unfailingly deferential. He says "golly" and "holy geez" and "gosh" and will sometimes get so caught up in talking to crowds of children waiting to see his son that he will assign himself the task of autograph courier, running back and forth between dressing-room and security area with small strips of paper, hockey cards and pens.

Those who have known Walter Gretzky during the astonishing two decades in which his son has risen from the novice celebrity who scored 378 goals for the Brantford Nadrofsky Steelers to the highest-salaried athlete on earth say that, through it all, Walter has never changed. He remains the Bell Telephone worker who built the backyard rink at 42 Viradi Avenue, Brantford, and taught his first-born such innovative maxims as "Skate to where the puck's going and not where it's been."

His headaches date from the time his son played pee wee. Walter Gretzky's Bell Telephone work crew was laying thick cable one day, with the truck moving as the cable spun off a large reel and was taken down into a manhole. The cable caught and Walter raced to stop the truck just as his foreman motioned the truck to continue. The cable snapped, striking Gretzky so hard on the left side of the head that it fractured his skull and destroyed forever the hearing on his left side. "That's why I'm continually moving this way," he says, leaning his head sideways into the conversation. "I always got headaches, all my life, right here," he says, tapping the left side of his head. "But I never get them any more. Not at all."

Walter Gretzky was painting at his mother's farmhouse in Canning, fifteen minutes outside Brantford, on a late

October day in 1991. His memory of what happened is only slowly coming back. "I don't remember this," he says, "but I'm told I called out." It is fortunate he did, for he was found in time, and an ambulance raced him first to the little hospital in nearby Paris, Ontario, and from there to the intensive care unit at the Brantford Hospital.

He was lucky again, for the neurosurgeon on call was Dr Rocco de Villiers. The brilliant de Villiers had not operated since August, when his daughter, Nina, had been abducted and murdered while out jogging, an unspeakable crime that had galvanized and outraged southwestern Ontario. The neurosurgeon buried himself in the work at hand, operating for five hours on the critically ill Gretzky. They drilled a hole the size of a quarter just above his left ear and were able to relieve the pressure of the bulging artery. Damage had been done, but a life had been saved.

Wayne Gretzky and his wife, Janet, left Los Angeles to be at Walter's bedside, where they joined Phyllis, Wayne's sister Kim, and his brothers Glen, Keith and Brent. They took turns, waiting, hoping, unsure that Walter would survive. For a week there was precious little hope to hold on to. Walter Gretzky's eyes sometimes opened, and it seemed he was looking at whomever was in the room, but he could not speak. He could not even signal to them with a squeeze of his hand or a movement of his finger. The family talked to him anyway. His eldest son told him everything was going well with the Kings. He said he'd had eight goals. (He lied: in the five games that had been played before Walter fell ill, Wayne Gretzky had failed to score once. But knowing how his father worried, he didn't want to cause any more stress if, perchance, he was able to hear and understand.)

Wayne Gretzky tried to express his appreciation for the

work of Rocco de Villiers. "I can't find the words," he said.
"I can't say enough about what he has been able to do and
the pressure he's probably been under and the stress he's
had in his own life." After five days, de Villiers told them
that he thought Walter would survive and that he would,
very slowly, recover much of what had been lost. He smiled
when he told the family that, speaking as a doctor and a
father, he was happy that, for someone, life was working
out as it should.

The calls were flooding in to the hospital. Prime
Minister Brian Mulroney called to wish Walter well, as did
Brett and Bobby Hull. Arsenio Hall and Bo Jackson and
long-time Red Army coach Victor Tikhonov wrote. The
cards and calls were welcome, not only by the father but by
the son, who was then at the beginning of what would
become the two toughest years of his career. In the Canada
Cup tournament that had been played just before the NHL
training camps began, Gretzky had been hit from behind
by Team USA's Gary Suter and he had hurt his back. The
back was not responding. He thought, for a while, that the
one positive result of the vigil at his father's bedside was
that it would rest his back enough for the oncoming season. It did not. He played the remainder of the season, but
his skating was laboured and his movements stiff. He led
the league in assists and won, again, the Lady Byng Trophy
for gentlemanly play, but it was being whispered that he
was fading fast, that he might even retire soon rather than
go on playing.

With his father slowly recuperating throughout 1992,
Gretzky decided in the summer to undergo surgery.
Doctors in Los Angeles repaired a herniated thoracic disc,
and the recovery period cost him nearly half the 1992–93
season. He played dreadfully on his return and was, once

again, being written off around the league. He was described—accurately—at the end of May as looking "as though he were skating with a piano on his back," and the description so infuriated him that his performance through the remainder of the 1993 playoffs now stands as one of the more remarkable accomplishments of his career. Nine months after back surgery, three months after returning to play, he led the Kings on a charge that took them to within a game of the Stanley Cup, which Montreal won—in part because of the critical penalty the Kings suffered when Marty McSorley was found playing with an illegal stick—and which, when it was over, saw that familiar name, Wayne Gretzky, at the top of the leaders' list for playoff goals, assists and points. Gretzky was back.

Yet it was no fairy-tale ending. He was back as a player, but life was far from perfect. His great friend Bruce McNall, the Kings' owner who in 1988 had brought him to Los Angeles, befriended him and become his partner in other ventures, was beginning his long downward spiral that would culminate in late 1994 with his pleading guilty to four counts of bank fraud involving $324 million. His long-time friend and business partner actor John Candy died in March of a heart attack. Gretzky's home was badly damaged and his growing family—which now included children Paulina and Ty—terrified by the January 1994 earthquake in California. His mother-in-law, Jean Jones, who often cared for the children—including the new baby, Trevor—suffered a broken collarbone and leg injury in a traffic accident. He was on the verge of a fabulous new contract and the Kings were getting new ownership, but the team was suddenly so bad that, a year after reaching the Stanley Cup finals, they missed the playoffs entirely. (And would miss them again in the shortened 1995 season.)

Even his greatest moment of 1993–94—the March 23, 1994, game in which he scored against Vancouver and passed Gordie Howe's career mark of 801 goals—was bittersweet, as his long-time friend and champion Howe refused to join in the league celebrations, arguing that the real record would need to include the 174 goals that Howe had scored while playing with his sons in the defunct World Hockey Association. Gretzky, to his credit, refused to get drawn into such an easy controversy—"To me, he was, and still is, the greatest hockey player that ever lived," he said of Howe—but he was deeply hurt.

There was more. He could feel some of his twenty-year lustre beginning to fade. He was, after all, the greatest hero of a country reluctant to praise. It was part and parcel of the Canadian dynamic, and in many ways Gretzky had escaped it longer than anyone who had risen to the top before. "This country," author Morley Callaghan once wrote, "has some kind of an ingrown hatred of excellence. The way to be ignored in this country is to seek and crave and love excellence."

Canadians who achieve international recognition—the singer Anne Murray comes to mind, the writer Mavis Gallant—could relate to what Canadian poet Elizabeth Brewster had meant when she wrote: "Next time I am born/ I intend to come/ from a different country." Since 1988, Gretzky had come from a different country, and he now understood the differences. His children could be children in California, not Wayne Gretzky's children, and that was an advantage. But he was still Wayne Gretzky, forever from Brantford, Ontario, Canada, and in some unfathomable way he was beginning to wear on people back home as he had in novice and pee wee hockey when Walter Gretzky would sometimes overhear parents from their own

Brantford team grumbling in the stands, "Why don't they take the little bastard off the ice?"

"With his Hollywood home," Richard Gruneau and David Whitson wrote in their 1993 book, *Hockey Night in Canada: Sport, Identities and Cultural Politics*, "appearances on such TV programs as 'Saturday Night Live', and his marriage to movie actress Janet Jones—a union referred to by more than one journalist as Canada's 'royal wedding'— Gretzky is both the working-class boy who made good and the Canadian who made it onto the huge stage of the American entertainment industry. Indeed, the Gretzky story is one of 'making it' in so many ways that even the dream merchants of 'boys' own' fiction could scarcely have made it up. In Wayne Gretzky, life surpasses the normal limits of fiction." And for an ever-increasing number of people, the normal limits of others' tolerance.

No image could avoid small chinks over a twenty-year period, but Gretzky's had probably come as close as humanly possible. There were the niggling details such as his now-uncomfortable friendship with Bruce McNall. Not only was McNall being exposed as a crook but he had some time earlier upset Canadians with his brief involvement in the precarious Canadian Football League. It was McNall who had formed a partnership with Gretzky and John Candy to purchase the Toronto Argonauts for $5 million. It was McNall who had then signed American college star Raghib "Rocket" Ismail to a ridiculous four-year $30.1-million deal, $20.7 million of which was guaranteed. The Argos had won the Grey Cup, but the investment was almost instantly sour. Ismail was a public-relations bust; the Argos were losing $3.5 million a year; and McNall, hailed only months before as the saviour of the troubled league, pulled the plug and the three investors bailed out.

Gretzky had also been pivotal in the discussions that had ended the brief NHL players' strike just before the 1992 playoffs, an act that some other players now saw as being too subservient to owners and that, thirty months later, had contributed greatly to putting owners in a position where they could lock out the league. A lockout, they said, would mean nothing to Gretzky, as he had his brand-new $5.6-million bonus from his new contract, regardless of whether there was a season. Canadian fans, furious at having no game to follow, were blaming outrageous contracts and bonuses—Gretzky's being the highest—with taking away the 1994–95 hockey season.

He was thirty-three and could not possibly have many years left to play or, for that matter, to make such grandiose money. But no matter how badly Gretzky wanted the season to begin, he would not get involved other than to say, repeatedly, that he backed the players one hundred percent and blamed the owners for not going ahead with the season. But it seemed he was more comfortable not saying anything at all, a position his friend Mark Messier articulated in an interview with the *New York Daily News*: "Sure, Wayne and I could go in and say, 'Let's do this and give up this and do whatever we need to get the games going.' Right now, all the other players might say, 'I'm glad they got the games going.' But I don't want to sit here ten years from now when players are saying, 'Yeah, Messier and Gretzky sold us down the road so they could collect their money.' So it's a bit of a Catch-22 because this isn't really mine and Wayne's and our generation's war. It's the younger generation's war and even the generations after that."

Out of such thinking grew the idea for the tour of Europe and taking the fathers. A fun trip, with hockey, but away from it all. There was some simmering anger in Canada about how Gretzky would rather go to Europe than barn-storm through his own country, but so what? It was true. He wanted to play at least once more against Europeans, and he wanted to show European fans the NHL that they had been reading about for years. He saw it, he said, as "a goodwill trip." He would put together a good team, but it would be made up of his old friends. They would be an ageing group—average age thirty-one—and they would, obviously, be the most expensive team ever assembled. Had there been a season, on the night that the Ninety-nine All-Stars took to the ice in Stockholm, Sweden, with Doug Gilmour in the line-up for one night, the annual salary level of the group would have hit $57,297,740.

Gretzky knew that they would be regarded back home as millionaire players in Europe on a lark, but since both points were essentially true, what could he do about it? He did not foresee the other criticisms. First, the gossip that came to them: that other stars' noses were out of joint because they had not been invited, that lesser-known play-ers were miffed because they had no option of playing in Europe. Then, the news angle that was pounced upon when Radio-Canada, the French-language CBC, decided to broadcast a couple of the European games back to Canada. Why, the francophone media asked, when there were no French-speaking players on the team? Gretzky responded that he had invited Mario Lemieux and Patrick Roy and he had Kirk Muller invite Vincent Damphousse, but all had declined.

But the explanations fell flat against the second onslaught, which included the remarks of Luc Robitaille, the popular star of the Los Angeles Kings who had been traded over the summer to the Pittsburgh Penguins for

Rick Tocchet, who *had* been invited on the trip. The trade, it was said, had been engineered by Gretzky, who has long been rumoured to be the real general manager of the Kings—he did, after all, insist that Marty McSorley be included in any deal that would take him to Los Angeles. Robitaille, who had been immensely popular with the Kings and who had won the heart of Canada in the spring when he scored the shootout goal that brought Canada its first World Championship in thirty-three years, had been stung by the trade and clearly blamed Gretzky. He dismissed the Ninety-nine All-Stars as a group of Gretzky sycophants, saying the only way anyone could have been chosen was to have been "*un teteaux*"—an ass-kisser.

The anti-francophone controversy quickly vanished, but it made escape to Europe all the more attractive to Gretzky. The love and adoration that poured from the fans was unreserved. In Helsinki, two young girls stood on the street outside the hotel all night long just to wave goodbye to the bus in the morning. In Norway, two young boys stood waiting with blank sheets of paper in the hopes of an autograph, and when Gretzky obliged on his way out from a practice, they ran together down a hill of new-fallen snow, waving their treasures in the air and shouting at each other until the one jumped into the arms of the other and they tumbled like tangled angels into the drift at the bottom of the hill.

Gretzky loved the trip. He loved the clinics when he could skate with the youngsters of each town they would play in. He loved the genuine autograph seekers, not one of them a dealer, most of them with slips of paper instead of hockey cards, all of them saying "Thank you" when he signed. He loved the cheers and the games, and he loved it that his old friends had all agreed to come and that four of them had brought their fathers.

"It's kind of like being a kid again," he said.

In Helsinki the Ninety-nine All-Stars put together a starting line-up that rang through the years: Fuhr in goal, Huddy and Coffey on defence, Messier at centre with Gretzky on left wing and Jari Kurri on right. They were all in their thirties now, all a little slower, all on a downward trend, but there was a moment just before the puck dropped when the left winger, 99, looked up at the clock, back at his defence, across to his centre and right winger and then down onto the still-freezing ice, which, had it been reflective enough, would have shown his smiling face. *This is the way it once was. This is the way I will remember it forever.*

At the end of that first shift against Helsinki Jokerit, he came off and looked to where his father was standing, too busy opening the gate to the off-coming defence to catch his son's look. Walter Gretzky had no illusions. "I just open the door," he said at the end of that first game, "and watch and listen." The next day, in Tampere, he joined his son for an impromptu press conference in the large twisting room off the main arena that houses the Finnish Hall of Fame, a full-sized Wayne Gretzky poster, Gretzky sticks and Gretzky sweaters from past World Championships and Canada Cups displayed prominently among the homages to the great Finn teams and players of the past.

"Mr Gretzky Sr.," a woman television journalist asked towards the end of the press conference, "what kind of son do you have and how did he become the ultimate hockey player?"

The question took Walter Gretzky by surprise. He had sat down at the table only because his son had pulled up a chair and told him to sit. Now he was being asked a question. His son pushed the microphone closer. The father cleared his throat and shook his head nervously.

"Wayne always did like hockey," Walter said, clearing his throat again, reaching. "Even when he was three years old. And it just kind of happened."

It didn't at all. But how could he possibly explain a lifetime in a news bite? How could he tell them about the backyard rink and the tin cans and Javex bottles that he would have his son skate around? How could he explain the value of practising a slapshot off a turned-over picnic table? How could he tell them about the sticks he would set about the ice for his son to hop over while he skated, the targets he would put up for him to shoot at? No wonder the son had once told radio host Peter Gzowski, "When the Russians came over here in '72 and '73, people said, 'Wow, this is something incredible.' Not to me, it wasn't. I'd been doing those drills since I was three years old. My dad was very smart."

Would these people understand if he told them that his son's signature sweater tuck—seen as vanity by so many—came from a father noticing his child was too short to shoot unless that side of his oversized sweater was tucked out of the way? How could he tell these people that he and his wife had once legally given their fourteen-year-old son away, making Bill and Rita Cornish of Toronto his legal guardians so he could play for a team more in keeping with his talents? How would they ever understand the battles that ensued over that act with the Canadian Amateur Hockey Association, battles that left tremendous bitterness within the Canadian minor-league hockey system and, some say, changed it forever? How could he explain how, two years later, after he carefully warned teams that his sixteen-year-old son was too young to go all the way to Sault Ste Marie to play junior hockey, the Soo took him anyway and he had to leave again?

"I try to move my son sixty miles down the road to play hockey and hockey says I can't," Walter Gretzky says of that difficult time in Jim Taylor's 1994 book, *Wayne Gretzky: The Authorized Pictorial Biography.* "Now we don't want him to play five hundred miles away from home and hockey says he has to. They were worried about a fourteen-year-old boy being away from home, but a sixteen-year-old boy is fine?"

He has been asked a question that no hockey parent can answer. He does not himself quite know how his son became "the ultimate hockey player", but he knows it has much to do with idle time and endless practice, that it happened more in the backyard and in the basement and in the neighbour's driveway than it did in any fifty-minute programmed drills at a hockey rink. Walter Gretzky is not the sort who can—or even would, if he could—quote philosophers like Jean-Jacques Rousseau, who believed that "the work of children is play." He has never read Swiss psychologist Jean Piaget, who says, "Every time we teach a child something, we keep him from inventing it himself." But he knows. He knows the value of child's play with no adult present to point out mistakes. He knows his son is special largely because he made sure that idle time was available, but he cannot talk about this any more than he could tell them about different types of intelligence, that his son's true IQ may be spatial and bodily-kinaesthetic and that nothing, not even endless practice and endless play, could bring that brilliance on if it was not already there, waiting to be tapped.

And if he tried to tell this woman what it was really like

some nights, she would never believe him. The question is asked on the assumption that people have been cheering Wayne Gretzky forever, but it is not so now and was never so before. Would she believe that they once spit from the stands at his ten-year-old? Would she believe that it reached the point where, after games, his son switched jackets with various team-mates in the hopes that he could make it out of the arena without being attacked?

Wayne tried to talk about this in his autobiography. "My sudden stardom didn't sit too well with the parents of the other kids," he wrote. "It was never the kids who were the problem. It was always the (alleged) grown-ups. They'd call me a puck hog. We lost six games all year, had our season's stats go up in the Hockey Hall of Fame, and they were worried about how much I had the puck. People would actually come to the game with stopwatches and time how long I held the puck. People would boo me. Once, at a big tournament in my own arena in Brantford, I got booed when I was introduced. That's tough to take when you're ten years old."

Not long before his aneurysm, Walter Gretzky did try to say what he felt about those first years. "No one writes about how bitter parents are," he told the *Toronto Star*'s Lois Kalchman in 1989. "I have been on both sides of the fence and the saddest part is they don't realize they have the best gift of all, a normal healthy boy. They are so busy resenting others who they think are better. They cannot accept that some boys are twice, three or four times as good as their son."

He remembered how glad the parents of his son's winning team were when he sent the boy off to live with the Cornishes in Toronto. He was tired of nervously walking the aisles and overhearing conversations he would have preferred to ignore, tired of his fellow parents refusing to cheer his son. The women, he says, were always worse than the men. And to this day, there are people in their home-town of Brantford that Phyllis Gretzky will not talk to—and will never forgive.

This early experience fundamentally changed Wayne Gretzky and made him what he is today. They talk about his goals, but for every goal he has ever scored he has two or more assists. The unselfishness is a trademark, as is the practised humility in the spotlight. He learned, even as a youngster, to credit the team and say nothing about him-self. He used to pretend he was not even aware of coming personal milestones when, in fact, he was acutely aware of every statistic, every record, every projection. This humility endeared him to many; to others, it grated. But he could not change. He was, by then, as much a product of Walter Gretzky's reaction to other parents as he was of his own phenomenal gift.

"You're a very special person," Walter told his young son when it seemed every media outlet in the country was seek-ing an interview with the ten-year-old phenomenon. "Wherever you go, probably all your life, people are going to make a fuss over you. You've got to remember that, and you've got to behave right. They're going to be watching for every mistake. Remember that. You're very special and you're on display."

"Thanks, Dad," the son wrote on the last page of his autobiography twenty years later. "You taught me to play hockey, yes, but that wasn't the half of it. You taught me to be fair, to do the right thing, to respect people and, most of all, to be a man. Not that it was tough to learn. All I had to do was watch."

But to answer all that in a question session where

everyone was already checking their watches—impossible. Better to say, "It just kind of happened."

The press conference over, Wayne Gretzky dragged himself out to the bus for the twenty-minute ride to the next hotel. It was early afternoon but already dark, and he was exhausted from jet lag and an early-morning departure and a clinic he had put on for the Tampere youngsters. He sat back in his seat, half closing his eyes as he turned towards the window and the passing factories and houses at the edge of the Finnish city, Christmas lights burning in every window.

A sharp turn in the road gave way to a field and two outdoor rinks glowing under streetlights, a gleaming celebration of swinging sticks and darting colours and utter, uncomplicated joy. Wayne Gretzky suddenly sat up, moving tight to the bus window, famous nose pressing against the glass, watching until the outdoor rink could be seen no more.

His voice was wistful: "*That* is real hockey."

A few seats ahead, his father was staring out at the same scene, the same memory.

"When I was a boy of fourteen," Mark Twain wrote, "my father was so ignorant I could hardly stand to have the old man around. But when I got to be twenty-one, I was astounded at how much he had learned in seven years." The players who had brought their fathers on this trip— Gretzky, Messier, Coffey and McSorley—were all of an age to appreciate those words. All now in their early thirties, they had to be thinking about careers winding down, what they would stand for, and why and how it had all begun.

Bringing the fathers along, said Wayne Gretzky, "was part of the reason for the trip," a reason that would grow each day with significance. It was, he said, "a way of paying them back" for all the years they put in when the players were too young to appreciate the sacrifice. All the 6 a.m. practices. All the times the car was cold. The times the block heater hadn't been plugged in. The scraped windows and shovelled driveways and new sticks and sharpened skates and bad coffee. This one was for them.

For Gretzky, who counts himself solidly against the notion that minor hockey suffers from parents' presence at every practice and every game, it was exactly the gift that their fathers would understand and appreciate best. "They love being at the rink even more than the players," he said, laughing about a meaningless afternoon practice where all four fathers could be spotted sitting behind the glass, watching as they had in Edmonton in the eighties, back in pee wee and atom in the seventies.

Mark Messier felt the same. Renowned for his single-mindedness on the ice, he found that, coming off at the end of shifts, he was suddenly acutely aware of how this time it was different. Paul Coffey felt it. Marty McSorley felt it. There was nothing maudlin about this feeling. This was not hockey's equivalent of Pete Rose, who after getting his record 4,192nd hit, looked up from first base and thought he saw Ty Cobb and his father cheering from the stands in heaven—"Cobb was in the second row, Dad was in the first." This was real, not of the imagination, and it was about satisfaction, not longing.

Paul Coffey could look into the stands and see his father and Walter Gretzky sitting together as they had back in Toronto nearly twenty years ago when Paul and Wayne had first played together on the Toronto Vaughan Nationals Junior "B" team, and as they had through the eighties, when their sons were winning Stanley Cups in Edmonton and again, briefly, in the nineties, when Coffey was a member of the Los Angeles Kings before his trade to Detroit. (A trade, incidentally, that had outraged Gretzky and proved, he liked to say, that he was not the general manager of the Kings that some said he was. Even so, the GM who agreed on the trade, Nick Beverley, was soon fired from his post.)

Jack Coffey had joined the tour in Oslo; he had been delayed in Toronto waiting for his passport. "It's awesome," the younger Coffey said. "It's a chance for all of us to play together again, but also for them to get together." They made an odd foursome: Doug Messier so intense behind the bench, Walter Gretzky so humbly standing off to the side of the bench, big Bill McSorley staring down with a huge, eternal grin on his face, Jack Coffey sitting erect, watching behind heavy glasses and an expression that rarely gave away what he felt.

A retired airplane assembler who has lived all his life around Toronto, Jack Coffey was perhaps the least involved of all the parents, by intent. A solid man with a droll sense of humour and deep pride in strongly held views—"I'm the original Archie Bunker!"—Jack did not feel he had much expertise to pass on in hockey. "I never got off the river," he says.

He had, however, played lacrosse as a youth, and coached his only son—there are also two daughters—for a couple of years. It was a happy arrangement, but he knew it could not go on. He found his single-mindedness made him an effective but eccentric lacrosse coach. He could not, for example, tolerate anyone else working a bench with him. So he decided that, for hockey, he would be able to handle only one role at a time. He could coach—though he would come to believe no father should coach his youngster once the child turns competitive—or he could drive.

"I gave one hundred percent to the driving," he says with a wry grin.

His son was a fine athlete, gifted in lacrosse and baseball as well as hockey, and Jack Coffey can recall only one contribution he ever made to Paul's hockey development, apart from the driving. He had long been a devout Toronto Maple Leafs fan and was particularly fond of big Frank Mahovlich, who he thought had a strong, long, fluid skating stride. He told his son to try to skate like Mahovlich, to make sure his stride was as long and strong as possible every time he moved. Jack Coffey's greatest satisfaction was overhearing his son, just home from practice, talking to his mother, Betty, in the kitchen. Jack Coffey laughs at the memory: "He'd say, 'My crotch is sore—I hope Dad's happy.'" Dad was.

The gruffness was a façade. Jack Coffey had one other bit of advice for his son—"Always have fun"—and many years later, on the night that he would play his one-thousandth NHL game, Paul Coffey would recall this as the most important instruction he was ever given for the game. Jack's son—like Walter Gretzky's son—was a phenomenon in Ontario minor hockey, a lithe, smart defenceman who could skate so well that those who once might have looked to Frank Mahovlich took to looking to Paul Coffey. His skating ability became both one of the great legends of the game as well as one of the great mysteries of hockey. He jams size 9 1/2 feet into size 6 3/4 skates. (He would turn to a larger skate later, when the season began, and became convinced that the new comfort was behind one of his finest seasons.) He refuses to use good, new laces and instead insists on worn ones. He—perhaps alone in hockey— insists that his blades be sharpened with no rocker curve to the blade, instead wanting the cutting edge on a flat plane.

Other players who have tried to follow this style have, inevitably, fallen flat on their tails.

Yet to see Paul Coffey on the larger European ice surface is to see skating the way it is usually done only in imaginations. He went over out of game shape, and the stride took three games to come back, but when it did, the sight was worth the admission: one man, effortlessly gliding so fast it seemed he could somehow accelerate by merely willing more speed upon himself. "My legs go, I'm done," he said at the end of the first game in Sweden. But he knew he was far from done.

He was, however, thirty-three. It had been more than fourteen years since he left for Edmonton, described by Peter Gzowski in his evocative book of those days, *The Game of Our Lives*, as "the shy, young Coffey. *The* rookie. Coffey was Edmonton's first-draft pick in the spring, and they expect wonders from him. So far, however, he seems bottled up, as tense on the ice as he is reticent off it." By the end of that 1980–81 season, Gzowski called him "among the most obviously changed of the Oilers. He has finally confessed that at the beginning of the year, when he was playing ineffectually and sitting out as many games as he was in, he was in constant terror of being sent back to Kitchener to play Junior 'A'; because of his youth, he could have been. 'And if I'd gone down there I don't know if I'd ever have made it back up,' he said. The confession would have been beyond him six months ago, when he would never have presumed to talk about himself—or, for that matter, to speak so long a sentence without pausing. Now he is out of his shell, an accepted member of the team."

The shell persists. It was, in so many ways, what made him special at first, a gifted young man with a nearly obsessive manner towards his game. "I guess I knew Paul would have a chance when he was about sixteen," says Jack Coffey. "He was playing for the North York Rangers, and the kids he knew were having a Hallowe'en party. He thought about it, but in the end he didn't go—he went out running instead—and he told me later that evening that he was glad he hadn't. When they start running the streets on their own, you know they're determined."

Paul Coffey followed Gretzky to the Soo and from there to the Oilers, but he arrived wise on the ice, sheltered off it. The team set him and Jari Kurri up in an apartment and, both suffering from extreme shyness, neither would ask any further help with even the fundamental basics of life. Close to Christmas the team trainer, Barrie Stafford, was reading the daily weigh-in charts and noticed that both were losing weight. He looked at the two room-mates and was shocked at how unhealthy they looked. It was only under cross-examination that the team found out that neither youngster could cook even Kraft dinner. If there wasn't a team meal or a road trip to provide a balanced diet, they ate nothing but Oreo cookies, dipped in milk.

Such youthful folly was part of the early charm of the Edmonton Oilers. Wayne Gretzky had a roughly similar experience with his first room-mate, Kevin Lowe. Stunned by the minus-forty-degree weather of his first Edmonton winter, Gretzky noticed that Albertans coped with the elements by letting their cars idle even while shopping, so they'd have a warm car to get into when they ran from the grocery store. Gretzky and Lowe took to letting their car idle constantly, often through the night, and only stopped when they found there was an experience worse than a cold car seat: an empty gas tank, with a dead battery.

"They were kids," Jack Coffey says. "Kids. They grew up together in Edmonton. They learned to play hockey together there. They could make mistakes and they were allowed to learn from their mistakes. That's what made them such a great team." Doug Messier agrees. His two sons—Mark and Paul, three years older—were both gifted hockey players, both bound, he believed, for the NHL. Paul ended up with the Colorado Rockies, a struggling team with an old-style coach, Don Cherry. The Rockies demanded a certain style—firewagon, bashing hockey— that did not suit Paul Messier's style. Financially strapped and desperate for fans, the Rockies had no time to be patient with young players and the mistakes they would make. Paul lasted nine games and was dispatched to the minors, and from there to play in Germany; his NHL career was over before it even began. Doug Messier believes absolutely that if Paul had gone to Edmonton instead, or any team willing to live with young mistakes the way the Oilers were, then Paul would have had a long NHL career as well. "I agree one hundred percent with that," says Paul Messier.

Paul Coffey was selected sixth overall by the Oilers in the 1980 draft. He went off to play for Glen Sather, a coach who cultivated an all-for-one, one-for-all ethos, and the young Oilers bonded as only rare, and successful, teams do: the New York Islanders of the four straight Stanley Cups, the various Montreal Canadiens dynasties, the Leafs of the sixties. It was Sather who took note of Coffey's heart-stopping speed and taught him to jump up into the play, becoming the dangerous fourth man on rushes with the speed necessary to get back if the rush was foiled. It was a new role for Coffey, something he had never done in junior, and it became his game. "Who knows," Coffey has said, "if I was picked by Washington with the pick ahead of Edmonton, maybe I would never have played this way."

He blossomed into an extraordinary talent among such talents as Wayne Gretzky and Mark Messier, but, being shy by nature and extremely reticent in interviews—a demeanour that, combined with his dark good looks, led many to see him as aloof—he was never able to gain the wide acceptance and celebrity of his more outgoing, more confident team-mates.

It grates the father to think that his son has never achieved the superstar acceptance that should have been his for years. Coffey has been three times traded (to Pittsburgh, Los Angeles and Detroit) and is seldom credited by the media for anything but his outstanding skating ability, and consequently his profile has long been sadly out of whack with his achievements. Jack Coffey can no longer listen to sports talk radio or read some newspapers. He lives in a city where the Leafs' Doug Gilmour—a fine player with one award (the Frank Selke Trophy as the NHL's best defensive forward) and two all-star game appearances—has usually been worshipped by the media, while his own son—seven all-star selections, two Norris Trophies as the league's best defenceman—is either ignored or questioned. He can't bring Detroit a Stanley Cup...he can't check...

But just consider the facts: Paul Coffey stands second only to Wayne Gretzky in the number of NHL awards he holds or shares. Gretzky has sixty-one; Coffey ten. He is the defenceman against whom all others must be measured, for at the time of the Gretzky Tour of Europe he had scored more goals (344), more assists (934) and more points (1,278) than any defenceman who went before, including his idol, Bobby Orr. He once scored forty-eight goals in a single season, *on defence*, one short of Gordie Howe's highest single-season total. He has won four Stanley Cups as well as the two Norris Trophies (a third in 1995) and has played in four Canada Cups. He has played more than one thousand games and compiled a personal record challenged only by Boston's remarkable Raymond Bourque, who leads Coffey in all-star selections (fifteen) and Norris Trophies (five) but has never won the Stanley Cup. It would be hard, if not impossible, to choose between the two, but Scotty Bowman, who has coached Coffey in both Pittsburgh and Detroit, has no qualms: "Since he came in the league, there haven't been any defencemen as good."

Jack Coffey, naturally, agrees. In Europe, far from the North American sports media and the carping talk shows, he found he could enjoy watching his son as he had not in years. The thunderous cheers as Paul Coffey was introduced each night, the gasps as he would suddenly fly across the neutral zone with the puck, gliding around a swift-skating European defenceman who could not understand how another player could move so quickly without moving his feet. It was fun again.

Twenty years after he decided he must not coach his own son, Jack Coffey has returned to minor hockey in a novel capacity, still stressing that "fun" is what matters most in the end. His thirteen-year-old grandson, Kevin, is playing pee wee, and the team had asked if Paul Coffey's father—who must, of course, know a lot about hockey—would help out at practice. He would not; but what he would do, he suggested, was save the coaches and managers a lot of headache. He thinks today's parents have gone insane, driven there by ambition and greed and the ever-increasing media emphasis on how much money NHL players are making. "They all think their son is Wayne Gretzky," he says, shaking his head. What he would do, he told the team, was act as "a sort of go-between," operating in that dangerous gap that separates team officials from parents. "If parents want to talk to the coaches," Jack Coffey says, "they have to go through me first. If a parent phones me up and says, 'My kid should be getting more ice time,' I'll say, 'Of course he should. And what would you suggest I do—stop sending little Billy out so your boy can have his ice time?'" He chuckles: "It makes them think."

He thought a lot about minor hockey in Europe. He thought about it when his son joined Wayne Gretzky in the morning clinics, NHL superstars showing eager Finnish, Norwegian and Swedish youngsters, sometimes as young as four, how to take a pass and give a pass and how to do cross-overs and how to stride and, perhaps, how to one day skate like Paul Coffey. It all took him back to those earliest years when his own son was just beginning to emerge as a player.

Over lunch one day, he sat with Bill McSorley and Walter Gretzky and began reminiscing about the glorious Edmonton years. He was talking about the 1984–85 Stanley Cup series, when the Oilers won their second straight Cup, this time against a feisty Philadelphia Flyers team. He had watched a tape of it the week before he left for Europe. "It was great hockey to watch," he said to the table. "They were having such fun."

"I don't remember," Walter Gretzky said matter-of-factly.

Jack Coffey decided to go back even further, back to when Paul Coffey and Wayne Gretzky were fourteen and both briefly members of the Young Nats team in Toronto. It was when the Gretzky Affair over the move from Brantford to Toronto was in full force.

"Remember the first time we met, Walter—that little restaurant on St Clair?"

"No, I don't."

Jack Coffey talked on, about how his son, Paul, had just

been called up. How the team went off to Switzerland—the first time father and son had travelled together to Europe—and how Walter Gretzky's son had been unable to go to Switzerland because the hockey bureaucracy had temporarily suspended him for daring to play outside his designated area.

Walter Gretzky looked up from his plate, smile crinkling. "Yes," he said. "Yes. I *do* remember."

Doug Messier had a far different perspective on his son than either Walter Gretzky or Jack Coffey could have on theirs. Messier had played the game professionally. His own father had switched from farming to the oil business, and he had grown up in Alberta in relative comfort and with opportunities. He could go to university if he wished; he could play hockey if he liked. And he had decided to do both.

He played for the Edmonton Oil Kings, became the property of the Detroit Red Wings and played briefly in England for Nottingham. But he also got an education, attending the University of North Dakota on scholarship and then moving to the University of Alberta, where he trained for a career in teaching. He struck an agreement with the Lacombe school district. The board would advance him a thousand dollars to use towards his education, and in return he would take up a teaching position in the district. But he found he was not yet through with hockey.

It was unlikely he would ever reach the NHL, even if Detroit had retained his rights. But he could still have a minor-league career. He gave the thousand dollars back and caught on with the Edmonton Flyers, which moved the following season to Pittsburgh. He wasn't keen on moving to Pittsburgh, so he was sent to the Portland Buccaroos, where he played for nearly eight years and was able to complete his master's in education at the University of Portland.

Doug Messier played defence. He was a physical player who could score points and, with his partner in Portland, Pat Stapleton, he was considered among the best of the minor-league defencemen. But he quit just when hockey was going through its biggest period of expansion, the NHL doubling in size and the new World Hockey Association starting up. By the time the WHA began in 1972, he was back in Edmonton to start his teaching career. Bill Hunter of the city's new WHA franchise, the Oilers, approached him about playing, but he was thirty-six and he felt it was time to get on with his life. Hockey was over.

Doug and Mary-Jean Messier had four children, two sons, Paul—born in England when Doug played for Nottingham—and Mark, and daughters Mary-Kay and Jennifer. The sons were taken with their father's game from the beginning. They would accompany him to the rink in Portland. They attended the hockey schools Doug ran. They played minor hockey in Portland and, when the family returned to Edmonton and Doug Messier "retired", he turned to coaching his elder son, Paul, who was a ten-year-old novice. He ended up, however, with two sons playing. Seven-year-old Mark came out to the practices and was, already, among the best on the ice. The team went to the city finals that year, and father and sons' hockey careers were, from that point on, inextricably connected.

As Paul Messier advanced in minor hockey, his father stayed on as coach. They were together up until midget, when Doug made a decision that had as much to do with his two passions, hockey and education, as it did with his own coaching career. He established a Junior "B" team in nearby Spruce Grove, and he took them to the Canadian Championship in the spring of 1975. Mark served as stick boy.

Doug Messier's idea was to preserve his sons for a college scholarship, if that was what they wanted. By not playing in major Junior "A", they would remain eligible for scholarships; if they took the usual route to the NHL, they would lose their college eligibility. He wanted them to keep their options open, as he had. "I was always a strong advocate of junior teams and against the major junior system," he says, "because education is not a big factor at major. I tried to stress the positive side of going to college on a scholarship."

It worked with Paul—he went off to the University of Denver—but it was a complete failure with Mark. "He just wanted to play hockey," says his father. At fifteen, the kid was not only good enough to play on the Spruce Grove Mets, he was able to dominate the league. "Everything happened so fast for Mark," says brother Paul. "He was playing Tier II and he was just too big for the league." At sixteen, Mark moved on to the St Albert Saints in a better junior league and from there jumped to Portland in the major Junior "A" Western Hockey League for the playoffs, where he scored an impressive four goals in seven playoff games. He wanted to move on immediately. He wanted the NHL.

Doug Messier had a feeling his son could do it. Edmonton radio personality John Short remembers talking to Doug Messier about his precocious fifteen-year-old star and how Doug accurately predicted that his son would not only make it to the NHL but would be a star in the league.

The reason, he told Short: "This guy will pay the price. Whatever is necessary is what he'll do."

Doug Messier found himself forced to reassess his idea of both sons winning hockey scholarships. At sixteen, Mark was already no longer eligible, having played Canadian major junior hockey. Mark was also so set on a professional hockey career that he could see little reason for wasting time on anything else, including school. "School just wasn't for me," says Mark Messier. "I knew it, and he knew it, too."

Doug and Mark talked it over and the decision was made. "We're pretty liberal," says Mark. "He basically just let us do what we wanted to do." And what Mark wanted was to quit and go, full out, for a professional hockey career. "He never really pushed us to do anything," Paul says of his father. "He let us make our own decisions." The Messiers began investigating the possibilities. Mark would not be eligible for the NHL draft for another year, but he was already over six feet and more than two hundred pounds, and both he and his father thought he was ready at seventeen. The World Hockey Association—by now in a bitter fight with the NHL over new young players—was willing to take youngsters at that age and then, if necessary, fight the NHL in court. Wayne Gretzky at seventeen was off to the Indianapolis Racers, where Doug Messier's old defence partner, Pat Stapleton, was coaching, and the older Messier felt his boy would be better off cared for by an old friend if Mark was determined to do it. By now there was no turning back.

Mark Messier, a centre, ironically ended up replacing Gretzky, who was sold by the Racers to Edmonton eight games into the season when the Indianapolis owners realized they were having trouble filling seats. Mark Messier played five games before the Racers folded entirely—the only cheque he received from the Racers bounced—and he was forced to return to a month of hockey with his old junior team, the St Albert Saints. The Cincinnati Stingers, another shaky WHA franchise, called, and Mark finished out the year with them, playing fifty-four games and scoring only once. But the important thing, the father thought, was that "he survived." He had proved he could play with men.

The WHA died at the end of that season. Most teams were wound down—Cincinnati included—and the Quebec Nordiques, Hartford Whalers, Winnipeg Jets and Edmonton Oilers were invited to join the NHL for a fee. Players who had played for WHA teams were subject to a draft, with Mark Messier going to the Minnesota North Stars, but a deal was quickly made with the Oilers. It turned out to be the best possible situation, for under Glen Sather, Mark Messier blossomed, just as did young Paul Coffey and the other members of the team whose centrepiece was the remarkable Wayne Gretzky.

In retrospect, Doug Messier had done the right thing. His son would go on to win six Stanley Cups, five with Edmonton and the sixth, and most dramatic, with the New York Rangers. Long before the first, Peter Gzowski had written of Mark Messier's "controlled fury" on the ice, and he had, presciently, observed, "So many of the other youngsters take their moods from him that there are those who believe he will one day be the captain of the Oilers." Captain of the Oilers, captain of the Rangers: two Hart Trophies as the league's most valuable player, the Conn Smythe Trophy for his dominating performance in the 1984 Stanley Cup, four first-team all-star selections and one second-team. Pressing on five hundred goals. More than thirteen hundred points.

But he would never be known for his numbers. Mark Messier would stand for *determination*. His father had seen it from his first, ill-fated intrusion into his son's hockey world. Mark was only six and playing atom, and the father noticed that his son, like the other players, would chase the puck down the ice but then stop and stand in front of the net rather than forecheck. "I took him aside and said, 'Look, if you're the first guy down, you *have* to go to the puck.' He just looked at me and said, 'My coach puts the fastest players at centre, and the centre is supposed to skate down and stand in front of the net.' I thought it was a pretty strange response. I'd played pro hockey! I knew far more about the game than his coach did. But that was Mark."

Determination. A force. A presence. He went to New York in 1991, to a team that had not won the Stanley Cup since 1940, and he brought them one within three years. He became a major New York celebrity—dates with Madonna, appearances on David Letterman's show—but he did not forget his role: to lead. And to lead, he helped rid the team of its coach, Roger Neilson, and took charge in a manner in which he at times appeared to intimidate his own team as much as their opponents. The day Neilson left, Messier taped on the dressing-room wall the inspirational words of Vince Lombardi, the late Green Bay Packers football coach who is generally credited with the oft-quoted philosophy, "Winning's not everything—it's the only thing." The team missed the playoffs that season but won the Stanley Cup the next.

He took charge in Europe, as well. The tour's official name at the outset had been Wayne Gretzky & Friends and, at Gretzky's request, had been altered to The Ninety-nine All-Stars, but everyone still referred to it as Gretzky's team: Team Gretzky, Wayne Gretzky NHL All-Stars, still Wayne Gretzky & Friends. And indeed, the star was Gretzky both on and off the ice. But on the ice they could just as easily have been called Mark Messier & Followers, for he set the tone. It was Messier who, in Stockholm, spoke out when it appeared as though this goodwill lark might have the potential to embarrass these NHL stars and their fabulous salaries and impressive records. They had lost in Detroit and in Tampere, where the star of the Finnish victory, twenty-one-year-old Sami Ahlberg, makes only $15,000 a year as a professional player. They had stumbled, but won, in Norway. Now they had arrived in Sweden to play the three strongest teams of the tour.

After the first period of the first Swedish game, played against Stockholm's Djurgården, the first-place team, it was clear that the Swedes were having the better of the play and that the outcome was merely a matter of time. It was Mark Messier who stood up in the dressing-room between periods and caused the room to fall silent. Coach Doug Wilson, who had never seen this effect before, marvelled at how little Messier said—"*Enough is enough!*"—but the effect was instantaneous. The NHLers went on to win 9–3.

Two nights later, in Göteborg, Messier was at it again, hitting hard the first player who moved, intimidating the Västra Frölunda team throughout the game and scoring the final, sealing goal. With four wins, the NHLers could not now be called losers. He had, once again, done the job people have come to expect from him. Finally, Doug Wilson, the team's coach, understood what had happened when, in playoff games between Wilson's Chicago Blackhawks and Messier's Oilers, it seemed at times as if Messier "just *willed* his team to win."

Twenty-seven years after six-year-old Mark Messier told

his father to leave the coaching to coaches, Doug Messier was, much to his own surprise, one of his son's coaches once again. It had been years since he had coached at any level. In 1982 he had left teaching and taken a job coaching the Moncton Alpines in the American Hockey League, but he had not liked it and had ended up in Germany, where Paul was having a successful European hockey career and where they were keen to hire a coach with Doug's experience. But he had soon returned and moved further and further away from any direct connection with the game. His closest contact was when he took over as Mark's agent after the death of Norm Kaplan, but that was about bargaining and numbers, not leadership and line changes.

Even though there was no real meaning to the European tour, Doug Messier was nervous. But soon the nervousness passed and he loved the practice drills and working the bench at games. "Once you're a hockey player," said Paul Messier, "you're always a hockey player." It gave Doug a perspective he hadn't anticipated. He had always known his son's capabilities. He had been at every one of Paul's Stanley Cup victories. Since he had become his son's agent, he had, time and time again, argued in meetings about the merits of his son's play and the intangibles of his leadership. But he realized now that he had no idea just what he had raised and who he was now representing.

"He's just a horse out there," Doug Messier said. "A horse. I can't explain it, but when the going gets tough, he just seems to become *bigger* out there."

It gave his son new perspective, as well. On the ice, Paul could think about nothing but the game. Skating off and sitting down on the bench, he had a new feeling to deal with. One that had to do with past victories, not the win he was trying to will tonight.

"I think about it," he said. "I sometimes look over at him and think how great this must be for him."

Sometimes it's hard to see the McSorley reputation in Bill McSorley's eyes. A big, rumbling man with a slow, rolling gait, he has eyes as soft as his voice: wide-open eyes filled with kindness and trust. They are laughing now—big, crinkling eyes that he sometimes wipes as he tells one of a dozen stories that, over time, have come to stand for the McSorley family's legendary toughness:

"We have this border collie and I was out planting with my son Jack when suddenly this dog takes off after a coyote that was out in the field. He just took off, barking and running and chasing that coyote straight into the woods. We didn't know what to do, so we unhitched the wagon and had our lunch and just waited. Pretty soon that dog comes racing back with his tail tucked between his legs and jumps right up onto the flat we were planting from and turns and starts barking at the woods. We could see the coyote again. He was watching. 'Jack,' I says, 'if I had a gun here, I'd shoot the dog and let the coyote go.'"

According to some of the McSorley children, he cheats himself on the telling. In their version, Bill McSorley puts a boot to the back of the dog and kicks him clear off the flat. "You yellow son of a bitch!" they say he shouted. "McSorleys don't back down from anything. Now get back in there and fight."

Apocryphal, perhaps, but the purpose of the story is to convey something about a most unusual family: Bill and Anne McSorley, farmers from Cayuga, Ontario, parents of three girls and seven boys, the seven boys born all in a row. It would have been eleven children, but an eighth boy died after only a few days from congenital heart failure.

It was a big farm, four hundred acres, and through it ran a canal that would freeze over each winter. Bill McSorley kept the frozen canal scraped and ploughed clean with his tractor and built a storage box down by the ice where he could keep the used hockey equipment and skates he would pick up at sales and auctions. "No one ever had to go without," he says. The boys were welcome to fight over first dibs on the best skates. If the fighting got too wild, Bill says, "I would kind of weigh in and get them straightened out," and then go back to his farm work.

It was a remarkable way to grow up, part Ma and Pa Kettle, part clan wars. The sports and fighting that seemed, at times, to tear the family apart were, in fact, bonding it forever together. "We learned to stick together," says Marty McSorley. "We learned to stick up for each other. We learned you don't squeal on each other. It translated into the way we acted when we played on sports teams. The best way to have respect on a team is to treat each other like brothers."

The kids remember how all ten of them would be crammed into the car for the Sunday trek to church and how one Sunday, coming out, they found the locals had taken Bill McSorley's big car and written "Just Married" all over it. They remember Bill McSorley's love of a good laugh as well as his absolute hatred of television. He didn't need the studies that showed the average North American child was spending 2.5 hours a day watching TV but only one hour for sports-visiting-church-outdoors-hobbies. He did not need American educator Urie Bronfenbrenner to tell him that "the primary danger of the TV screens lies not so much in the behaviour it produces as in the behaviour it prevents."

"If we were watching TV there was hell to pay," remembers Marty. "If we were skipping out on the chores and down on the canal, well, then he'd be more lenient."

The family was almost fanatical about hockey. Wednesday nights and Saturday nights were devoted to the Leafs broadcasts—the one time Bill McSorley encouraged them to watch television—and the living-room would brim with McSorleys gathered to watch the broadcast as if it were, Marty says, "some kind of religion." They played on the canal in summer and up in the old chicken house during the rest of the year, a tennis ball instead of a puck and a couple of nets Bill built for them out of two-by-fours and chicken wire. A neighbour claims, "There's still blood on the walls from some of the games they had up there."

The athletic ability the children got from their mother, who had once been a provincial softball champion, and from Bill McSorley's own father, who had been a local hockey player of some renown and who spent the remainder of his life brooding about not having gone away to try his hand at professional hockey. "Some people, they build on it," Bill McSorley says of his father. "Some let it eat away at them. My father was one that it ate away at. He almost needed a piece of paper so he could keep a list of all the things he was upset about."

It made the old man a fierce, driven competitor in everything he did, including farming, and Bill could not help notice that his father's personality would often flash in his children. He found the old man's hair-trigger temper in his son Chris, who had a minor-league career and is now an associate coach with the Las Vegas Thunder of the International Hockey League. "For Chris it was never hockey," Bill McSorley says. "It was war." "A father is a strange thing," the American poet Robert Tristram Coffin wrote, "he will leap/ Across a generation and will peep/ Out of a grandson's eyes when unexpected/ With all the secrets of him resurrected./ A Man is taken by complete surprise/ To see his father looking from the eyes/ Of a little boy he thought his own/ And thought he had the breeding of alone."

In his son Marty, however, he found a mix. His own big gentleness at times, his own enormous strength, his father's drive, Anne's quick intelligence. It did not show up in school. By the time Marty was twelve, he had his mind firmly on one thing: hockey. Once, in grade seven, his teacher, Tom Brophy, took him to task for not completing assignments.

"Marty," he asked, "whatever are you going to do with yourself if you won't do your homework?"

"It doesn't matter," the youngster replied with total confidence. "I'm going to play in the National Hockey League."

It wasn't, of course, quite as simple as that. If the NHL were filled with those who said they were headed there, half the country would have been locked out in the fall of 1994. Marty McSorley was big, and he was tough, but he was not that good. But because he was big and tough, he had an instant role. The Cayuga teams did not have a lot of players to draw from, and when Cayuga played the other small towns around Hamilton, Marty was given ample ice time. When they played out of town, he would leave the ice only when the referee could tolerate no more.

Marty's early memories almost always concern fights. Little wonder. Cayuga was considered a scrappy minor hockey organization determined not to be beaten by the bigger, often equally tough, teams around the loop. And because there were so many McSorley boys, there were

always one or two on every team. It was impossible to find
a game without a McSorley, and because they were big and
prided themselves on their toughness, they could usually be
found in the penalty box or at the bottom or top of a pile
of swinging fists. The McSorley file is one of the thickest to
be found in the Cambridge, Ontario, offices of the Ontario
Hockey Association.

Marty McSorley remembers a number of brawls where
his father—then in the prime of life and weighing 260
pounds—would have had enough and would simply wade
into the fight, his rubber boots slipping. The son remembers being trapped at the bottom of one huge pile when he
was fifteen and playing Junior "D" and how, magically,
bodies began flying off him until he found he was staring
up into the familiar face of his father, reaching down to
haul him up by the scruff of the neck. He remembers
another battle involving a younger brother, Jerry, when a
team that vastly outnumbered the small Cayuga team was
baiting them and starting what amounted to an ambush.
"Dad came out onto the ice. He broke up the fight and
then he turned and ordered the coach to get the players off
the ice. That was the end of that game."

Bill McSorley would help his son, but he would not
advise him. "Dad never pulled me aside and said maybe I
should try this or that," says Marty. "Never." He offered
what he could: a rink to play on, some equipment and his
undying support for whatever his son wanted.

It was around this time that Bill McSorley remembers
his son's first experience as a labour negotiator. Long
before Marty became one of the NHL Players Association's
key bargainers in the 1994–95 owners' lockout, he was a
sixteen-year-old farm-hand sitting across the table from the
farm's owner, his father. Bill was adamant that his children

all have chores and all do them diligently. And he insisted that they have the proper equipment for working around the farm. Marty and two younger brothers needed new work boots, and since they cost close to seventy dollars a pair, their father thought it reasonable that they pay for the boots themselves. It would teach them value. And it would ensure that they kept good care of them. Not so, Marty argued. "You want us to work on the farm, you pay for the boots. It's your responsibility, not ours." In the end, Bill agreed. He paid for the new boots.

Marty McSorley desperately wanted to make it as a hockey player. The oldest of the seven brothers, Paul, had been given a brief tryout with the Toronto Marlboros of the Major Junior "A" league, and he had become a bit of a hero around Cayuga even though he had come up just short. Chris, too, was a promising player and but for a car accident when he was coming of draft age—someone ran a red light and struck the Volkswagen he was in—his story might have been different. Marty had the necessary drive, and he was convinced he knew how to go about it.

He would make it as an enforcer. He played a year of Junior "B" in Hamilton and then got invited to try out for the new Belleville Bulls expansion Junior "A" team. He set off for training camp more determined than ever. He would do whatever it took. "I had two fights my first morning of camp," he remembers. "I had two fights in the afternoon. I had a fight the next morning. I had another fight that afternoon. My hands were so beat up I could hardly hold anything.

"I called home and my dad came on the line. 'You can always come home, son,' he said. 'There's a fork and shovel in the barn. They'll be waiting there for you.'"

Marty McSorley hung up, iced his aching hands and

prepared for another day of fighting. That next day the Belleville manager, John Mowat, came up behind the bench, patted the big kid from Cayuga on the back and said, "They need your size on this hockey club."

The Belleville coach, Larry Mavety, turned McSorley into a classic role player. He was the designated fighter, the one who would be sent out to mix it up when the coach thought his own team needed a start or the other team needed to come to an abrupt stop. McSorley was eager and willing and asked no questions. Put me out, Coach, I'm ready to go.

Marty was a late bloomer. He attracted no notice, apart from his eagerness, when he was the age when others were drafted into Major Junior "A". He was a fringe player, a role player. But he was still coming. He was still growing at twenty-three, his weight finally settling at 230 pounds. The Pittsburgh Penguins, attracted by his size and willingness to scrap, signed him as a free agent and sent him to the Baltimore Clippers of the AHL to work on his defensive skills. Pittsburgh then brought him up and tried to turn him into a right winger, but nothing anyone could do could help this terrible team—Mario Lemieux would not arrive until the next season—and he was soon back in the AHL. He was "just a big, raw talent," says Bill McSorley.

But then Marty got lucky. He was a throw-in on a deal in which the Penguins acquired a goaltender and he ended up going to the Edmonton Oilers at the beginning of the 1985–86 season. The Oilers had just won two Stanley Cups; Wayne Gretzky was entering his prime; and Glen Sather was still willing to live with the mistakes young men make. McSorley's role was to be the tough guy, but he was also encouraged to play and to develop. Sather even let him practise on a line with Mark Messier and Glenn

Anderson—two swift-skating, hard-shooting scorers—and, gradually, Marty began to emerge as a hockey player. "Marty McSorley was an up-and-down player until we got him," Gretzky wrote in his autobiography. "Pittsburgh had bumped him down to the minors. He was a star with us."

He was also Gretzky's protector, a job he inherited from Dave Semenko. It was a happy relationship. McSorley gave Gretzky ideal protection during his most productive years and, from Gretzky, he learned how to play a game he had, for the most part, been too busy fighting to give the time it needed. "It helped to see great players and how the game was broken down," he told Stan Fischler for Fischler's 1991 book, *Bad Boys*, "how it was played at a high level and the things that were done behind the scenes. It improved my game tremendously because I had the chance to improve and to watch firsthand all of that and try to incorporate some of it into my game. I knew that I couldn't incorporate all of the things that Mark Messier does or all the things that Jari Kurri does or all the things Wayne Gretzky does. But little bits and pieces I could pick up.

"I learned to read the game better. As a tough guy I learned when to fight and when not to fight. I learned there are times when you've got to take a punch in the face, there are times when it's important not to take a penalty, and times when it's important to push back for the team. A tough guy had to work hand in hand with the other nineteen guys on the bench and on the ice. You are a piece of the puzzle."

When Wayne Gretzky was traded to Los Angeles in August 1988, he insisted that McSorley be an integral piece of the new puzzle. (McSorley today insists that the trade was Gretzky and Mike Krushelnyski straight up for the

Kings' Martin Gelinas and Jimmy Carson—and $15 million cash for Marty McSorley.)

In his second year he won the Stanley Cup with the Oilers and played far more than the usual thug role, a role that teams traditionally shelve as they enter the playoffs. In twenty-one playoff games he scored four goals and had three assists, a significant contribution.

They won that Cup in Edmonton's Northlands Coliseum on May 31, 1987, against the Philadelphia Flyers, with Bill and Anne McSorley sitting in the stands. The final score was 3–1, but for Bill, the best memory began only when the buzzer had sounded and the game was over.

"I had been sitting with Anne and I got up and walked down to the glass, right where the Zamboni went in and out, so I could watch the presentation. Anne was just to the left of me and I looked back at her to wave and then they swung the doors open. There was this big pool of water there from the Zamboni and I remember stepping back from it so I wouldn't soak my good dress shoes.

"Suddenly there were all these security people pushing me back and I looked and there was John Ziegler coming along and right behind him was the Stanley Cup. He looks at me and he winks. And Andy van Hellemond—he'd refereed the game—he's coming off and he sees me there and he nods. You know, like he understood.

"Then all of a sudden Marty's there and he's pulling on me. He's saying, 'Dad, you gotta come with me to the dressing-room!' I didn't know what to do. I looked back for Anne but everybody was standing up and I couldn't see her any more. Marty just keeps pulling on me, right out onto the ice."

It was a moment captured live on "Hockey Night in Canada." The big, reluctant farmer with the snow-white hair being yanked out onto the ice by the huge Edmonton defenceman, the older man looking awkward and then, suddenly, overwhelmed by the emotion, his eyes filling with tears as they made him touch the Stanley Cup. The tears rolled down his big cheeks and onto his good dress shoes. He could feel the third-period snow from the ice soaking through. He didn't care. All he could think about was where he was and that his son was hugging him and yelling in his ear:

"We got our name on the Cup, Dad! We got our name on the *Stanley Cup!*"

They found Anne McSorley and brought her into the dressing-room so she could touch it, too. Marty McSorley hugged her and kissed her and told her the same thing: "We got our name on the Cup! *Our* name! You! Dad! All the kids! All of us! Because this is for all of us!"

The season ended and another one was to begin. It was October, a brilliant Indian summer day in Cayuga, a Sunday, and Anne McSorley had an unusual request for her husband. Would he drive her up to Hagersville? At first it made no sense to Bill. They had two cars; Anne never asked for a ride when she could drive herself. But she didn't want to go herself. She had been a registered nurse—though ten children left her little time to work outside the farm—and she knew something was wrong. She had recently undergone a series of tests. "I've got blood trouble," she told her husband. She already knew.

They diagnosed leukaemia, and she underwent treatment at the Hamilton Hospital. At first everything seemed so hopeful, but soon there was no hope at all. The Oilers won a second Stanley Cup in the spring, but it did not hold the same joy for Marty. He could think only of his mother and how long she had left. She went down quickly, and died in September.

When Marty McSorley got his ring from the Oilers, he handed it over to his father. Perhaps, he thought, it would bring him some comfort.

The Ninety-nine All-Stars spent fifteen days in Europe. They played twice in Finland, winning once and losing once. They played in Norway, where they almost blew it against a hastily assembled Norwegian all-star team. They played much better in Sweden after Mark Messier told them "Enough is enough!"; they won twice and lost only once, to a Malmö team reinforced by the addition of thirty-five-year-old Mats Naslund, who had played only two meaningless old-timer games before scoring twice against the Ninety-nine All-Stars. Counting the loss back in Detroit against the IHL Vipers, the richest team in the history of hockey had compiled a 4–3 record over seven games. Not brilliant—but great fun.

They flew to Freiburg, Germany, to close out the tour against another hastily assembled all-star squad, this time made up mostly of second-level German league players and a few better players from nearby Switzerland. The NHLers had flown in thinking more about the shopping than the hockey. They arrived in Freiburg and set off immediately for a seven-hour round-trip bus ride to a Hugo Boss factory outlet for suits and shirts, by now far more interested in what they would be taking home than in what they would be discovering in Germany.

When they played that final night it was a rag-tag contest, with the Gretzky team seemingly intent only on causing as few whistles as possible. They knew they had to get the game over with quickly in order to make their flight, which was to leave from Basel, Switzerland. Under

Swiss regulations, if the plane did not take off by 11 p.m., it would not take off at all. They would be stuck an extra night at an exorbitantly-expensive hotel in Freiburg.

The first goal was an inside joke. At 6:09 of the first period, a puck flew out of a corner, and settled on Brett Hull's stick. He shot, the puck bounced crazily and fell in the net. For Hull—who had NHL seasons of 57, 54, 70, 86 and 72 goals heading into this trip—it was his first goal of the trip. Out of shape and unaccustomed to the bigger ice surfaces, the contribution of the NHL's premier sniper had been nil until Freiburg. After two weeks of frustration—"I can't catch the little buggers!"—Hull's reaction was not to cheer but to laugh. On the Gretzky bench, they broke up.

But they had misjudged the team; they had misjudged the crowd; and they had misjudged the significance of this visit. This may have been a quick trip to a factory-outlet town for them, but to the people of Freiburg it was history. They stood—more than four thousand of them—and sang and waved their team flags and cheered every play, every introduction, every goal from both sides. Those who had been hockey fans all their lives had never imagined that they would one day see Wayne Gretzky play, and not only Gretzky but Fedorov, and Hull, and Coffey, and Messier.

The fathers began to feel that this was different. Jack Coffey kept talking about the rink: ice cold, open doors, few seats. "This is old-time hockey," he kept saying with a laugh. "This is just like the rinks everyone started out in." The crowd somehow lifted the German players. The NHLers were ahead 5–1 in the second period, but then, with the waves and songs and cheering behind them, the locals began to surge ahead. One goal, two, three, four. After each Freiburg goal, the speakers burst with the strains of classical music. It was 6–5 in the third period with the Germans pressing, then 7–5 with two minutes left in the game.

It was time for the Germans to pull their goaltender, but this was not the place, nor the occasion. Instead, the German coach deliberately sent an extra player onto the ice. Under European rules—even though they were playing under NHL rules so they could speed up the game by having goaltender Grant Fuhr eliminate the icings—the punishment for such a "mistake" would be a penalty shot, and the Germans not only insisted on calling it, they insisted that Wayne Gretzky, who has scored on only one penalty shot in his career, take it. It was, one said later, to be a "tribute" to him.

The "tribute" caused an awkward moment, with no one sure what to do. Gretzky skated in and, as he admitted later, he tried to give the young German goaltender a thrill by letting him say forever that he had once stopped Gretzky on a penalty shot, but the young goaltender fluttered and seemed deliberately to let the puck into the net. The crowd roared its approval. They had come to see the Great Gretzky score, and now they had seen it. Final score, 8-5 for the Ninety-nine All-Stars, with "99" scoring the final goal of the night.

The NHL players had not anticipated the emotion that followed. They had been cheered at every stop, but never like this. The horn blew to signal the end of the game and the crowd rose in its entirety and sang to the players. Youngsters flooded onto the ice and began hugging their heroes. In the stands, older men stood staring down onto the ice, weeping with abandon.

"They weren't the only ones," Bill McSorley said later. "They weren't the only ones."

The players raced for the airport, and on the Swissair bus for the ride across the terminal to their waiting charter, Walter Gretzky sat beside Doug Messier, the two "assistant coaches" at the end of their unexpected assignments.

Messier slapped Walter Gretzky's thigh. "Well, partner," he said. "We did all right."

Walter thought about it a moment—a door opening on a new treasury of memories—and then the crinkled grin. "Yeah," he said. "We did all right, didn't we?"

The Promise

Regina, August 22, 1994

They go every day right after supper, the blowing snow sharp against bare skin in winter, the sun soft and soothing in summer. If weather permits, they walk, but weather in Saskatchewan is stingy with permission. They prefer to walk in summer, for there is something about being so small under such a large sky that helps keep things in perspective.

On a warm August evening, the sun over Regina takes on a certain glow as it slants over Wascana Lake and the verdant park that surrounds the Legislative Building and includes a protected waterfowl area. Here is the optimistic prairie light that forever promises better tomorrows, and it plays easily on the faces of the tall, muscular man with the rolling shoulders and the trim red-haired woman who walks by his side. They move briskly, sometimes talking, sometimes in silence, their thoughts already with the one they go to see every night, right after supper.

As they near the lake, a small flock of Canada geese rises and passes over their heads in a ragged chevron. Larry and Terry Hornung stop and watch, shielding their eyes against the sun while they listen to what seems an endless argument over order and direction. There is something so magnificent about these large dark, white-throated birds and the way they slide through the air, something so admirable in the way the older, stronger birds move out in front while the fast-growing goslings follow. The sounds are of parental guidance, for Canada geese are unusual in that the young will stay with the parents long after they have learned to fly, parents and offspring hanging on to something they recognize as protecting. The Canada geese of Wascana Lake are even more unusual, for they do not fly south and they do not go north. They stay right where they are, no matter the conditions, every day of the year.

The Hornungs walk from the townhouse they moved into after the accident to the Wascana Rehabilitation Centre, where their son, Brad, has been living for most of the past eight years. They come in through the front doors and go up in an elevator to where a walkway takes them high past the theatre, dozens upon dozens of people in wheelchairs forming a half ring out from the stage for an evening concert that is about to begin. Men, women, the elderly, children. Car accidents, diving accidents, farm accidents—the sheer number chilling to those who do not come each day, those who, unlike Larry and Terry Hornung, do not each day consider how shockingly frail is the human spinal column, how close at hand lies the impossible.

For Brad Hornung, sitting now in his room, waiting for his mother and his father, it happened—as it always happens—so unbelievably fast that he has now spent eight years trying to pry the seconds apart. Those seconds piled into each other when he crashed into the boards at the Regina Agridome on March 1, 1987. He knows the Regina Pats were on a power play with two players from the Moose Jaw Warriors in the penalty box. He knows he received a pass and began carrying the puck up the right boards. He knows he cut for the net and saw his Pats linemate, Craig Endean, open, and that he dished off to Endean in the hopes that Endean would have a better shot at the goal. The pass was no surprise. Brad Hornung was known as a playmaker. "That," he says now with a laugh, "is what you say when you can't score goals." It is what happened next about which he is still not completely sure. But nor is anyone else.

Approximately six thousand people were in the Agridome that evening. One was Dale Eisler, the respected political columnist of the Regina Leader Post and the Saskatoon Star Phoenix. It was the only game he made all year, much to his regret, for Eisler loved the fast, furious junior hockey of the Western Hockey League. He liked the hometown Pats and the stylish players like the young comer Brad Hornung. It was an excellent game, barely seven minutes into the second period when Dale Eisler saw Brad Hornung make the last pass of his life.

"It was a two-on-one," Eisler remembers. "He was on the right and he passed off across the ice. He seemed to be looking back as he went around the net, looking back to see, I guess. It wasn't a really vicious cross-check or anything. But you knew instantly. You knew."

Theoren Fleury, now an NHL star with the Calgary Flames, was on the Moose Jaw bench when it happened. He knew there had been a hit, but it didn't seem like anything that should have resulted in this. He thought at first maybe Brad Hornung had just "lost his balance." Whatever, the Pats' forward had gone head first into the boards. Simple, instant and, said Fleury, "one of the scariest things I've ever seen."

Ken Edwards was sitting behind the Moose Jaw net when it happened. Edwards, secretary-treasurer of the credit union up in Raymore, had played senior hockey all of his life and was now following his son's promising career with the Warriors. The father tried never to miss a game if it was within driving distance, and it had taken only an hour to come down to Regina. It was a good game, so far, for Troy Edwards.

Troy was at the end of a difficult shift, successfully killing off the penalties, when he made a dash for the Warriors' bench, only to turn back suddenly when the Pats turned over the puck and began another rush. Troy took the puck carrier—the right play—and stayed with him as Brad Hornung cut towards the net. It happened so fast that Ken Edwards was never quite sure exactly what happened. "The kid went into the boards and I expected him to get up like they always do—but he didn't. I felt sick to my stomach."

There were two who were directly involved: Brad Hornung, who went down, and Troy Edwards, who had been chasing. Hornung lost the precise memory of it. He believed, for a long time, that it had happened differently, and was surprised later by the details. Troy Edwards knew the details perfectly; he was surprised by the results.

"I remember it," he says. "I remember perfectly the period leading up to before I hit him. I remember hitting him.… It was a five on three. I was killing the penalty. The puck went into the Regina end and I remember thinking, 'Okay, let's make the change now.' But they turned it up so quick. Suddenly they're back in our end and I didn't think I could make it to the bench in time for the change. I decided to go back. I followed Brad to the net. That's what they tell you to do. 'You go with the guy to the net.' All I remember after that is skating by and looking down. He didn't look good.…"

Troy Edwards was mortified by what had happened. He got off the ice, went to the visitors bench and sat, crouching inside himself, watching just over the top of the boards, saying nothing. No one said anything. The bench, like the building, had gone completely silent. Troy Edwards could see the panic when the trainer got there and the doctors rushed out onto the ice. He knew there was blood. He knew they'd cut Hornung's throat. He figured, correctly, that the young Regina centre had swallowed his tongue. He remembers being so thankful that doctors had been there and something was being done. The kid would be all right. Soon this nightmare would be over.

Larry Hornung was also sitting in the Agridome stands. As soon as Brad went down he stood up, knowing instantly. He had played too many years of high-level hockey—two years with the NHL's St Louis Blues, five years with the Winnipeg Jets of the World Hockey Association—not to know. "I knew there was a problem when he didn't get up right away," remembers Larry. "So I went down."

Larry never got to his son. Brad was already surrounded by the doctors, and the security staff was pushing people back so they couldn't see. But Larry had seen enough to know it was bad. It was as if someone had turned a bucket of blood over onto the ice. One doctor was inserting a breathing tube through the emergency tracheotomy, another was massaging the youngster's heart. A minute ago Brad Hornung had been in the prime of life, cutting towards the Moose Jaw net; now he was behind the net, with no vital signs. The doctors were afraid they were losing him.

Terry Hornung was at home, listening to the game on the local radio station, CKRM. She rarely went to her son's games. She had been twice, but being there made her too nervous. She was petrified Brad would be hurt by the speed of the game and the way Western juniors have of hurling themselves towards nets and checks and unforgiving boards. It was easier to listen while doing something else.

But she knew, too. The silence, for one thing. The radio carried no buzz from the crowd. Dale Eisler remembers: "It was stone silence. It was the strangest feeling. Twenty minutes or so and not a sound—just this enormous pall over the crowd."

Terry was getting frantic. She had no idea what had happened. Just that her son had gone head first into the boards and wasn't getting up. "People out there," play-by-play broadcaster Kevin Gallant told her, "you'd better start praying for Brad Hornung." She had already started.

Brad's grandfather, Bud Miller, was already on his way to pick Terry up at the house. He, too, had been at the game, sitting beside Larry. He knew he could do nothing but get to Terry as fast as he could and then to the hospital. He was already out in the parking lot of the Agridome, desperately running for the car.

A friend grabbed Larry and told him he'd take him to the hospital. They could follow the ambulance. They, too, ran for the parking lot, jumped in the car and roared off with the horn blasting to clear the way. It was a short distance, almost next door to the Agridome, but the trip seemed to take forever. "I was trying to remember every prayer I'd ever learned," Larry says. He was scared. He had good reason to be scared. Ahead at the hospital, the doctors in emergency were once again worried that the youngster was slipping away from them.

Brad Hornung himself had "no awareness," he remembers. Months later, when he saw a tape of the hit, the scene made no sense to him. "For some reason," he says, "I had always envisioned it on the other side of the net." After that, he thought he could "remember pieces. The ambulance. The hospital. The feeling that something's gone wrong."

Something had gone terribly wrong.

Doctors who worked on Brad Hornung as he lay on the ice and later as he arrived in the emergency ward of the Plains Hospital held out little hope at first. The young man's neck was broken. His heart had stopped. His lungs would no longer function. He had suffered an injury of devastating proportions, the effect of which is usually death.

Medical tests have determined that 150 foot-pounds of force are necessary to break the human neck. When Brad Hornung—five foot ten, 175 pounds—struck the boards at a skating speed of approximately ten miles an hour, his helmeted head suffered an impact of six hundred foot-pounds, meaning the effect was equivalent to a six-hundred-pound force hammering into the back of his neck. His spinal cord had been crushed by the force: his third cervical vertebra had snapped on impact and the cord had burst under compression. That he was still alive was due entirely to the speed of the tracheotomy performed on the ice, the effectiveness of the heart massage and the respirator that was able to restore his breathing and keep oxygen moving to his reluctant heart once they got him to the hospital. He was fitted with a halo, which was fixed to his skull with stainless steel screws. He was completely paralysed. But he was alive.

How could it have come to this? The snap of a finger, the snap of a spinal column. Only hours ago he had been a dark, handsome seventeen-year-old with a smile for stardom. His fluid skating, his play-making ability, his drive and his enormous heart more than made up for the size that once made some scouts wonder. He would be eighteen soon, eligible for the NHL draft, and he was already counting on it. People said he would make it, just as his father had made it a generation earlier.

In 1969, the year Brad was born in Fort Erie, Ontario, Larry Hornung was playing for the Buffalo Bisons of the American Hockey League team. Brad was Larry and Terry's first child and, as only first children can, Brad's arrival had changed them instantly and forever. "No man can possibly know what life means, what the world means, what anything means," Lafcadio Hearn once wrote, "until he has a child and loves it. And then the whole universe changes and nothing will ever again seem exactly as it was before." In Fort Erie in 1969, they knew their whole universe had changed. They had no idea that it would change that completely again, in Regina in 1987.

At the age of three, Brad took up his father's game. Like so many good minor-league professionals who had come just short of the NHL, Larry Hornung had been picked up by the new World Hockey Association that began rivalling the NHL in 1972. He had gone to the Winnipeg Jets, moved his young family, and life in Winnipeg was filled with promise. Brad first skated at the Winnipeg Jets' annual Christmas party, a determined, tousle-haired youngster who insisted on going out with his father and the other men who played for the Jets. "He didn't want off that ice," Terry remembers. "He just wanted to skate."

It was a wonderful time and place to be a kid. The Jets were the toast of Winnipeg, and the team's great hero was former NHL superstar Bobby Hull, who had his own youngsters fighting to get on the ice at that Christmas party. St Louis Blues superstar Brett Hull was seven that year, and the Hull children—Bobby Jr., eleven, Blake, ten, and Brett—were determined to use the ice as much as the Jets themselves.

"The Winnipeg Arena was my playground," Brett Hull wrote in *Shootin' and Smilin'*, the autobiography he wrote with Kevin Allen. "The Hull boys were at the rink all the time, always in everyone's hair. Jets practices were happy hour. We were friends with anyone who would give us a stick. When the team finished practice, the Hulls would begin."

Brett Hull today has no memory of Brad Hornung, who would have been so much younger, but he has distinct recollections of Larry Hornung: big, strong, gentle and "a great guy" with the many children who were always around the arena. Unlike some others, Larry never resented the special attention, and extra ice time, given the Hull youngsters and whatever other kids happened along. "My dad ran the show," remembers Brett Hull, "and whatever he said, goes." This meant that even the very young Brad Hornung, like the other boys, could still play on the rough ice at the end of practice and on the fresh ice before practice so long as he stuck to the only rule Larry had for his son: "When they came on the ice, I had to get off." It was a thrill, and a privilege, and he knew it from the first moment he skated with his father.

Brad began in the Winnipeg minor hockey system and, by his own account, wasn't very good for the first couple of seasons. Then, "one year it clicked into me to skate around guys instead of going right through them." Brad Hornung the playmaker was born. His father retired from the game and the family moved briefly to the small Manitoba community of Baldur near the North Dakota border, where Larry was briefly involved in a hotel and Brad was an instant "superstar" in the weak local hockey league. Soon, however, they were headed farther west to Regina, where Larry, a big, easygoing man with an understanding manner found a good life after hockey. He got a job as program director with the Drug and Alcohol Rehabilitation Centre in Indian Head, some forty miles east of Regina. The family moved into the city, and at the age of sixteen, Brad Hornung became a junior with the Pats.

He was only in his second season when he cut towards the net against the Moose Jaw Warriors.

An hour north of Regina along Highway 6 lies the small town of Raymore. It is both typical and atypical of Saskatchewan communities. Typical because of the railway tracks, grain elevators, churches, Elks Hall, post office, Co-op store, Saturday farmers' market, credit union, hotel, Chinese restaurant, streets lined with Manitoba maple, pioneer museum, John Deere outlet, a few garages, a hardware store, a small pharmacy and the "nuisance grounds" on the edge of town. Atypical because Raymore is thriving.

Raymore is the "R" stop on the old Canadian Pacific rail line that no longer stops for passengers. The line still goes through Punnichy, Quinton, Raymore, Seimans, Tate—P, Q, R, S, T—and on west through the alphabet, but places like Tate are remembered now only by the old-timers and the local historical clubs. Tate is now a ghost town, a few rusted cars hidden in the Saskatoon bushes and the tiny post office serving only wasps. Raymore is at the opposite end of this prairie scale: the high school and grain elevators are full. The province has built an extended-care home in the town, and the farmers who have grown old and either handed off or sold off are moving in, meaning Raymore is a rare Saskatchewan town where the population is on the increase. There is a pool for the kids. And the rink is in good repair.

It was to Raymore that a young hockey player named

Ken Edwards came in 1954, the year the town put up the new rink. Edwards was from Lestock—the "L" on the old CPR—and his English father had been a section foreman on the line and, later, a farmer. As a youngster, Ken had been typical of Saskatchewan youth of the time, spending every possible moment away from school and chores on the frozen sloughs batting around hockey pucks and, when a puck wasn't available, whatever happened to be round and frozen and free. He played the same game Gordie Howe played in the 1940s, the game thousands of prairie youngsters played since the 1930s, the game that somehow became part of the Canadian genetic code.

Though Ken Edwards was a fine hockey player, he was an even better baseball player in a rural community that prided itself on the quality of its ball and the abilities of its players. At the age of twelve he'd been invited to work out with the local junior team and permitted to hang around so long as he didn't mind sorting bats and shagging balls. By the time he was of junior age, he was the best ball player in town, a star in summer and a fine defensive hockey forward in winter.

Sparkie Loreth, Raymore's legendary sports promoter, had already scouted the youngster down in Lestock and he invited Ken Edwards to come to town to play hockey for the Rockets, hoping to talk him into staying on for summer ball. Loreth was a character, a man of vision even if the vision spread no further than up and down the railway line. He saw Raymore as the community that would take more pride in its sports than any of the other towns, and he knew that pride would be reflected in other areas and, eventually, Raymore would become the town where new people wanted to settle.

To Sparkie Loreth, improving the team meant improv-

ing the town. He brought in hockey players such as Ken
Edwards and he even hired a playing coach to come up
from the United States. The new coach's name was Steve
Gaber, and he brought with him a new way of shooting—
the slap shot—that was only beginning to make an appearance in the National Hockey League with Bernie "Boom
Boom" Geoffrion of the Montreal Canadiens. The Rockets,
at one point, were well ahead of the rest of the hockey
world in embracing this new shot, and while Ken Edwards
played for the team, they won five provincial senior hockey
championships, an astonishing feat for a community with
a population under two thousand.

Loreth persuaded the youngster from Lestock to stick
around and play for the ball team in the summer, and since
Ken Edwards was pretty well going to be playing sports for
Raymore year round, Loreth also lined up a job at the local
Credit Union. Edwards took both positions, became a key
player for the hockey and ball teams and rose to secretary-
treasurer of the credit union. He came for a season and
stayed forty years in Raymore. "I just loved the people," he
says, still a little surprised that four decades could pass so
quickly. "Here I was, this young kid just out of high school,
and they took me in. I got into the credit union and I
found I liked nothing better than helping people, so I was
happy to stay."

Four years later, in 1958, Edwards felt himself established
enough to ask his old high-school sweetheart from Lestock,
Leonore Nofield, to marry him, and Leonore agreed. Soon
the Edwards were a growing family in Raymore. Todd,
Twyla, Rhonda and Angie all preceded Troy. Robyn, the
sixth, was the last. It was, in many ways, a typical, innocent
prairie childhood for them: school, church and the out-
doors. Ball in summer at the town diamond, and skating

and hockey in winter either down at Stevenson's slough just off Second Avenue or at the rink. The two boys were hockey crazy, playing after school and all day Saturday and Sunday afternoon and even in the evenings with wooden spoons and a ball in the hallway of the Edwards home.

"The slough was maybe a thirty-second walk from the house," remembers Troy. "All the neighbours would be down there, all my friends. If the town rink got chewed up we would move back onto the slough. And we would start on the slough—it always froze up before the rink. We had natural ice at the rink. There would be nine or ten kids in a game. It was a great place to learn how to stickhandle."

Sometimes, if the kids were lucky, Ken Edwards would carry his skates and gloves and a stick down to the slough and come on with them and teach them a few tricks. Because he was a local hockey star, the kids looked up to him, even idolized him. Troy Edwards would later discover that the whole town felt this way about the man who ran the credit union. He was a hard worker and well respected. But he would find that out about his father only as he himself grew older. When Troy was a child, his father was a hockey player first, a banker second.

Ken pushed his kids, but in a quiet way. It was clear that he expected them to excel and to work the hardest, and the expectation—and fear of disappointment—alone drove them. He would work with them, and he would go with them. If the teams needed a driver, he would supply the car and driver and gas. When Troy made junior with the Moose Jaw team, Ken and Leonore would make the two-hour drive for the home games. And after the game, whether in a blizzard or in fifty-below temperatures, a two-hour or more drive back, and up for work the next morning.

A simple, straightforward life. But few large families can slip through life without injury. In 1974, when Troy was only five, his popular thirteen-year-old sister, Twyla, took suddenly ill with meningitis and died. It was unexpected and shattered the Edwards family. It still chokes family members to talk about their daughter and sister. Thirteen years later, the Edwards' tragedy gave them a special appreciation for what the Hornungs were going through in the days and weeks and months that followed the shriek of a referee's whistle seven minutes into the second period, Regina Pats versus the Moose Jaw Warriors, March 1, 1987.

They understood, all too well, the searing, spinning helplessness parents feel when, for the first time, they cannot magically make everything all right again for their child.

Rarely is a parent's desperate urge to fix as publicly displayed as during the televised 400-metre track event of the 1992 Barcelona Olympics. British runner Derek Redmond tore a hamstring running the semi-final. He fell to the track, clutched his injury and valiantly rose again in tears to continue hobbling down the track, determined to finish. By any measure it was already an act of heroism. But it became something unforgettable when Redmond's big, middle-aged father, Jim, burst from the stands, wrestled past the security guards and ran to meet his injured son. Then, with Derek's head buried protectively in his massive shoulder, Jim Redmond half dragged, half carried his son to the finish line.

Larry Hornung was big and strong. He would give his son his legs if he could. His arms. His lungs. His spinal cord. He would do anything, if anything could be done.

But for a long time it was doubtful that anything could be done.

Dr Chris Ekong, the neurosurgeon who had read the initial X-rays and placed the halo on Brad, had been the one to break the news to the family. Ekong had explained in detail. The break, the effect on the spinal column, the fact that Brad would be a quadriplegic—if, in fact, he survived the coming days. It was so much simpler for the team doctor, Dr Gil White. He knew who he was dealing with; he knew Brad, he knew his intelligence, and he knew the youngster's remarkable maturity. He hadn't even started the explanation when Brad forced a question out through the respirator tubes: "How's my brain stem?"

The Hornung family was devastated. Brad's younger sister, Leanne, had fainted when she first saw her brother locked in the halo, with tubes running into his throat. The patient, however, was remarkably calm. It wasn't just that Brad could not move. There was an unusual peace about him, as well. He did not seem afraid. He did not know what the others were trying to deal with at that moment— that he might die within hours—but he did not seem worried.

It came from being young and in remarkable physical health. "Brad once told me," says Terry Hornung, "'It's a good thing it wasn't you or Dad or Leanne that it happened to, because you wouldn't have made it.' He thought that his physical conditioning saved him." Perhaps it had. He had surprised his doctors by making it through the first few days. But that initial surprise was nothing compared to what was yet to come.

Brad Hornung despised the respirator. He hated the sound, he hated how it made talking all but impossible. He had been told why it was necessary—the brain could not get instructions down to his diaphragm muscles—but he was convinced the condition was temporary. "Somehow," he says, "I thought I wouldn't need it."

The machine required constant monitoring and there were always technicians around. There were constant tests—"It didn't work very well," Brad remembers; but, in fact it was his own breathing that wasn't working very well—and he began to be more frightened of the machine than of his own body. Even with the shattered spinal cord, he felt he still had some say in his body. He felt he had none in the workings of the omnipresent, depressing machine.

"The first two or three weeks I was confident," Brad remembers, "but by the sixth week I was starting to wonder. Maybe I *will* need it."

In the third week of April, hospital technician Chris McCuddon, who had become a friendly fixture in the injured hockey player's hospital room—"a very special person," says Larry Hornung—took a gamble.

"I'm going to shut off the machine," McCuddon said. "And if you need me, I'm here."

Brad Hornung stared from his bed, then nodded. McCuddon switched off the power and sat at the edge of the bed, ready to move the moment the youngster showed any distress. The machine shut down, the room going eerily silent, then even more eerily filling with the softer sound of human lungs at work. Brad Hornung was breathing on his own.

It lasted six minutes. McCuddon switched the machine back on and everything went back to the way it had been. But everything had also changed. McCuddon went off to tell the neurosurgeon on duty, Dr Brown, and the doctor came running down the hall to see for himself. "He started jumping up and down," remembers Brad. "He looked at me and gave me the thumbs-up sign."

Suddenly, there was some hope. He could breathe on his own. And in late June, Dr Ekong removed him from traction, took off the dreaded halo and fitted Brad with a neck-support brace. On the surface, things were improving. But reality was also setting in. The traction ring and halo vest had proved ineffective in stabilizing the bone at Hornung's third spinal vertebra. Probably no movement would be coming back.

The emotional story of spinal cord injuries is hope, and even though it runs in each direction it usually crashes. Hopelessness eventually rises to acceptance. Hope usually descends to reality. For those with no personal experience of such circumstance, its pervasiveness is almost incomprehensible. In the United States, some two million Americans a year suffer head injuries from accidents that happen in cars or water, on skateboards, bicycles, football fields, hockey rinks—even sidewalks. About a quarter of that number—five hundred thousand—are injured severely enough to require hospitalization. A mere 3.5 percent suffer some sort of lifelong disability. That tiny 3.5 percent, however, adds up to seventy thousand Americans a year. A college bowl filled with lives that are far too often shattered. A small city of the impossible, each one of them certain that such things happen only to other people.

In Canada, there are more than thirty-five thousand survivors of spinal cord injury. Most are caused by traffic accidents, but sports—led by diving—is the number two cause. Someone's spinal cord is injured in hockey approximately once every three weeks.

One would think, with such a population, that the partially paralysed would have found an easy place on the map, but such has not been the case. The Presidential Library in Washington, D.C. holds thirty-five thousand photographs of former American president Franklin Delano Roosevelt; only two of them show him in the wheelchair in which he moved through the final years of his presidency, and neither of them was ever published during his life.

It was not until the end of World War II, when injured veterans returned from overseas, that North America began to accept that life can exist without natural mobility. Such pioneers as Clark Harrison—a sniper's bullet had paralysed him from the chest down—did much to change the public perception with his speeches and colourful exploits. He learned to fly a plane by hand controls and flew solo to Alaska to raise money for rehabilitation research. In 1988, the year after Brad Hornung's injury, Harrison set out to fly alone back to the same battlefield where he had been shot; he crashed into the wilds of Greenland and survived with nothing more than a cut on his face. He died, at sixty-four, a year later from the flu.

In the time that Canadian hockey was recoiling from the injury to Brad Hornung, Vancouver native Rick Hansen was winding down his twenty-six-month, thirty-four-country Man in Motion tour to help raise public awareness of the needs of the handicapped. "If we don't even raise a thousand dollars," Hansen had said at the outset, "it will still have been a success because we have reached a billion people."

It was a resounding success. Hansen raised $20 million that would go towards public awareness campaigns and helping the handicapped. He took his chair up onto the Great Wall of China, and in Beijing the country's largest department store installed a ramp so others in wheelchairs could come to shop. In St John's, Newfoundland, his visit led to more than forty inquiries on how to build ramps. In White Rock, British Columbia, an elementary school raised enough money to make the local beach accessible to wheelchairs. In Saskatchewan, a program of school instruction on the disabled went into planning, the aim being to integrate disabled students into health and physical education classes. Hansen's visit had been critical, organizers said, but the impetus also came from a massive outpouring of sympathy for Brad Hornung.

The Man in Motion tour was about hope, and Brad Hornung had started breathing on his own only weeks after Hansen's triumphant return to Vancouver. How could Brad not begin hoping?

The moment the technician switched off the respirator and Brad began breathing could be described as a quantum leap in his quality of life. That it happened at all is remarkable, for progress is rarely so dramatic for those who have suddenly become quadriplegic or paraplegic. In a matter of weeks he went from being expected to die to having his own expectations, his own ambitions. That he would want some control over his life is only natural, for the most thundering realization for anyone so injured is to discover, on first waking, that from that point on they are dependent on others as they never before imagined possible. It is no longer a case of deciding to move, to eat, even to use the bathroom; it is, from that point on, a collegial, shared decision of at least two, often more.

Californian Sam Barukh, a former weightlifter who lost his lower-body movement in a truck accident and then became a nurse, once described the feeling: "At first, it was like being a baby, an infant. I couldn't even move my arms. You can't just say, 'Have a great attitude.' It is a living loss, not to feel orgasms, not to have bowel and bladder control, it's a heck of a loss....

"The biggest mistake is someone standing in a full body saying, 'It isn't so bad.' You find out that, at between twelve and sixteen months, people realize that this is not going to go away. People come to grips with that in their own way: some get religious, some get psychiatrists, some get dope.... But my experience is that life is precious, and people would do anything to save it."

Hope is both inspiring and cruel in this world. Failed experiments date back to at least 1874, when an electrode was inserted into the brain of a paralysed woman and the effect on her limb movement studied but not understood. There have been instances when dramatic medical cures for paralysis have been announced only to be found fraudulent after word, and rabid hope, has already been spread.

Real hope comes in minute measure. At the Miami Project to Cure Paralysis—an organization founded in 1985 by a wealthy Washington businessman whose spinal cord was crushed—scientists have been working with experimental walkers that use electricity to stimulate muscles and transmit orders. They study the regeneration of nerve fibres and are enthusiastic about the future injection of Schwann cells—helper cells that key regeneration—into spines that have been severed or severely injured.

Other research projects are looking into transplanting foetal cells to replace lost neurons and new drugs that might reduce damage if administered within hours of the trauma. About five hundred scientists around the world are working with neural prosthetics, and in Europe, "bionic" devices that allow patients to void their bladders on their own are already commercially available. Biomedical engineers in Cleveland have developed a complicated device that gives quadriplegics enough hand motion to allow them to eat and brush their teeth and even answer the telephone.

Long before the Hornung family dared even think about the possibilities science may one day offer, they passed through the cruel reality of false hope. In the early days following the accident, when they were still in the unavoidable phase of wishing everything could miraculously go back to how it had been, Larry would come to his son's hospital room and, each time, gently touch Brad's toe or hand, a small way of saying hello. One day the leg began moving when he touched the toe, another day the arm moved when he touched the hand. Larry and Terry were convinced feeling was coming back in their son. He was healing. For weeks they waited, praying, only to find out the reaction, an involuntary spasm, was common with spinal injury.

It was only when he began breathing on his own that they saw how great small miracles would become for them: the first time he breathed, the first time the hospital staff had him sitting up in a chair when they arrived to visit, the day he began training on his electric wheelchair…

"We were seeing progress," Larry remembers. And, to them, it was magnificent. It was a beginning.

Gradually, Brad Hornung became aware of his new life and began to understand that it was a life with its own possibilities as well as its obvious limitations, even with its own humour. There was even a quadriplegic cartoonist, John Callahan, whose bizarre sense of humour graced his autobiography, *Don't Worry, He Won't Get Far on Foot.* And there were athletes, great athletes like Hansen, who were able to continue as great wheelchair athletes, and athletes like Brad Hornung whose athletic days were over, apart from being a spectator. They all shared the same shock, the disbelief, no matter where or how the injury had occurred. And they all had to realize that it had indeed happened, and had been an accident, and that life must go on.

When Jack Tatum of the Oakland Raiders hit Darryl Stingley of the New England Patriots in August of 1978, both knew instantly—just as Brad Hornung and Troy Edwards knew instantly—that something had gone wrong. Stingley was running a simple pattern. Tatum was making the tackle he was supposed to make. But it went wrong. At twenty-six, at the top of his career, Stingley's head snapped back and, in the span of that silent snap, he was left a quad-riplegic. "We just sort of hit head to head," Tatum tried to explain to the news media immediately after the game. "When he went down there was no question that it was serious. He never moved—never. You can't take a thing like this lightly, but you have to go on playing. You tell yourself it's part of the game, you know?"

Part of the game... Most spinal cord injuries result from car accidents and diving accidents—and, in the United States, from gunshot wounds—but it is the sports accidents that garner most of the attention. Though the result is the same no matter how it happens, there is something about athletic accidents that makes them seem not only more preventable than car or diving accidents but somehow less acceptable. There is little point in blaming the individual; there may, however, be something to gain in the future by critically analysing what happened on a sports field or an ice rink.

In the United States, the sport that attracts the attention and blame is football. Six million high-school students play interscholastic sports each year, and, according to the National Athletic Trainers' Association, some 1.3 million injuries come out of such seemingly harmless activity. More than a quarter of these injuries—330,000-plus—happen playing football, and of these, thirty-six will paralyse a youngster. In Canada, it is hockey. The difference between football and hockey—both contact sports where helmets are mandatory—is that football spinal injuries have been happening for decades and the situation is improving, while in hockey spinal injuries are a relatively new concern for the game.

Ironically, the very thing that is intended to protect against head injuries has a corollary connection to the spinal cord injury statistics. According to a Vancouver Sun article by Robert Mason Lee, in the three decades leading up to 1975, the year the Canadian Amateur Hockey Association made helmets mandatory for all hockey players, there does not appear to have been a single hockey spinal injury in any Metropolitan Toronto hospital. There are no figures from across Canada, but if there were any such injuries they were extremely rare. In 1975, the first year of the helmets, there was one, the next year two, until by the 1980s a pattern of fifteen a year had settled in across the country. In the three hockey seasons that followed the injury to Brad Hornung, sixty-two Canadians would suffer spinal injuries playing the same sport, and a third of them would end up in wheelchairs for life.

The hockey careers of approximately two hundred Canadians have now come to an end through spinal injuries, forty or so left quadriplegic and six who died from the same respiratory failure that set in on Brad Hornung in the spring of 1987. At eighteen, Hornung was a typical victim, for seventy-five percent of those injured are between the ages of eleven and twenty, at the dawn of what should be a bright, active life.

The helmet was intended to stop head injuries in both

sports, which it did. However, in both sports *spinal* injuries increased. When it was realized that in football those injuries were coming from players using their helmets as offensive weapons to butt opposing players, the practice was forbidden, with severe penalties applied. The effect was immediate: instead of thirty quadriplegic cases a year in American football, there were now ten. In Canadian hockey there are about four, but given the relative numbers of participants, the risk of paraplegia is three times greater in hockey than in football.

Changes in equipment have become a double-edged sword for hockey. As players became more "armoured", the style of play changed, the art of bodychecking all but vanishing as the sticks came up and "in-your-face" checking— full body attack, with raised gloves and stick leading the charge—became a taught and approved method instead of the charging penalty that would have resulted in earlier years.

The two players who were closest to Brad Hornung when he hit the boards—Troy Edwards, who was chasing, and Craig Endean, who had taken Hornung's pass—are agreed that the equipment alone has changed the manner in which the game is played. "Since we started wearing eye-shields, the sticks have come up," Endean told a Regina reporter. "Before that, everybody had respect for each other's face." Edwards, who now coaches an élite bantam team, thinks the game has changed radically just in the few years since he himself was a bantam. The youngsters seem armoured. The style of checking that comes up right through the system has changed. The attitude towards size and strength and intimidation has become so much a part of the Canadian minor hockey system that, he says, "the game is going the wrong way." He does not, however, know what can be done to change matters.

Nor does Larry Hornung, who also feels the equipment, the attitude and the lack of stringent rules have changed the game. He speaks almost wistfully of a time when players had "respect" for each other's eyes and faces. He himself did not wear a helmet until his final year of professional hockey, and by then the game had changed dramatically from when he first started playing. Sticks were higher. Players were bigger and stronger. The rules of the game had changed in the way they were called, if not written. He knows today's game could swiftly be repaired by a return to that respect. He knows that eliminating the helmet under the current style of play would be virtually impossible. There can be no turning back.

The problem, as Dr Tom Pashby, the leading expert on hockey injuries and the man who introduced the face mask to the game, told the *Sun*'s Lee, is that "players think they're invincible." But they are far from it. In 1972, Pashby began keeping track of eyes lost because of hockey injuries. And though the numbers dropped dramatically as masks and visors become mandatory, by early 1995 he was up to 284 cases of blindness, usually resulting from stupidity. While the full mask caused a total elimination of lost eyes at the lowest levels, the explosion of recreational hockey—older players, older reflexes, older habits—brought a whole new danger group into Pashby's continuing study.

An eye can be saved by merely putting on a mask. A neck cannot be saved by merely putting on a helmet. A helmet absorbs twelve percent of the impact. A helmet that would protect a player hurling into the boards as Brad Hornung did that night in Regina would have to be so huge and light and absorbent that its existence is impossible. "And that's not realistic," says Pashby. "No piece of equipment is going to protect against broken necks, so players must be taught to play the game properly."

Two years before Brad Hornung became a national story, the Canadian Amateur Hockey Association banned checking or pushing from behind. In effect, the CAHA was reintroducing a rule that had, for reasons forgotten, been dropped from the rules of hockey in 1916. The initiative had some effect, but not enough. The injury to Hornung, as well as injuries to others, caused the rule to be toughened in 1989. As Vancouver *Sun* columnist Archie McDonald had written shortly after the accident, "We can't alter the tragic circumstances that changed the lives of two junior players but we can try to rehabilitate hockey."

One step was the stiffer rules from the CAHA (now known as the Canadian Hockey Association) that made checking from behind a five-minute major penalty and a game ejection. The federal government department overseeing amateur sports ran a dramatic poster campaign featuring an empty net and a youngster in a wheelchair. "The one who did this to me got two minutes," says the boy. "I got life." As well, the Hockey Development Centre for Ontario began distributing thousands of copies of Mike Bossy's video, "Smart Hockey," in which the former New York Islanders star talks about the proper ways to check and campaigns against checking from behind. Bossy's own career had ended because of back problems connected to playing hockey. He had also come to believe that the situation was worsening: "In my mind, there is a definite correlation between violence on the ice and violence in society. I think what it all boils down to is respect for another human being. I think when you respect someone, you don't want to hurt them, no matter how much you want to win. Nothing is worth paralysing someone or killing them."

The greatest influence on minor hockey behavior, however, continued to be the National Hockey League, where
nothing was done until the 1991–92 season, when checking from behind finally became a major penalty with an
automatic game misconduct. The NHL move was prompted,
in no small part, by the frightening check on Wayne
Gretzky during the 1991 Canada Cup when a player on
Team U.S.A. propelled the game's greatest star head first
into the boards. Gretzky was fortunate: he instinctively
put his hands up to cushion the blow. Dr Charles Tator,
chief of neurosurgery at Toronto Hospital and head of
SportSmart Canada, said at the time that, but for this
split-second good fortune, Gretzky would have received "a
serious spinal injury." Gretzky could not complete the
tournament, and his back problems accelerated to the point
where he required major back surgery before returning
partway through the 1992–93 season. Never a fluid skater,
Gretzky's mobility never fully recovered.

Despite the new rules, the injuries still mounted. In
1990, Mel Unruh, a midget "AA" player from Aldergrove,
British Columbia, was rendered a quadriplegic in a similar
check. The fourth and fifth cervical vertebrae were severely
damaged, causing Unruh to lose all control and most sensation below the shoulders. The resulting lawsuit—Unruh
sued the player who hit him, his own hockey club and officials, the Pacific Coast Amateur Hockey Association, the
B.C. Amateur Hockey Association and the CAHA—went
all the way to the B.C. Supreme Court. All defendants but
the opposing player were dismissed, but the damages
assessed against the youngster who hit Unruh with a
"thoughtless, not vicious" check amounted to $4 million.
The settlement sent a chill and a warning through
Canadian hockey.

A U.S. study of handgun victims with spinal cord injuries—like hockey players, they tend to be both young and male—estimated the lifetime cost for treatment at between $4.2 million and $7 million. Unruh was considered somewhat fortunate under the circumstances. With some shoulder movement, he could operate an electronic wheelchair. Bright in computer technology, he could apply his intelligence without requiring much body movement, and this, plus his determination to lead a productive life, may have reduced the potential award. As one of his lawyers, Robert Gibbens, said at the time, "It may seem like $4 million is a lot of money. But not when you need daily care, and not when, in all likelihood, it will have to last the rest of your life."

This is the rub: the dramatics of the injury propel it to the front pages, for a brief stay; the reality of the injury, improved care and modern technology mean that long after the papers lose interest and the name fades, life goes on. A different life, but a life just the same, every bit as precious.

The adjustment is so painful and difficult that it cannot possibly be conveyed in words to those who have not gone through it. When, in 1992, another young British Columbia player, eighteen-year-old junior Bill Zapf, ended up a quadriplegic after a check from behind, his father, Gene, put into words what all hockey families must feel when they go through this rare, but so very real, trauma: "If this had happened in a car accident, I might be able to accept it. It would be easier to take. But not like this. Not on the ice. This is supposed to be a game."

The game of March 1, 1987, began again not long after the ambulance carrying Brad Hornung had sped off to Plains Hospital. The referee had seen the play behind the net, but he hadn't called a penalty on it. Perhaps, like so many others in the building that night, he wasn't exactly sure what he had seen. The game continued. Moose Jaw killed off the remaining time on the penalties and went on to win 6-3. But no one took any joy in it. "I just felt sick," Ken Edwards remembers. "Sick." So, too, did six thousand others.

Troy Edwards couldn't even keep track of the score. All he could think about was Brad. During a break in play towards the end of the game, the word he was praying for came back. "I heard he was okay," Edwards says. "Someone told me he was sitting up. I felt so high—he's *okay*! Then the next report was that he'd broken his neck. I went down to the ultimate low."

Troy went home to Raymore for a few days. His Moose Jaw team-mate and close friend, Kevin Herom, drove him and stayed the first few days with him. Troy stayed secluded in his parents' house and refused to let anyone see or talk to him. "I wanted to put it in perspective," he says. "I had to understand how my life would change because of this. I knew it would be dramatically—but not the way it did."

He tried to stay away from the news but it was hopeless. He was the news. Brad Hornung was the news. Yet, except in the eyes of sportswriter Gregg Drinnan of the Regina *Leader Post*, it seemed they were but bit players in a larger story. Drinnan had written with compassion for the two young men. Others had written with passion as they attacked the game, attacked the system that allowed something like this to happen, attacked Edwards as a dumb product of the system who was himself being controlled by the system. And it was not a local story; it had become a national story, with feature coverage everywhere from television to *Maclean's* magazine. The national stories, however, always seemed to attack the game. Troy Edwards could not read them. Some his family kept from him. But he saw enough to forever lose respect for journalists.

"They have a story to do, I know that," he says eight years later. "But a lot don't take into consideration the human factor. Not just me, but for Brad, too. They were just using us to make the game look bad."

The coverage made no sense to him. He was the villain, even though he had never intended to hurt anyone. As a kid, he had always been the one coming to the rescue of those being bullied, those in need. "I was always the one who would jump in," he says. "I took more abuse myself than I would let others take." And he says, with a full appreciation of the terrible irony in saying so: "I hate to see others get hurt."

He hated, in particular, what the public debate was doing to Brad Hornung. If Edwards had become the villain, then Hornung had become not only the victim but a statistic rather than a person, an incident rather than a human. "Here you've got a guy paralysed for life," Edwards says. "And they're making a big deal out of it for what it means to hockey—not to him."

Troy Edwards decided he would quit hockey. After the Moose Jaw–Regina game, he would never again play. That was it. He could never go back. His father, Ken, did not like to hear this, but he had no idea what to do about it. So he talked with an old friend, Wayne Back, who said that it was important to think about how some good might come of something so terrible. Perhaps Troy could help someone. Perhaps there would be some educational value in this tragedy. If it could prevent another incident, then something of value would have been gained. Ken Edwards told this to his son, but Troy didn't see how there could be any value in what had happened.

A few days later an old coach of Troy's, Gord McMurchy from nearby Semans, called on the Edwards house. He and Troy chatted casually and, of course, the conversation got around to Brad and how he was doing in the hospital. "I'd like to see him," said Troy. McMurchy said that sounded like an excellent idea. He said he'd been reading an article about a pro football player who "always wondered why that guy who hit him never came to see him." It wouldn't be right if Brad ever wondered the same thing.

Troy contacted Doug Sauter, Brad's coach with the Pats. Sauter had seen the tragedy for what it was and had said so publicly: "There are three victims here—Brad, Troy and the game of hockey." He was the perfect person to engineer a meeting. It had to be quiet, no one in the press could ever know, no one at the hospital should know, but Brad Hornung would have to agree. "Doug Sauter is a big, burly guy," says Edwards. "You'd probably think not very emotional." But in fact he is very emotional. Even before they reached the hospital room, the big coach was in tears.

It had to be a short visit. Brad had little strength; there were tubes everywhere and the dreaded respirator sighed by the side of the bed. With Sauter's hand on his shoulder, Troy Edwards walked to the bed, looked down at the young player staring back and tried to say something. But it was Hornung who wanted to speak, even though he wasn't supposed to talk.

"He looked at me," Troy remembers, pausing for breath. "He could barely talk. I could barely hear him. He told me… 'Keep playing. Don't quit.'"

Brad Hornung remembers the moment as well: his big coach there crying, and Troy Edwards, tears in his eyes, sorry, but *there*. "I was glad that he was able to do that," says Brad. "I could see that he was hurting. I felt bad for him."

Perhaps the most remarkable part of this story is how Brad was able to accept what had happened without bitterness. He could not blame Troy Edwards, as a few others had. He could not even blame the game, as so many others had. "It didn't even cross my mind," he says. Resentment, he says, "is unnatural. I don't even know where it comes from."

"Brad was raised to be a lot more mature than that, I hope," Larry adds.

Maturity is one thing. Acceptance is another. In many ways, Brad Hornung handled it better than anyone else in the family. His parents had cried and prayed and would wake in the middle of the night and not be able to go back to sleep for wondering what they could have done to make it so this would never have happened, what they could do now to take it back to the way it was.

"For the first time," Larry says, "it dawned on me that one of my kids might have a problem I can't fix."

Yet the greatest neurosurgeons in the world could not fix it. Love could not fix it. The feeling of helplessness, of doing the wrong thing out of love alone, is always with us. All a family could do was comfort and be there. They could be there, and feed him, and help him adjust, but they would have to adjust, as well. And it is never easy, not for anyone.

"It's like a broken heart," says Terry Hornung. "A pain in your heart."

Larry squeezes his hands, hoping to somehow form the words that cannot possibly tell what it was like.

"It's like a hole right through you," he says finally. "A

hole right through you—and a cold wind blowing through."

It took Troy Edwards years to come to terms, even partial terms, with what had happened. From March 1, 1987, on, not a single day passed without him thinking about Brad Hornung. He would pull up in a shopping area and the mere sight of the blue-and-white sign for handicapped parking would send him back to that night in the Agridome. Why was he able to park where he wanted and run in whenever he wished? What struck Troy as a five-minute inconvenience—running down to the convenience store for a paper—would require days of planning for Brad Hornung.

Because of what Brad said to him that day in the hospital room, Troy Edwards eventually came to terms with returning to hockey. It was his game, after all, the game he loved. And his anger with the media had to do with them using Brad and him to attack the game, after all. The game was just a game—like Doug Sauter said, the third "victim" in this thing—and his leaving it would only justify those who said the system had created this situation. The system hadn't. God hadn't. It had just happened and would never be fully understood by anyone.

He played out his junior year and, as a twenty-year-old, got an invite to the Edmonton Oilers camp that fall. The 1987 Canada Cup had been played earlier that month, and several of the Edmonton stars—Wayne Gretzky, Mark Messier, Paul Coffey—were missing from camp, but it was still the thrill of a lifetime for the youngster. One day coach Glen Sather put Edwards on a line with Marty McSorley and Jari Kurri; he can remember every second of every drill they tried.

The Oilers liked Edwards enough to send him down to their Cape Breton farm team for a longer look. But he still had no contract offer. He was big enough for professional hockey—just over five-ten and 205 pounds—but, again in Cape Breton, he wasn't quite there. "I could pass and score okay," he says, "but just okay. I didn't make it for a reason. I could do a few things good. I could do everything fairly well. But I couldn't take it to that next step. It was close."

He went home and then, for several months, he went off to play in the International Hockey League for the Milwaukee Admirals, but it was not a pleasant experience. "We were brutal," he says. "We were losing every game. Everybody was down in the dumps. I figured there has got to be more than that to life." He decided to quit and look for something else. "The day I quit pro hockey," he says, "I think my dad felt bad."

He enrolled at the University of Regina, playing hockey for the varsity team and working on his degree in business administration. He got a job in pharmaceutical sales and began playing senior hockey for his father's old team, the Raymore Rockets. The Rockets were delighted, and pulled out the No. 4 sweater for the third time. Ken Edwards had worn the number for seventeen years and, when he retired as a player in 1971, the team had quite appropriately retired his number. They took it out of retirement when Todd Edwards joined the team a few years later, and after Todd wore No. 4 while winning two more provincial championships for the Rockets, they put it away again. When Troy Edwards came back home to play senior hockey, it seemed only right that he wear the family number, and only proper, as well, that another provincial championship soon followed.

Ken Edwards still remembers what it feels like to hear a

cheer rise in the Raymore rink after a goal, the way it seemed to burst into the rafters. After he retired from hockey he stayed on at the credit union and was delighted when his hockey-playing sons came back to wear his number and hear the same delighted, appreciative hometown cheers that had once been meant for him.

Like any player of achievement, Ken Edwards had come to love that sound. But after Troy came back to play for the Rockets and the team headed out of town to play in one of the other Saskatchewan communities that are renowned for their good character and decency and kindness, there was a new sound, one that cut so deep to the bone that Ken Edwards soon began to wonder how his son could go on playing.

He had never heard such things before. He could not even say what it was they were saying except to pass the comments off as catcalls. He could not himself repeat what others—often the very people he had dealt with when they were buying new machinery or selling off a quarter section—were shouting at his son. Women with white hair, older couples with, surely, children of their own and their own heartaches. Grown men with their own real and never-realized dreams. Churchgoers hanging over the boards and screaming, *screaming*.

"*Killer!*"

"*Backstabber!*"

"*MAIMER!!*"

Troy Edwards heard the very first call, and heard every call that followed. He was devastated. He tried to shut them out, but could not. He could not believe what they were saying any more than, when he looked into the crowd, he could believe who was doing the yelling. They looked like the people he had grown up around. They *were* the people he had grown up around.

"I'm a twenty-one-year-old kid trying to come to grips with what had happened," he says, "and I couldn't understand how people could be so mean—just to try and get someone off their game."

The shock was so great, particularly the attacks from older people, that he says he eventually "lost respect for the human race." He believed for a long time that it was a passing thing, that eventually the name calling would stop, but it did not stop. It got worse, the seething crowds convinced they were getting to the star of the powerful Rockets. They were.

After four years he had come to the conclusion that the game he loved was, in this situation, unlovable. "The doors are closing on me," he said. He began to plan his retirement from senior hockey.

How could it not get to him? The opponents he found on the ice he could deal with. If they try to hurt you, you slip out of the way. If they do something illegal, then the officials, if they are doing their job, will catch them. You can answer back with passes and checks and goals, your final statement on the scoreboard. But how do you keep the others out of your head? How, when they scream all night from the stands and are still screaming when you hurry out into the parking lot? What can you do but throw your equipment and sticks in the trunk, slam the door tight, keep the windows up and drive away from it—perhaps for ever? The others could drive back home thinking of how the game went; every night, without exception, Troy Edwards drove home thinking of Brad Hornung.

It was years before he could talk about how he felt with anyone but family and closest friends. His old hockey friends who went on to professional careers—Theoren

Fleury, with the Calgary Flames, Mike Keane and Chris Odelein with the Montreal Canadiens—seemed to understand best of all. They knew how easily it could happen. They had all been in situations when there is contact, and one goes down, and all know that quick rush of private relief when they see there is movement in the one left lying on the ice.

Troy Edwards travelled constantly in his jobs, first as a pharmaceutical representative, and now as a sales representative for Labatt Breweries. He had so much time to think, and he slowly came to a realization that much of his problem in dealing with what had happened had been the lack of anyone with direct experience to tell him what to expect. In those first few days at home in Raymore, he had convinced himself that this memory, like all memories, would fade with time, the pain would ease. Never for a moment did he suspect it would take on sharper edges with time and hurt in ways he could never then imagine. If only he had spoken with someone who would understand, not just sympathize. He had no one. But perhaps, he began to wonder, he might be able to help someone else.

On March 15, 1994, another Moose Jaw player, Jason Yaganiski of the junior Canucks, cross-checked seventeen-year-old John Millikin of the Notre Dame Hounds, and Millikin spilled head first into the boards, snapping his neck in much the same fashion as Brad Hornung. Millikin, too, was left a quadriplegic.

The story rang with cringing familiarity. Young Millikin's mother, Susan, at home when the phone call came in with the terrible news: her son had suffered a fractured fifth cervical vertebra. Her reaction: "You kept thinking, 'Maybe, maybe, maybe…maybe it's not as bad as they say.' But it was. It's happened. You can't look back."

When *Calgary Herald* sportswriter Tom Keyser spoke to the injured young man, Millikin sounded like a young Brad Hornung, worried about how terrible Yaganiski felt. "He didn't mean it to happen," Millikin said. "But it did." The injury had, once again, rekindled the debate over checking from behind. "They can't make kids like John a quadriplegic and then just say: 'That's the way it is,'" said Susan Millikin. "Hockey's a great game, but it doesn't need checking from behind. It has to be stopped. And it will be stopped."

The parallels were remarkable. The injury, the forgiveness, the debate. Millikin, like Hornung, had even weathered an early crisis in which he had stopped breathing. The prime minister had called. Bobby Orr and Don Cherry had written. Calgary Flames captain Joe Nieuwendyk had come twice to visit and talk. A trust was under way and a fundraising dinner being planned. "He's a tough kid," Cameron Millikin, his father, told Keyser, "an inspiration to us—he'll make it."

With such support, he would. Troy Edwards read the stories and hoped that young Millikin would be as strong and determined as Brad Hornung. But he couldn't help wondering about Jason Yaganiski. The only consideration he seemed to get was as the perpetrator. There was talk about "dirty" checks; there was outrage over such tactics; there was determination that such checking must be stopped—as it must—to prevent any more Brad Hornungs or John Millikins. But what about preventing any more Troy Edwardses or Jason Yaganiskis?

Troy knew immediately he had to get involved, and he went to see the distraught young man. They spent two hours together. Knowing firsthand that sympathy can only do so much, Troy chose another route: blunt reality. He told Yaganiski that the road ahead was going to be tough on him, and that he had better realize that he, too, was a victim in this terrible tragedy. He was lucky that, unlike young Millikin, he would not spend the rest of his life in a wheelchair, but he would spend the rest of his life thinking about it. Every day. Every morning on first waking. And it would not go away, no matter how much wishful thinking Yaganiski did, no matter how hopeful he became that time would eventually erase it. Instead, time would enlarge it.

"I think about it every day," Troy told the young man. Yaganiski knew that he would, too.

Edwards told the young man that his strength would come from his family. He warned him that there would be friends who would disappoint, and others he would lose. Still others would never mention it. But, even if they could not talk about it, those who truly mattered would be there for him. As he explained to Yaganiski, "Some people just don't know what to say."

The hardest part of the discussion turned out to be Troy Edwards admitting out loud what he himself was only now coming to terms with: no matter how much either of them—or Brad Hornung or John Millikin—might wish, there could be no turning back of the clock. Ever.

"You can't spend your time wondering why," he told Yaganiski. "If you do, you'll drive yourself crazy."

The one journalist in the country whom Edwards still trusted heard the story and called. The *Leader Post*'s Gregg Drinnan, almost alone, had understood what both Brad and Troy were going through back in 1987. Now it was 1994, perhaps time again to talk, to see it all in perspective, perhaps time to send a message out to others who, like Jason Yaganiski, were in need now or might, God forbid, be in need sometime in the future. They talked, and

Drinnan wrote another understanding column. He talked about the 1987 incident and how a brave young man named Brad Hornung had forgiven the player who had hit him. He talked about the peace of mind that a mature, generous Hornung had given Troy Edwards back then and how now, seven years later, a mature, generous Edwards was helping out a youngster in similar need. He talked about how, the previous spring, Edwards and Hornung had again been in contact when Troy's mother had suffered a stroke and was, briefly, recuperating in the same Wascana Rehabilitation Centre where Brad now lives. He told about how they had got together and "had a real good talk."

Troy Edwards spoke reluctantly. He made it clear he was not asking for sympathy. He had not gone to Drinnan with the story. He had not sought any publicity. He had sought, instead, a young man in the same desperate need that he had been in back in 1987. The vast majority of people who read the story realized the courage that it took for Edwards to do this, just as they instinctively understood the courage Brad Hornung had shown from the moment he realized he could not move. Most people took this as a good sign, a necessary sign, that the human side must be seen and that such tragedies must be prevented, at all cost, because of what they do to two lives, and what they do to young men, not just a game.

A few, however, did not understand anything at all. The next game Troy Edwards played in, they shouted from the stands: "Paralyser!"

A year later, he is even more reluctant to discuss the matter. It is, perhaps, too difficult to explain, though he does understand how much other families going through what the Hornungs and Edwards are still going through could be helped by the sharing of experience. He knows from his own vital encounter with Jason Yaganiski.

"Maybe he didn't know what to expect," Troy explains. "I wanted to tell him, 'People are going to rip you apart, and you are going to be remembered for this and for nothing else.'

"I don't ever want to take away the fact that Brad Hornung has gone through a lot or that he suffered far, far worse than anyone in this. But there's a lot about the other guy, too. It's not as bad, but it's tough.

"He reminded me of a young Troy Edwards. He loved the game. He never meant to do it. It was kind of like he was waiting for me with open arms. 'Help me, help me.'

"I told him what to expect."

His father and mother came every day. His real friends came constantly at first and regularly from then on, their friendship deepening. His family moved to just off the Wascana Parkway so they could walk over on good nights, have an easy drive on bad ones. His grandfather also came every day, and after Brad's grandmother died in 1987, he, too, moved closer to the rehabilitation centre to make visiting simpler.

It was some time, however, before Brad was able to move into the rehab centre. Two weeks after he began breathing on his own he was taken out of intensive care and moved to a seventh-floor room at Plains Health Centre. A better room, but the same institutional food, which he despised. His mother began bringing meals, eventually every meal. She would even bring along his favourite bacon and cook it in the microwave that had been installed for the use of the heart patients down the hall. He gained back all of the twenty-five pounds he had lost in the initial weeks of the trauma. And, as time passed, he gained an uncommon perspective on what had happened to him.

By the first summer he had already come to terms with the fact that he would be paralysed from the neck down for the rest of his life. "You have to accept it," he told a reporter. "Life goes on and you do the best with what you have. At first, it was a time of change, shock really. But it's got easier because you get used to the adjustments. Like everybody else, I have my good days and bad days. But I don't have many bad days. Being alive makes me feel good."

It was a short but remarkable interview. Brad Hornung was then nineteen years old, a hockey player who had just lost the thing he had believed he loved best in life, and yet there was not the slightest trace of malice. "It did us both good to talk," Hornung said of Troy's visit. "I guess it was harder on him than it was on me. It was a freak accident. It could happen to anybody. It could have been me doing that to someone else."

He spoke out against checking from behind, but in a manner rarely heard. "It's a dangerous situation," he said, "but most players use common sense. I don't think they hit a guy from behind with the intent to hurt anyone. That's just the way the game is played." Common sense—strict rules against checking from behind, player education, attentive officials—would be the appropriate way to make the game safer. But to condemn the game wholeheartedly was unfair.

Over all, his recovery was astonishing. From death he had reached life. From helplessness he was moving towards independence. A tutor was helping him finish grade twelve. He planned to go on to university. A special wheelchair had been ordered and he was anxiously awaiting its delivery. He was reading about the scientific progress in spinal repair.

"There's a lot of research going on," he said, "and if it happens, great. If not, I have to live the way I am now."

He spoke like a young man whose world was opening up—not closed down, as so many had presumed. University. A job. Moving out. A van. "I'm at the stage like a few other people at eighteen who are not sure what they want to do."

No one, not his family, not his friends, could understand where such strength came from. Looking back so many years later, he believes he knows: "The lessons I learned through hockey helped me. You have to sacrifice." He smiles. "I got all the clichés."

All the clichés—and none more important than *one day at a time*. He realized that, without even thinking about it, he had become a young man who shared the values of his father, the values so treasured in the hockey culture. "The work ethic," Brad says. "And what it means to be involved in a team sport. That was so valuable." As far ahead as he could see, he had hard work facing him. And a new team, anxious to work with him.

He could no longer play hockey, but he found this far easier to accept than he would have imagined—had he ever imagined such an impossibility. The messages of his father made more sense now than ever. "I was always told if something goes wrong at school, you can forget about hockey. His advice was invaluable. He taught me that there was more to life than hockey." He would, he decided almost immediately, become a fan. He watched the 1987 Stanley Cup playoffs from intensive care, still awake when Pat LaFontaine scored in the third period of overtime to end one of the longest playoff games in NHL history. The only thing he could not do was cheer. But by the following season, he was going to some of the Pats games. It was the first year that checking from behind was no longer allowed in the Western Hockey League. He knew why.

In becoming a fan and no longer a player, Brad Hornung found that his attitudes towards hockey took new form. He began to see how the images of professional hockey reflected back on minor hockey, how the pressure placed on so many youngsters by demanding parents is too much and too often destructive. "I feel sorry for some kids," he says. "You see the way some parents act around their children and you have to ask yourself, is it worth it?" Like his father, Brad believes the CHA is doing its best to bring in new rules such as the one he helped initiate and to promote fair, clean play.

"Somehow," says Larry Hornung, "we have to make it so the boys respect each other more."

Both agree that the improvements in protection created their own unsuspected threat. The helmet, Larry says, gives young players "a feeling of invincibility" that, combined with youth, cannot help but create danger no matter what the rules or the teaching. One thing that particularly worries Brad is the sense that the game continues to speed up, the players continue to grow, yet the dimensions of the rink remain static, and increasingly dangerous. And despite the best efforts of the new rulings, he still sees checking from behind, both accidental and intentional, and not always called by the officials. "It pinches my heart and my throat every time I see it."

Sometimes, when Brad Hornung is watching "Hockey Night in Canada" on his television in the Wascana Rehabilitation Centre and Troy Edwards is watching the same game in his small apartment in the basement of his parents' Regina home, they will see the same play and feel the same emotion. Sometimes, Troy will be playing a game in the Highway Hockey League in a small town like Southey or Lumsden or Strasbourg and he will see a deliberate attempt to injure—often aimed directly at him—and it will be one more push towards his coming exit from the game.

He keeps going because he cannot stop them from yelling at him or attacking him, but he can prevent them from taking over his life. It's his life, after all, not theirs, and they know nothing of it. They can hurt him, but they cannot run him. He will make his own decisions about hockey.

Troy Edwards now coaches a bantam team in Regina as well as plays senior hockey for Raymore, but he has become convinced that, even in the few years since he and Brad Hornung were bantams in Saskatchewan, the sticks have come up higher, the checking style is different, the danger level increasing.

He has not been alone in thinking this. The Canadian Hockey Association was slowly coming to the conclusion that, even at the lowest levels, coaches and managers were turning to size and intimidation over skill. "In branch or regional championships at the bantam and pee wee levels of play," said a discouraged CHA president Murray Costello, "...the recruitment of size for intimidation and neutralizing skills is proving successful."

Several key CHA members had noticed another development, one so appalling that it at first seemed impossible to imagine. The CHA had been working for years to strengthen the critical checking-from-behind rules, and for some time they had felt there was great progress. An illegal check from behind now meant five minutes and expulsion from the game. Real punishment for a real crime. But word began trickling back from the regions that some coaches at these same innocent levels were teaching their youngsters to turn their backs on an opponent who was driving at them in the hopes that a five-minute penalty would result and the other team's player would be thrown out of the game. For the sake of the most meaningless of advantages, they were deliberately encouraging children to put their very lives in danger.

One bantam coach in Regina, Troy Edwards, found that he was preaching constantly to his players: "Don't hit the kid from behind... Don't hit the kid from behind."

"Sometimes I'll hear myself on the bench," he says. "Something will happen on the ice and I'll grunt or groan or say something like 'Thank goodness' when I see the kid's going to be all right. I wonder if sometimes they hear me."

Before the accident, Brad Hornung had been a typical eighteen-year-old in control of his life and enjoying the gifts of athletic ability and popularity. Life had moved so quickly, so smoothly, that he had given little thought to what it meant or why he should have considered himself lucky. The accident forced time upon him, time for reflection that is given to few eighteen-year-olds, and it changed him. He came to believe that he and his friends were fortunate to be able to play a game as difficult and fast and graceful—and, of course, tough—as hockey. He was lucky to have the family he had and the friends he had made. He noticed that, when his team-mates came to visit, they would come in groups. "They seemed to feel better if they came together," he says. "No one ever came by themselves." He understood.

Eight years after the accident, he had become a young man very much in control of a life that, at one point, seemed without control at all. The financial concerns had been eased somewhat by insurance settlements and a CKRM radio telethon that raised more than $200,000.

The family remains deeply appreciative of the way prairie support was extended to them.

Today, thanks to the Brad Hornung Foundation, Brad lives in comfort in the Wascana Rehabilitation Centre and may, one day, strike out on his own. He has a television on which to watch his beloved sport. He has a sound system for the music—Def Leppard, Odds—he loves. He has the van to take him to the odd movie and hockey game. And most importantly, he has his chair, a hugely expensive wheelchair that is controlled electronically by what little movement he still has. With electrodes placed in pads on the headrest, he can move it and turn it by pressing back slightly with the back of his head. It took a long time to adjust and there were accidents—"I took out a salad bar one day"—but eventually he became very adroit at control and now moves about the centre at will. "It's good here," he says.

In 1994, he went to Florida with one of the nurses and her husband, the three of them travelling around the state taking in ball games and other sporting events. The bond the family formed with the doctors and nurses and therapists at the rehabilitation centre has even had an effect on the life of the Hornungs' other child: Leanne now studies speech therapy at the University of Minnesota in Duluth.

Brad has his computer system, which is designed to work through Morse code rather than typing, the signals sent by Brad puffing into a tube for a dot, sipping for a dash. He is transferring his university courses from audiotape to computer file and plans to graduate with a degree in history from the nearby University of Regina.

His textbooks, as well as the works of fiction he loves to read, must first be torn apart and then refitted with special spiral binding so he can read from a stand and turn the pages with a special pointer that is attached to a mould he holds in his mouth. "Just like when he was in hockey," jokes Larry. Brad talks about one day getting a job. He stares out the window towards the provincial legislature and says he might even run for office. He laughs. "I wouldn't even have to get a lift."

There are posters on the wall—a signed Pete Rose, a signed Carol Alt (sent by the model's husband, former New York Ranger Ron Greschner)—photographs of the New York Islanders and of the sprawling Hornung family reunion. There are plaques to recognize his election to the Pats' Hall of Fame, the retirement of his sweater, No. 8, from the Regina Pats, and the founding of the Brad Hornung Trophy for the Western Hockey League's Most Sportsmanlike Player. There is a print on his wall of wild horses running free. The familiar poster "Footprints" has a place of prominence on the far wall: "The Lord replied, 'My son, my precious child./I love you, and I would never leave you./During your times of trial and suffering,/when you see only one set of footprints,/it was then that I carried you.'"

"The first time I read that," he says. "I took it pretty hard." He had to read it hundreds of times. As word of the tragedy spread, cards and letters began flooding in from all over the world. Old women sent him prayers, schoolchildren sent him drawings. The deluge overwhelmed the Hornungs. On average, ninety pieces of mail arrived each day for Brad, and often a copy of "Footprints" would be somewhere in the stack.

"I started putting them all in scrapbooks," says Terry Hornung. "But I had five filled and I realized I hadn't even made a dent in the pile. I gave up." She could not get over the outpouring of sympathy, the compassion. "I think so many people thought it could happen to them just as easily," she says. She kept every piece of mail that arrived, filling up huge boxes in the Hornung basement and thinking that, one day, she would reread them all and sort them. That day is still far off; the letters, sent to ease pain, now cause pain with the reminder.

The letters arrived when there seemed to be no hope. Before he could breathe again, before the chair, the movement to the rehab centre, the van, the room, the new life. Over time, the relationship within the family returned far more to normal than any of them ever anticipated. "It's the same," Brad says. "It's still the same. There's times they're mad at me and times I'm mad at them."

"I don't think anything's changed," says Larry.

Terry laughs: "He doesn't even think there's anything wrong with him any more."

Seven years later, they find it odd to talk about Brad as if he were two separate people, the hockey player before and the quadriplegic after, for quadriplegia is now seen by them for what it is: a condition. And the human persists despite the condition. Their son is still with them and, in some ways, he has given them what they tried to give him. After the accident, Brad Hornung had three futures in his hands, not just one, and he has allowed them all—himself, his parents—to have real futures, not lives dedicated to and dwelling in the past.

His is not a story of one person and two lives, two different people in one body, the one living there before the accident and the other after. It is, as it has always been, Brad Hornung. He is still handsome, funny, smart and ambitious. His parents were proud of what he did in hockey, but there was always something about his excellence there that could be explained by gift. It came naturally.

Puffing and sipping to control a computer does not come naturally. Reading by turning pages with a mouthpiece does not come naturally. Learning to control a wheelchair with the subtle flex of the only muscles that will flex does not come naturally. Going to university and aiming for a job in the real world does not come naturally. But it is all coming. And because of spirit, not gift. This came to Brad Hornung through such extraordinary effort and determination that his parents now stand in awe of their son.

"I'm more proud of this," says Larry. Scoring goals and making a team and turning professional and carrying a Stanley Cup around an ice surface all pale in comparison.

Beyond the window, the lingering summer sun is finally setting. In the rich, almost liquid prairie light, the geese take off again from Wascana Lake, their flight plan bringing them directly towards the Wascana rehabilitation centre where, directly in front of the huge window in the cafeteria sitting area—their shadows play on the glass, their calling penetrates—Brad Hornung stares, smiling.

"This," he says, "is the best view in all of Regina."

His parents nod in agreement.

They are staring at their son, sitting with their backs to the window.

The Gift

There is something about the retired gentleman going through the cafeteria line in a shopping mall at the edge of Bloomfield Village, just off Interstate 75 at the northern reaches of metropolitan Detroit. The others in the line—many of them also retired—cannot help but notice him, recognition building. He wears no identifiable uniform: blue jogging pants and matching nylon jacket, running shoes with the laces loose. But there is such familiarity in his *lines*: sloping shoulders, sloping nose, the big, easy smile that serves as handshake and calling card and, after a moment of staring, confirms to the onlookers that this is Gordie Howe, Detroit, and history.

He has come here on the afternoon of the last day of the year for a long lunch with his wife, Colleen, and three of their grandchildren. In a few hours it will be the New Year's Eve of the year in which he will turn sixty-five—Gordie Howe, old-age pensioner—but he will spend it neither celebrating nor reflecting. Instead, he will drive back down I-75 to the edge of the Detroit River, where he first stood in the early fall of 1946, a seventeen-year-old who would be described in the Red Wings press guide as "shy and afraid of the opposite sex", and who would not even dare think how long he could last. Longer than anyone, it would turn out.

But he would not be thinking of that. His mind would reflect back on those times only when he took a visitor down into the bowels of the Joe Louis Arena and showed where workers had stashed the huge green turn-off sign that once told freeway drivers which exit to take for the Detroit Olympia. He would talk, briefly, about rats, about how in the early days the players would sleep in the arena during training camp and how he would keep a hockey stick by his cot not because he was dreaming of playing in the NHL but because he would sometimes have to kill the rats that were running over the sleeping players and scrounging through their clothes. Sometimes, they would even play hockey using a dead rat as a puck.

It would be forty years or more before he would realize that the rats he should have been worrying about *owned* him, but that was so long ago. What matters now is that he is one of the few former NHL stars who can watch his own son wear the colours of his old team. Mark Howe will play this night for the Detroit Red Wings. And if Gordie Howe does not feel old on this, the eve of his sixty-fifth, he certainly would if he knew that his son was on the verge of becoming the oldest player in the National Hockey League—just as he himself had once been.

He and Colleen have brought Mark's children along to the lunch: Travis, Nolan and Azia. Gordie Howe is complaining about his knee—oddly enough, the one injury he managed to avoid in thirty-two NHL and World Hockey Association seasons, 2,186 regular games, 235 grinding playoff matches. He hurt it roaring down a water slide with Nolan on his lap. It is so sore and strained he can hardly skate.

Nolan and Azia's older brother, Travis, is fourteen. He has the Howe lines. He also smiles easily, and he has a story to tell about his father and grandfather and the game they all love. Travis's bantam team, Detroit Little Caesars Pizza, has recently held its annual fathers-sons game. This year—

Travis's first with the team after the family moved to Bloomfield Village from a suburb near Philadelphia, where Mark Howe had been playing for the Flyers—the annual game added a "grandfather" division and invited out Gordie Howe. It was the first time since 1980, when both were with the Hartford Whalers, that Gordie and Mark had played on the same team. It was the first time that Travis, who dreams of one day playing in the NHL, had ever been on the ice at the same time as his father and grandfather.

It was "awesome," says Travis. He knew how good his father was because he had seen him play in the NHL. But it was his grandfather who had astonished. "He was making these behind-the-back passes," the grandson says, "doing all kinds of amazing things."

But the most amazing moment of all was when the biggest kid on Little Caesars Pizza bantams made the mistake of skating into a corner with Gordie Howe, "Mr. Hockey", "Number 9", "Elbows".

"Grandpa flattened him."

The man who put Gordie Howe back on the ice with his sons has just come from the doctor. It is a brilliantly warm July 1994 day at Glen Lake, on the eastern edge of New York State's Adirondack Park. Bill Dineen's shoulder is acting up. They think the problem comes from a back operation he had the previous summer. The back troubles, they think, come from seventeen years of professional hockey, twelve of them spent in the minors, more than thirty addresses from Quebec City to Seattle. "It's the old injuries," he says, "catching up."

His sons are also catching up. Kevin Dineen of the Hartford Whalers and Philadelphia Flyers has come down the lake in his new ski boat. Gord Dineen of the New York Islanders, Minnesota North Stars, Pittsburgh Penguins, Ottawa Senators and now the Denver Grizzlies of the International Hockey League has put out the Cokes and the deck chairs and the sun umbrella on his cottage lawn. Bill lives across the lake in a handsome geodesic home with his wife, Pat. Near Bill and Pat, another son, Peter, has a place, and sister Rosemarie has just bought nearby. Oldest son Shawn spends his summers here. And if the youngest, Jerry, moves into the Glen Lake area, the Dineens will all be "home" for the first time in their bizarrely nomadic lives.

Bill Dineen is talking about Gordie Howe. He is talking about the year 1953, when he was a quick little winger and had just joined the Detroit Red Wings. Gordie Howe was already a star as one member of the incredible Production Line: Howe, Sid Abel and Ted Lindsay. Howe had scored forty-nine goals the previous season, the highest number in a career that would, bewilderingly, never contain the fifty-goal season that would eventually separate the coming superstars from the pack. In Bill Dineen's eyes, Gordie Howe was a god, and he would one day come to represent the same for Bill Dineen's hockey-playing boys.

Bill's father, Matty, had played defence for McGill University and even had a tryout with the old Montreal Maroons of the NHL before deciding on a career as a civil engineer. He had worked as an engineer throughout Quebec—Chicoutimi, where Bill was born, Val d'Or, where the father played senior hockey and the youngster played in the minor organization—before settling in Ottawa, where he worked on the central heating plant that runs through the rock under Parliament Hill.

Bill Dineen was small, but a very good player. This was

in the years before youngsters under ten were effectively
"culled" on the basis of size by frenetic minor hockey orga-
nizations, and little Bill Dineen thrived on the open-air
rinks of Ottawa and in the city school leagues. By the time
he was fifteen, the scouts were calling on Matty Dineen,
and it was at this point that Bill was grateful that his father
had played the game himself and understood how frail the
dreams of a youngster and his family can be.

"My father used to come and watch the games," Bill
says, "and after, all he'd talk about was how much better
hockey was in the old days. He'd always say, 'Nobody can
bodycheck any more.'" His father supported but would
never push, even when the scouts seemed to be begging the
boy to sign. Matty Dineen was more interested in education, and when the opportunity arose for Bill to head off to
St Michael's College in Toronto to go to high school and
play junior hockey, he encouraged his son to grab it.

"The night I turned sixteen I was put on Cleveland's
negotiating list," Bill says. The Cleveland Barons were an
American Hockey League team—back then, AHL teams
could claim one junior, NHL teams could claim three—
and "they'd tie you up forever." Cleveland then traded the
youngster's rights to Detroit of the NHL, and he stayed on
the Red Wings negotiation list for four years, the team continually scouting him and periodically in touch with his
father. The University of Michigan offered a full scholarship, and, at his father's urging, he accepted. But Detroit
would not give up. "They tried to sign me," Bill says, "but
my father kept telling them I was going to go to school."

But, somehow, hockey got in the way. In his last year at
St Mike's, the Barrie Flyers picked him up for the junior
playoffs and they won the Memorial Cup. Bill Dineen, it
was said, was a real NHL prospect. While he was packing

for the University of Michigan, the Red Wings began applying pressure. They brought Bill and his parents down to Detroit, wooed the entire family, and in the end, "My dad basically left it in my own hands." Detroit offered summer school, which he tried for three years, but eventually gave up in favour of hockey. "It was what I wanted to do," he says.

Bill Dineen had one of those familiar NHL careers that can be described in two completely different ways. He came off a Memorial Cup championship and joined a team that would immediately win two Stanley Cups. He would score seventeen goals in his first season with the Red Wings and come third in the Calder Cup voting for rookie of the year. The New York Rangers' Camille Henry would win the trophy, Dineen's Detroit team-mate Earl Reibel would place second, Dineen third and Montreal's magnificent Jean Béliveau fourth. "I'll always remember that," says Dineen. Better than the magnificent Béliveau. If he remembered nothing else, it would have been a glorious NHL career.

But, like so many short professional hockey careers, it had a flip side. He had, at the end of that first season, a shot at twenty goals, which back then was considered the dividing line between the better players of the league and the journeymen. He also had a bonus clause in his $6,000 rookie contract that would mean extra money if he reached this unexpected milestone. With three games left in the season, Detroit general manager Jack Adams, who had drawn up the contract, inexplicably benched Dineen until the playoffs. The press wondered why. (Back then, a player wouldn't dare speak out.) His chance at twenty goals was lost for the sake of a few dollars. His confidence rattled, he would never have as good a season as that first.

At the end of that first year, Adams sat down with his promising young winger and had a heart-to-heart chat. "He told me, 'If I could have had a blueprint of the year I expected from you and compared that against the year I got from you, I wouldn't have changed a thing—I'm going to give you a hell of a raise.' I would get $6,500 for my second year, another $500. They were even going to boost my meal money from $5.50 to $7.00 a day. I was going up.

"At the beginning of the next season we were on a train to Montreal for a game. Everybody had gathered in the smoker car for a beer. Jack Adams and [coach] Jimmy Skinner were at the other end and Ted Lindsay holds this meeting at the other to talk about how some of the older guys were trying to get a players' association going. They'd already had some effect. Meal money had been increased from $5.50 to $7.00 and minimum wage from $6,000 to $6,500.

"I was sitting there and I couldn't believe what I was hearing. I was still making minimum wage!"

It was an astonishing revelation for the youngster. He immediately knew he had been conned, and that Jack Adams was simply using the players' naivety and small-town respect for authority to his advantage. With the empty eastern Ontario landscape slipping by in the background, Dineen looked around the smoker car: the cagey, brassy Lindsay, so willing to challenge authority, soft and quiet Red Kelly, smooth Alex Delvecchio, the volatile goaltender Terry Sawchuk, and, beside Sawchuk, Gordie Howe.

Howe was older than Dineen and the other rookies but he had this boyish, trusting air about him that made him somehow seem younger. He had just won the NHL scoring championship for the third straight year and his second straight Hart Trophy as the NHL's most valuable player. He had already been five times named to the all-star team. And yet he carried absolutely no air of stardom. They called him Blinkie. He had little education. So unbelievably shy was Howe that the day he was to begin grade nine, he had walked to the edge of the schoolyard, stared for a while at the laughing, confident youngsters heading in through the immense doors, and turned and walked back down the street, never to return.

The experience with Jack Adams made Bill Dineen wonder if stars like Howe and Lindsay were treated the same. He knew that Lindsay would never allow himself to be taken, but he had no idea about Howe. He did not know that Adams and Howe would gather in Adams's office year after year after year, with the boss the press called Jolly Jack and Jolly John and Happy John saying, "Go ahead, Gord, just say what you're worth," and Howe, convinced he was pushing the outer edges, would ask for a $1,000 raise and get it. He had no idea that, each year, Adams would, in confidence, tell Howe that he was the best-paid player in all the NHL but that he must never tell anyone, otherwise jealousies would tear apart the team. Howe never mentioned his salary to others, convinced for more than a decade that he was the top-paid player in the league—when he wasn't even the highest-paid on his team. It was not until 1968 that he learned otherwise in a conversation with new Wings defenceman Bobby Baun, when Baun let Howe know that the Wings were paying him $67,000 for the season. Howe was then making just under $50,000.

Had Bill Dineen turned to the great Howe on that 1954 train ride to Montreal and asked Howe if he had any contractual problems, Howe might have confessed that there was one thing that would bother him all his life. Jack Adams had promised him a Red Wings windbreaker if he would sign his first contract. To no one's surprise, Jolly Jack had reneged on the deal.

It was a moment Bill Dineen would file away. Twenty seasons later, when circumstances would produce a situation neither Bill Dineen nor Gordie Howe could possibly have imagined as that train sped into Montreal, the revelation about money and fair treatment would become the second most important factor in a decision that would make hockey history.

The Gordie Howe legend, like the Wayne Gretzky story, has long since become part of the hockey lore of Canada. It is better known, by far, than the story of the voyageurs and explorers who opened up the country, or of Lester Pearson, who won the Nobel Peace Prize. Howe and Gretzky speak to the deepest values of the country. They are who we are—or at least who we wish to be.

Gordie Howe was born in Floral, Saskatchewan, and grew up in Saskatoon. He was the sixth of nine children born to Ab Howe, a labourer who had come to Canada from Minnesota, and Katherine Schultz, the daughter of German immigrants to the Canadian prairie. A brusque "man's man" with little patience, Ab Howe's influence was both genetic and psychological, producing in his son a fascinating blend of power and meekness. "He was clumsy and backward and bashful," Ab said in an early radio interview. "That's why I thought he'd never amount to anything."

Gordie's mother, a kind-hearted woman, offered total support to her son, no matter what. He did poorly in school, largely because of his nearly debilitating shyness, and it bothered him. He would come home from school and he and his mother would cry together in the kitchen over how it had gone. It seldom went well: the school made him repeat grade three.

It was his mother's kindness that inadvertently gave Gordie Howe a new lease on life. A woman in the neighbourhood with a sick husband and a new baby was desperate for help feeding the child. She came to the door with a gunny sack filled with mostly useless items, and Katherine Howe, though she had little money, gave the woman some change. Inside, amidst the clutter, was a pair of old skates. Gordie grabbed one, his sister, Edna, the other, and off they went. The skate was too big for him, but he knew immediately that he had found something that held neither shame nor failure. He bought the other skate off Edna for a dime and never looked back.

It is difficult for those of us who did not grow up in the Canadian prairies during the 1930s and 1940s to understand how deeply the winter game penetrated. The adults listened to Foster Hewitt's Saturday-night broadcasts of the Toronto Maple Leafs games with the same dedication and faith they reserved for church the following morning. And the children played.

"We lived for hockey," says author Barry Broadfoot, who grew up in Winnipeg. "We played on the Red River when the ice had barely formed and we had to skate all the time because if we didn't, we'd go through the ice, and some of us did. We started on bobskates at age four and always bought second-hand skates—no tube skates then—two sizes too large so we could grow into them and they'd last three years, about a dollar a pair. We played road hockey with a puck that was a frozen horse turd shaved to look like a puck, but when you slapshot-ed it, it sailed off like a dart.

Yes, the slap shot. Bobby Hull didn't invent the slap shot. We did.

"We also bent our hockey stick blades into an 'arc' by steaming them in a pail of hot water on the stove made from two Imperial Oil 45-gallon drums cut and welded together and fitted with a door for the six-foot poplar sticks in the clubhouse—which was a boxcar we bought from the CNR for ten dollars and the city fire department flooded down the ground to saturation and it froze, and then they laid down four inches of water, which was then the ice surface. You never saw such large cracks in your life. And we got water from lengths of hoses from a nearby house. The land was donated by the city because there were hundreds of lots which had not been sold or just given up because the owners during the optimistic twenties could no longer pay the three-dollar annual taxes.

"Everything was scrounged. We played in thirty-below Fahrenheit and we played sixty minutes. Six to a team. You know, the old business about pads made of *Liberty* magazines, which sold for five cents. Our distinctive uniform was merely a crest hand-sewn by one of the mothers and sewn on our windbreaker or sweater. We froze our hands, our feet, our testicles and our faces. I once froze my feet so badly that for twenty years after whenever I took a bath my feet swelled up and turned white.

"We played teams in our own league. We played other districts. The whistle was a bell. Know why? If the referee—who could be a father or just one of us—put a whistle to his mouth, the skin would freeze to it. Clang-clang."

When Gordie Howe found hockey, he found himself. He could skate and he could stickhandle, and he was big. But he was not then tough. What he became as a player had to do with the effect of his father. "The first time he tried to join one of the small teams here," Ab once said, "they sent him home because he wasn't dressed properly or something, and I was hopping mad. Ever since then I've always told him to never take any dirt from nobody, because if you do, they'll keep throwing it in on you. That's the way life is."

According to Roy MacSkimming in his 1994 biography of Howe, *Gordie: A Hockey Legend*, the young Howe was like his father on the ice, but off the ice he was like his mother. "It would be a rank cliché to compare Gordie Howe to Jekyll and Hyde," MacSkimming wrote. "But it wouldn't be so far off the mark." Off the ice, with his mother smiling as she prepared supper in the background, Gordie Howe would sit for hours at the kitchen table practising his autograph, constantly asking his mother which style she preferred. To this day, Gordie Howe's signature is the most legible known to collectors.

By the time he was fifteen, NHL teams were already sending telegrams off to the Howes to let them know their youngster was being watched with interest. Katherine wrote back to each team, begging them to desist. The war was on, and two of her older sons, Vern and Norm, were fighting overseas. Every time a telegram came to the front door, she was convinced it was announcing a death, not an opportunity. If they wanted to make contact, she told them, they'd have to come in person to the front door. She had barely mailed off the letters when the knocking began.

The New York Rangers and Detroit Red Wings were the most persistent. The Rangers took Gordie off as a sixteen-year-old to a training camp at Winnipeg, but he was homesick and soon returned to Saskatoon. The Red Wings got him to Detroit, signed him up—largely on that promise of a red windbreaker—and sent him first to Galt, then to Omaha. At seventeen he was declared too good to keep out of the NHL.

Here, the lore of the man changes to the lore of the league. He was a sensation with the Production Line. Scoring champion, best player and, in 1950, very nearly one of the game's great tragedies when he and Toronto's Ted Kennedy may or may not have collided and somehow Howe ended up with a fractured skull. It was never determined whether the damage had been done by Kennedy's stick or by the boards, but it hardly mattered. There were moments when they first got him to the hospital that doctors were afraid they were going to lose the emerging star. But he survived, returned, and went on to a brilliant career. He was the league's best—six scoring championships, six Hart Trophies, twenty-one all-star selections—and also the league's toughest, a title claimed in a famous battle with New York Ranger Lou Fontinato during the 1958–59 season. Captured in a Life magazine photo feature, the blood, gore and damage Howe's fists did to Fontinato's face is still a conversation piece in NHL circles nearly four decades after the heavyweight championship of the league was decided in a few brutal moments.

His number, 9, became the most familiar in the game, partly because his main rival, Maurice Richard, wore the same number for the Montreal Canadiens. It was always presumed that Howe chose the number because of Richard and because No. 9 would come to mean the best player on a given team—even Wayne Gretzky had sought the number, reluctantly agreeing to 99 because an older player on his Sault Ste Marie junior team was already wearing the Howe-Richard number. But this is not at all how it came about. "I never went after it," says Howe. "I was offered it by Jack Adams, but I said I was fine with 17, the number I was wearing. But then I learned the lower the number you had the better chance you had of getting a lower berth on the train rides, so I took it for that reason."

He was widely considered the most phenomenal athlete of his time. "He could have been a star in any sport," Jack Adams once told the well-known sportswriter Trent Frayne. "Look at those shoulders, see how they slope from his neck. He used to hang from a door-frame when he was a kid developing those shoulder muscles. He could have been a prizefighter, he could have been a ball player."

In fact, he had been a terrific ball player and says he was once put on the New York Yankees protected list after a game at Indian Head, Saskatchewan, when he hit for the cycle. Howe, however, underplays the baseball talk. "I don't understand it," he says of the Indian Head game. "The ball looked as big as a basketball to me." His field work, he says, left much to be desired. "Fly balls looked like yo-yos to me," he says. "I was always back on my heels." Even so, he became friends with Detroit's Al Kaline and would some-times take batting practice with the Tigers, his powerful swing only lending credence to the story that he could have played any professional sport he wished.

Life seemed perfect in Detroit in the 1950s. He married Colleen Joffa, a Michigan native, and soon there were newspaper photographs of hockey's greatest star hoisting his young boys, Marty and Mark, high over his familiar head. Colleen Howe, a fiercely determined woman, did much to bring Howe out of his shell. He developed a rep-utation for dry humour, and people began looking at him in a different light.

Ted Lindsay was one whose perception of Howe changed dramatically. They had become linemates, and also fast friends. Red Kelly told Roy MacSkimming, "You never saw Ted without Gordie—they were like *that*." But they were not the same. Lindsay was ambitious beyond hockey—he had already started up his own business—and felt he was slowly educating his friend. Howe even became a partner for a while in the business interests; the Red Wings frowned upon this and set out to discourage him. Lindsay was also giving more and more time to building a players' association, absolutely convinced, and absolutely correct in thinking so, that the owners were taking unfair advantage of the players.

Jolly John Adams wasted no time in taking action. He traded Lindsay to Chicago after the 1956–57 season and, at the start of the 1957–58 season, the Detroit players became the first to withdraw from the fragile association. When others followed, the union was doomed, and would not rise up again for a decade. Lindsay always believed it had failed because two key Detroit players, Kelly and Howe, had not been there when he needed them. "Two key guys folded," Lindsay told MacSkimming thirty-seven years later. "Some people can stand pressure. Some can't." Howe felt he simply didn't appreciate the situation at the time and, in later years, became deeply involved with such "union"-like matters as players' pensions.

The Detroit dynasty had been broken by Adams. The 1955 Stanley Cup—again with Bill Dineen in the line-up—would stand as their last victory until well into the 1990s. The Red Wings would come last in the league their first year without Lindsay and rarely rise again to the top of the league. Howe, however, would continue on as one of the league's premier attractions. He would score one hundred points in 1962–63 and win his last of six scoring titles. He was considered on the downhill side of an illustrious career.

Colleen Howe—ably described by MacSkimming as "a woman ahead of her time"—attempted to help her husband cash in on some of his celebrity. She negotiated a $10,000-a-year deal with Eaton's for product endorsement and public appearances. But still he was not making nearly what a star of such long standing and durability deserved. When Bobby Baun brought Howe the shocking news that he had, essentially, been had all through his career with the Red Wings, it was pretty well too late for Gordie Howe to recoup. He played a few more years in the newly expanded league, but Detroit could not capitalize on the opportunities provided by expansion. When the Red Wings weren't in last place, they would finish second-last. He made the playoffs only once in his final five years.

The old injuries were hurting. His hands suffered terribly from arthritis. In the spring of 1971, Katherine Howe struck her head in a fall and could not recover. Shortly after the death of his mother, Gordie Howe announced his retirement. He was forty-three years old. It was considered time.

Besides, the boys were growing up quickly. Marty and Mark had been followed by Cathy and, a year later, by Murray. All three boys were playing hockey, all three showing great promise. The Toronto Marlboros of the Ontario junior league were wooing Marty and sixteen-year-old Mark to join the team.

Gordie Howe remembered what he had been like at sixteen and had left Saskatoon. He remembered how naive he had been and how much he had learned. Never again would a Howe be taken as he had been so taken by Jack Adams.

He helped the boys negotiate their deal with the Marlies. They would sign, but at his insistence they had one particular demand from the team.

They wanted team jackets. Up front and right away.

Bill Dineen lasted four and a half years in the NHL. His Achilles' heel turned out to be one joint higher: his knee. He hurt his knee twice while with the Red Wings, the first time in a wrenching fall that left him unable to play. "Detroit then accused me of faking it," he says. "They asked for a second opinion." A second opinion confirmed that there was real damage, but permanent damage had been done to his confidence. His own team didn't trust him. When he hurt his knee again, he hid the injury. He wouldn't even go to a hospital. He says, "Point of pride, I guess." Point of fear, more like it. He knew that if he was sent down, he might never return. The third time his knee went, he was in the minors, playing for the Buffalo Bisons in the American Hockey League. Again, he refused to go to the hospital. When the team got back to the hotel, "I couldn't move off the bus."

Yet he would spend many, many more years on buses. He had hoped to return to the NHL after Detroit traded him to Chicago and the Blackhawks sent him down, but he couldn't get back onto the big team. His final chance came in 1960, when Punch Imlach invited him to the Toronto Maple Leafs training camp and Dineen performed better than even he expected. The Leafs set out on a ten-game exhibition swing, and it seemed everything was coming back together. "Punch told me I'd made the team," Dineen recalls. "He even called me up in the plane and I sat right next to him when he told me. I said, 'That's great.'"

He went home, lined up a place to live in Toronto, and told his wife, Pat—who, like Colleen Howe, had met and married her husband in Detroit—to come along with the growing family. Then Imlach took him aside and told him the Leafs had "had a change of heart." And that was the end.

Suddenly the education he had passed over at the University of Michigan took on new meaning. He was only in his mid-twenties, he had his high school, but he also had a family. Shawn was two and Peter was a newborn. Soon there would be Rose, Gord, Kevin and Jerry. "When you've got kids and you're not making a lot of money," he says, "you've got to keep going."

Keeping going meant one of the most peripatetic minor-league careers in hockey. He played in Buffalo, Cleveland, Rochester and Quebec City of the AHL; he played in Seattle and Denver, where he finally retired as a player at age thirty-nine. And then he took up coaching, which he found to his liking and in which he found some success. The late Ottawa television sportscaster Brian Smith had Dineen as a team-mate in Denver and as a coach in Houston, when both were with the Aeros of the World Hockey Association, and Smith remembered him as fiercely competitive, funny (sometimes outrageously so— Dineen once dressed up in the full uniform of the other team and went out onto the ice to practise with them), kind, caring and well liked by his players. "The finest person I have ever met in professional sports" is the way Smith described Bill Dineen. Unfortunately, being well liked by your players does not guarantee a career. The nomadic life continued for the Dineens; at one point, Pat Dineen remembers, she was filling out a passport application and had listed twenty-eight past addresses on the form. It wasn't until Bill became coach of the Adirondack Red Wings in Glen Falls that they felt a sense of permanence. They began renting a little white and blue cottage at the far end

of the lake, then decided to buy and stay, no matter what
the future held.

"People would say, 'Where are you from?'" says Gord
Dineen after a refreshing dive into Glen Lake. "We never
knew what to say."

"Now it's here," adds Kevin.

By the time Bill and Pat Dineen reached Seattle there
were five boys and a girl, and all of them were interested in
skating. They began in Seattle and continued in Houston,
where in 1972 Bill was hired on as the coach of the
Houston Aeros of the new World Hockey Association.
Rosemarie wanted to become a figure skater (she would
later become a registered nurse), but all five boys were determined to make it as hockey players. It baffled the parents.

"I don't think either Bill or I were obsessed," Pat Dineen
told a Houston newspaper. "They seemed to want it themselves…. They took the initiative and worked and developed their skills." How could they not, though? Hockey
was at the core of their family life and, with so many
moves, the large family became its own travelling neighbourhood, with the Dineen youngsters always together,
always playing the same game: hockey.

It did not much matter that Bill Dineen was so busy
coaching that he came to think of himself as not properly
involved in his children's upbringing. He left the organization and discipline up to Pat; the entertainment the kids
took care of themselves. And if they wanted to do little but
play hockey, well, whatever they wanted to do was fine
with him. He would never push. He would, he felt, act
more like his own father, Matty, had, and hope that education would win out over hockey. "My dad took that to an
extreme," says Kevin. "Sometimes he wouldn't even *talk*
hockey unless we pushed him."

He wouldn't talk because he was afraid of influencing them too much. He was afraid that he would be the cause of them making a decision they'd later regret. If they were going to join the crazed life he and Pat had lived, they would have to make that decision themselves. He loved hockey. He loved the people and the game and the experiences, but it wasn't for everyone. It was tough to be a fringe player, barely hanging on, forever worried about what was going to happen next. It was easier for the real stars: they, at least, could pretty well count on where they'd be come September each year.

He joined legendary Montreal defenceman Doug Harvey in Houston. Harvey was to be assistant coach and head scout. A hard-drinking, fun-loving man who would eventually drop out of hockey and die too young of his excesses, Harvey was an instant hit with the sports fanatics of the Texas city. "I remember going with him while he gave a speech to some service club," remembers Dineen. "Doug stands up there and says, 'You god-damned dumb Texans, you wouldn't understand this complicated game anyway.' I was laughing my head off."

Dineen and Harvey knew they would need an attraction to sell the game in Texas. Together, they had attended the 1973 Memorial Cup tournament and, like everyone there, they had been astonished by the play of a seventeen-year-old with the Toronto Marlboros—Mark Howe, Gordie's second son. "He was just outstanding," remembers Dineen. Marty Howe, more than a year older than Mark, was also a fine player with the championship Marlies team, but Mark had the same presence that had been his father's signature. He was going to be a star—at any level. And every scout in the building knew it.

"I thought, 'Well, I'll go down and see if Gordie's there,'

Bill Dineen recalls. "I went down and ran into Colleen, and we talked for a while. It seemed to me that they were both about ready to play pro. I remember Colleen said, 'Oh, it's such a shame.'

"The next week or so was the draft. I talked to [WHA president] Gary Davidson about it. The kids were American. They were also pros—even if it was just fifty dollars a week. We thought maybe we'd take the chance and see what happened."

There was little doubt that the NHL was also eyeing the Howe boys. Mark was about to turn eighteen. The NHL had its draft at twenty, with exceptions being made for precocious nineteen-year-olds. Mark would, therefore, likely go in 1974, at nineteen. But at eighteen in 1973 he was legally entitled to make his own decisions. Perhaps if the WHA dared, drafting an eighteen-year-old would stand up in court if the NHL challenged. Dineen and Harvey talked it over and decided to gamble. Bill was sure he had two aces to play: the opportunity for Mark Howe to turn professional a year earlier than the NHL would then allow, and a hunch that his old friend might be open to a suggestion that would stun the entire hockey world, both NHL and WHA.

"I figured I would have to run it by Gordie first, so I called," Dineen says. "I know he likes to tell this story about him saying, 'What about a third Howe?' and how he can remember the sound of the phone hitting the ground first and then me second. But that's not quite true.

"He did say, 'What about a third Howe?' But that was just exactly what we expected. We knew he would want it. We knew that was the way to get to him."

Bill Dineen knew because of his own sons and the way he felt about seeing them following his chosen game. He

knew because he had seen the look in Colleen Howe's eyes
when she had said "What a shame" at the Memorial Cup.
He knew because he had seen Mark Howe play—and he
knew what any father who happened to be Gordie Howe
would be thinking to himself but afraid to say out loud.

"Just instinct." Bill Dineen chuckles. "Just instinct."

It was a most propitious telephone call. Gordie Howe was
miserable in retirement. He had been inducted almost
immediately, and most appropriately, into the Hockey Hall
of Fame, but it seemed he had himself become a plaque to
hang on the wall and invite people in to stare at. The Red
Wings had promised him a front-office job with meaning,
but he could find no meaning, and the salary was considerably less than he had been making as a player. They
wanted him for figurehead reasons only, for public relations
work, for handshakes, for luncheon appearances at the
local service clubs. He thought he would be helping to
make player decisions and working with the players out on
the ice, but his presence was so intimidating to younger
players, so distracting, that at one point the Red Wings for-
bade him to go out onto the ice and asked him to stay clear
of the dressing-room. They told him to keep Colleen away
from the rink and the junior team that the Howe boys were
playing on, even though Colleen had been fundamental to
establishing the Junior Red Wings. She, too, wanted to be
more involved than the organization was willing to allow.

Bill Dineen had wisely hit upon the two things that he
knew would work. He had appealed to Gordie Howe's long
history of being financially whipped by the Red Wings. He
says Howe was making $28,000 at the time. The Aeros
were willing to pay the threesome a $2-million package
spread out over four years. And, most important, he had

appealed to Gordie Howe's crazy dream of one day playing a game with his sons, an entire forward line of Howes.

Mark Howe later told a television interviewer that his father had been the main push behind his signing. Gordie had told Mark, "You're going to make more money at eighteen than I made in twenty-five years playing in the NHL. If you don't sign, I'll break your arm and sign for you."

It was supposed to be for one year. It was, everyone knew, supposed to be a gimmick—the Grand Old Man of Hockey skating with his sons—but it didn't work out that way from the first drop of the puck in Houston. With the Howes leading the way, the Aeros won the league championship and the now-long-forgotten Avco Trophy. Mark was the rookie of the year, and the old man, Gordie, came third in league scoring and was named the league's most valuable player. Bill Dineen's reward was a bit more earthy. When Houston held a parade to honour the winning team, they put the victorious coach in a low convertible—only to have a passing elephant offer his own pungent version of a ticker-tape parade.

It had been nineteen years since Gordie Howe had played on a winner, but winning like this was beyond his wildest imagination. He would play as long as he could. As long as he could with his boys. The Howes stayed together seven years, four with Houston, two with the Hartford Whalers of the WHA and one final year after Hartford was admitted to the NHL for the 1979–80 season. He played in the NHL all-star game that last year, a special honour granted to the fifty-two-year-old grandfather, and he used the opportunity to pass on a key piece of advice to the teenager who would soon challenge his title as the greatest player the game has known: Wayne Gretzky. Howe had noticed what everyone else had seen in the youngster—the hands, the eyesight, the ability to go to where the puck would eventually arrive—but he had noticed something else, too, and did not like it. "Quit your whining," he told Gretzky. It's unbecoming to the great players, he told him. Howe, so sore from arthritis that he could sometimes barely grip his stick, played the entire season without complaint, turning every reference to his age and health into a joke. "If I dyed my hair," he said, "they'd want more speed."

The memories of those who covered those years pulse with the sense of what it must have meant to Gordie Howe. They remember a teenaged Mark being down on the ice under a larger player who was pummelling away with his fists, and Gordie suddenly reaching down, bare-handed, placing two fingers in the thug's nostrils and bodily lifting the player off the ice. "The guy's nose must have stretched half a foot," an amazed Marty Howe told a reporter. "It seemed like the right thing to do at the time," added his smiling father.

Harry Neale, the popular analyst on "Hockey Night in Canada", was coaching Hartford when the Howes arrived from Houston. "There was one moment in a game in Houston I'll never forget," Neale told Dick Irvin for his 1993 book, *Behind the Bench*. "A beautiful story. Gordie was on right wing and Mark on left wing. Gordie got the puck on the far side and Mark is heading up the ice, right in front of our bench. Both Mark and Marty always called him 'Gordie' when they were around the team. I don't know if they had an agreement, but that's what they called him, always 'Gordie'. Anyway, on this rush, when Gordie got the puck, one of their defencemen fell down. Mark yelled for the puck. I guess he was excited because he yelled 'Dad!' instead of 'Gordie' and some of the guys on the bench could hear it. Gordie looks up and hits him with a perfect pass, right on the tape. Mark goes in and scores, puts it right over the goalie's shoulder into the top corner. [Dave] Keon and [John] McKenzie were sitting on the bench. They heard it, and maybe only a few others in the rink heard it, and they saw 'Dad' put the pass right onto his son's stick. I never thought guys like Keon and McKenzie were all that sentimental, but they had a look on their faces that showed they knew they had seen a moment that very few people experience. They talked about it and it was lovely, just lovely."

But it was not always so easy to coach the Howes. "When it came to handling the boys, Gordie never said a thing," Neale told Irvin. "I didn't play Marty much, and one night after a game Colleen Howe was waiting for me. When I came out she said, 'When I come to a game I come to see my *three* boys play.'"

The Howes were an instant sensation in Houston and an even bigger draw in Hartford. There was even talk of a fourth Howe joining. Murray, it was said, was a sure bet. He was fast, smart, flashy—and he was a Howe. "Wait till you see Murray," they used to say. "He's going to be the best."

How could he miss? He could, if he did not grow. Murray Howe was small all through his hockey career, and far too small when it mattered most: five inches shorter than his father and fifty pounds lighter. Yet he so desperately wanted it. Colleen remembers once taking him to a fortune teller who told the young man he had a most promising future, but it would lie in either journalism or medicine. He cried all the way home.

Murray tried to change fate. He worked with weights and he learned karate and he ran until he threw up and still he ran some more, absolutely convinced he would end up in the National Hockey League when the hurt was finished. But the hurt only grew, and eventually he had to face the obvious. He quit junior hockey and concentrated, instead, on school. He went to the University of Michigan, where, in 1978, he tried out for the school team but was cut. People felt sorry for him, but they completely misread him. He had no time to concentrate on hockey. He had decided to become a doctor.

In his freshman year, Murray set down on paper the confusion that had been tearing around his head since he set his mind on the NHL and his body stubbornly refused to cooperate. He was assigned an essay; it was to be personal and students were allowed to use a pseudonym. He entitled his essay "The Road to Nowhere", and though his name was not on it, anyone reading it would recognize Murray Howe as the main character.

He wrote about his father and the natural expectations that he, as a son, would follow. He wrote about being a superior player at a very young age and how, as the competition increased, there came a day that comes to so many dreamers when he had to deal with the fact that he was simply not as good as his early promise. He had become "the benchwarmer. The loser. The extra burden."

The loser... It was a self-condemnation that speaks to the irrational emphasis we place on excelling in hockey above all other pursuits. In Canada, it has been said that parents would rather have their child grow up to play in the NHL than become a doctor. An exaggeration, perhaps, but it illustrates the perceived returns from hockey: fame, respect, riches, accomplishment. For a youngster growing up in hockey's First Family, the pressures seemed doubled. Merely to keep pace, Murray Howe felt he had to be a superstar. And yet he also knew it was a hopeless chase.

Finally, a school friend gave some simple advice—Do whatever you are best at—and Murray Howe sat down at his study desk and compiled a list of the main concerns in his young life—school and hockey—what he took from them, and what they gave him. In school he was getting straight As; in hockey he was getting only criticism. In school he was praised; in hockey he was humiliated. In school he was able to offer help; in hockey he needed help. How could there even be a debate?

"All my life I had been struggling for something I couldn't get," Murray Howe wrote, "on the road to nowhere, and there right behind me was my gift, my talent that I had never once considered.... I changed my priorities in life that night to happiness first, education second, and hockey third."

He never forgot what his parents had told him: "Whatever makes you happy is what we want. We'll still let you in the door." He excelled in medical school and specialized in radiology. He married and began a family. Studies were difficult and the hours spent as an intern long, but he never let go of the game, continuing to play shinny hockey with friends and colleagues late at night in empty suburban rinks. At times, he felt he was learning a new game. "No body contact," he says, "a six-pack in the dressing-room at the end of the game. It's a lot of fun."

The night he scored six goals, he laughs, "I felt like Gordie Howe."

When Bill Dineen talked Gordie Howe into coming out of retirement and joining his sons Marty and Mark on the Houston Aeros, it did not occur to him that Howe would have a profound effect on the Dineen family as well as on the Houston team. He had decided to woo Howe for many reasons: one, the Aeros desperately needed a major attraction; two, he honestly felt Howe still had a year of good hockey in him; and three, he needed someone to set the tone for this young hockey club. In his own long career he had come across three such role models, and Howe was the only one who might still play. He needed a special kind of player, someone who could "carry himself well in public, do whatever's asked of him. It rubs off on the young guys."

But Gordie Howe's influence also rubbed off on the very young guys. The young Dineens were rapidly growing up. Shawn and Peter were already showing signs of being fine players with real prospects, and Bill found he couldn't keep the two younger ones, Gord and Kevin, off the Houston ice. When Gordie Howe got there, he encouraged them. "We used to play keep-away with Gordie Howe," remembers Gord Dineen. "You're a ten-year-old kid—that leaves quite an impression. He carries such a presence."

The idea that the two men they admired most, their own father and Gordie Howe, could have what appeared to be such marvellous lives in hockey profoundly affected the ambitions of the Dineen boys. Shawn went off to the University of Denver on a hockey scholarship, then played four years in the minors, including Toledo of the International Hockey League and Moncton and New Haven of the American Hockey League. Peter took the junior route, leaving home to play for Kingston in the Ontario Hockey Association, then being drafted by the Philadelphia Flyers and spending time in Maine, Moncton and Hershey of the AHL before briefly playing for the Los Angeles Kings and the Detroit Red Wings of the NHL. Gord also chose the OHA route, heading off to play for Sault Ste Marie before the New York Islanders took him in the second round of the 1981 entry draft. Kevin also went off to play Junior "B" in Toronto and then went on to the University of Denver on a scholarship. He was drafted in the third round of the 1982 draft by Hartford, played a year for the Canadian Olympic team and then went to the NHL to stay. Jerry, the youngest, won a scholarship to Plattsburgh, near his parents' Glen Lake home, and played four years of intercollegiate hockey.

It is easy to understand how daughter Rosemarie once stood up at the dining-room table and screamed, "Unless your mind's like a hockey puck around here, nobody pays attention." Hockey was the family obsession, partly by default—five hockey-playing boys versus one figure skater—but partly by design. Bill Dineen appreciated what hockey had given him. He liked the idea that he had played the same game as his father; he was astonished that his own sons, growing up in places like Houston, Texas, wanted the same.

They could not get enough of the game. In Houston, when they weren't on the ice at the beginning or after the Aeros practices, they were shooting pucks on the smooth cement of an outdoor cafeteria nearby, baffled Texans often stopping to ask what on earth they were doing. They made up games wherever they were, whatever they were doing. "We're pretty competitive in this family," says Gord, "no matter what it was, whether getting the last hamburger on the plate or what." Bill and Pat catered to them all, whether it was hockey or figure skating or baseball or any other activity in which they expressed interest. The parents' philosophy was simple: "Just let them go, and then go watch them play." They went out for football—the game that is to Texans as hockey is to Canadians—but found it boring and mild in comparison. "After hockey," says Gord, "it was nothing."

Because Kevin and Gord were so close in age, they were sometimes placed on the same team, at times with disastrous results. They sometimes fought each other in the warm-ups. They played tricks on each other. Kevin once removed Gord's skates from his bag, scraped them dull on the cement and placed them back in the bag so that Gord would fall down and have to sit out—and Kevin, of course, would then have extra time. Once Gord's skates were repaired, he deliberately began skating offside on Kevin every time Kevin carried the puck. The game ended in chaos, with the two best players on the ice, both on the same team, standing in the opposition end firing the puck back and forth at each other's head.

They fought, just as the McSorley boys all fought in Cayuga, Ontario, just as the Sutter boys all fought out in Viking, Alberta. At the time, it exasperated, infuriated and worried the parents; in time it took on another light, once the parents realized the children were growing up, maturing and, sometimes mystifyingly, taking on the very values they seemed to spite.

Bill Dineen still tells the story of the trip the family took out west one summer, driving from Toronto to British Columbia in a big station-wagon, when Gord and Kevin, then both young teenagers, got into a terrible fist fight over a matter no one can even now remember. He had stopped at a hardware store in Fernie, just over the Alberta–B.C. border, merely to pick up some bait and a few hints on where he might look for some mountain trout. "There must have been about forty people in the store at the time," remembers Bill, "and there was this big commotion up at the front. Everybody was at the window looking out at this station-wagon rocking back and forth in the parking lot. The kids were really going at it, and this guy next to me says, 'I've never seen anything like that before.' I said, 'Yeah, I wonder whose kids they are.'"

Things have a way of working out, often much to the surprise of those who least expected it. Gord and Kevin Dineen grew up to be the closest of friends, as well as virtual neighbours on the lake and, for more than a decade, colleagues in the NHL. It is a reality that still causes their father to shake his head. "I never did think they were going to be pro players," says Bill. "I don't think there was a lot of talk about any of them."

Gord grew up to be one of the most popular players in professional hockey. When he played with the Ottawa Senators during the 1993–94 season and captain Mark Lamb was traded during a contract dispute, a leader was needed for this dispirited team, one who could be positive and remain calm when surrounded by panic. Gord Dineen was the obvious choice. He moved on to Denver in the IHL and was soon captain again.

Kevin Dineen also made his mark in the NHL. He had always been a defenceman until, in 1983, coach Dave King of the Canadian Olympic program transformed him into a forechecking right winger. From a checking role he gradually changed to a goal scorer, scoring twenty-five, then thirty-three, forty, twenty-five and forty-five goals. The forty-five-goal season in Hartford during the 1988–89 season—and his playing in the annual all-star game—was a highlight in what is now a three-hundred-goal-plus NHL career. "It was *shocking* to the rest of us," says Gord. Adds Bill: "I think that's why he did it—to prove us all wrong." For his charity work, particularly for Crohn's disease, colitis and ileitis, Kevin was named NHL Man of the Year in 1991. He has suffered himself from Crohn's disease, an inflammatory bowel condition, since 1987, and at one point it threatened his career.

It was not easy. None of the Dineen boys was as obviously gifted as, say, Mark Howe, who was destined to succeed from the moment he made the U.S. Olympic team at age sixteen. But then, Bill Dineen was hardly comparable to Gordie Howe, even though Kevin Dineen insists that, of all the hockey-playing Dineens, "Dad was the best." The Dineens all had to work hard to accomplish anything. And, at times, it seemed the dream made little sense. Gord distinctly remembers a talk with his father when the family was living in Houston and Gord, at fourteen, was just beginning to imagine what hockey might mean to his future. "I asked him if he thought I could play pro hockey. He told me how many kids there were up in Canada and how good they were."

But the Dineen boys had no real choice. It was still the 1970s and hockey was little known in the United States and little played, especially at the élite level for teenagers. If they were going to test themselves—and if they were going to develop—they had to go north. When hockey failed to pan out in Houston, Bill Dineen began bouncing around hockey again, once more coming in contact with the Howe family in Hartford. The Dineen youngsters were moved from a middling hockey program to one that was, in Bill's estimation, of "poor calibre". Gord was soon off to the Ontario junior leagues and Kevin left for the minor hockey program in Detroit. "For me to get any better," Kevin says, "I *had* to go to Detroit." To get better, he had to play against better players.

Gord Dineen was stunned when he got to Canada and discovered he could not only play, he was good enough for the best junior league. "I always underestimated myself," he says. "I always thought there were better players in Canada. We were able to progress because we found out that

Canada had all these great players at pee wee and bantam, but they didn't get any better."

Their dad considers this the secret to the boys' success. They had this fear that everyone else—everyone else in Canada, at least—was going to be a better player. And they had grown up around hockey, they knew what was required. "It was important to keep everything in perspective," says Bill. "They never dared think, 'I can get away with going two-thirds speed.' They were motivated. Each one of them, even after they were drafted, continued to improve. None of them had a big ego. They could handle the setbacks better than other kids."

There were indeed setbacks. Between 1982, when he first went to the Islanders, and 1995, when he ended the season playing for Denver in the IHL, Gord Dineen was dispatched to the minor leagues ten times. Three times he was connected to Stanley Cup–winning teams, twice in Pittsburgh and once with the Islanders, but he never fully felt part of the celebrations. He was the one moving back and forth between the minors and the big team, the one they called on first to help when there were injuries, the one they sent down first when the injured came back.

When the Stanley Cup Champion Pittsburgh Penguins were invited to the White House for a reception with President George Bush, Gord Dineen found he could not take up his invitation. He hadn't been on the ice for the victory; he didn't feel he deserved to go. When the Ottawa Senators wanted him to play for their AHL affiliate instead of the NHL team he would eventually captain, he did not like the demotion one bit. "But my dad played seventeen years of pro hockey and twelve of them were in the minors," he said, "so I can't really stick my nose up in the air and say I'm too good to play there."

Kevin Dineen was more fortunate. He played twenty-five games for Binghamton in the AHL in his first year as a professional, but then never returned to the minors. He played seven seasons in Hartford and then, in November of 1991, he was traded to Philadelphia. It was a trade that delighted Kevin, for he was going to be joining his father in a way: Bill Dineen was then scouting for the Flyers. Kevin was going from a troubled franchise where there was little fan support to one with a long tradition of success and a tremendous fan base. With young players like goaltender Ron Hextall, Mike Ricci, Steve Duchesne and Mark Recchi, the Flyers seemed to him a team heading in exactly the same direction he himself hoped to go. They also had excellent draft prospects, with Swedish sensation Peter Forsberg taken in the previous June draft.

And the Flyers had veterans like Mark Howe on defence, the smart, smooth-skating Howe who once was a kid himself with the Houston Aeros and who would play with the much younger Dineen boys who kept hanging about the rink. Now Mark Howe struck Kevin as ageless, just as a generation ago Howe's father had seemed to Dineen's father. Mark Howe was then thirty-six; he was in his tenth season with the Flyers, where he had three times been named to the NHL's first all-star team. Mark Howe's one great frustration was that, unlike his father, he had never won the Stanley Cup, despite two gruelling final series against Wayne Gretzky's Edmonton Oilers. Howe was determined to win a Cup before he was finished—and such determination was exactly what Kevin Dineen hoped to find on his new team.

Dineen's career in Philadelphia was less than a month old when the Flyers fired coach Paul Holmgren for failing to bring the youngsters along as quickly as management wanted. It came as a shock to Dineen, but was nothing compared to the aftershock. He arrived at the rink to discover Holmgren was out and practice cancelled. In the dressing-room, defenceman Kjell Samuelsson told him, "Bill's going to have a meeting."

"Bill who?"

Samuelsson turned, surprised. "Your *dad*! You knew that."

He did not know. Bill Dineen had been working as a Flyers scout—usually travelling, rarely around the actual Flyers players—and neither he nor his sons ever expected he would be coaching in the NHL again. But the organization had come to him in desperation. They had been insistent, and after he had agreed to do it for a while, management asked him to keep the news quiet so it wouldn't leak to the media. Bill had told Pat, but no one else in the family—not even the son who would be playing for him.

Once Kevin got over the shock, he thought the idea "was kind of neat." It meant that the Dineens had joined a rare category in hockey history: NHL players who become NHL coaches with their own sons on the team. It had happened previously to the Patricks, Lester and his sons Lynn and Muzz, in New York. It had happened, briefly in Montreal, to the Geoffrions, Bernie "Boom Boom" and his son, Danny. Now the Dineens were together in Philadelphia.

It was, at first, a strange experience for Kevin. Like the other players, he began calling his father Willie, sometimes by an older nickname, Foxie, and as one of the team leaders, he sometimes had to act as go-between for his teammates and his own father. "He was approachable," says Kevin. "The lines of communication were always open." The players loved "Willie" and found his style unlike any most of them had ever encountered. When author and broadcaster Dick Irvin was interviewing for his 1993 book on coaches, *Behind the Bench,* Los Angeles Kings coach Barry Melrose gave Bill Dineen credit for teaching him "that you don't have to be an asshole to be a coach. Players don't have to hate you to play hard."

As for coaching his son, Bill found no awkwardness whatsoever in the situation. "With Kevin you know what you're going to get every night," he says. The problem, however, was not his son—nor even his son's team-mates. The problem was impatient management. Bill Dineen had no sooner finished out the season for Holmgren when the Flyers ransacked his promising young team to complete the second-biggest trade in modern hockey history, the June 30, 1992, trade that sent Quebec draft choice Eric Lindros to the Flyers for Hextall, Duchesne, Ricci, Forsberg, Kerry Huffman, Ron Simon, the team's first-round draft choices for 1993 and 1994 and $15 million (U.S.) cash.

Bill Dineen has no comment on the enormous trade other than to say it was "tough."

"It *was* tough," agrees Kevin. "I was one of the guys. And we went from a team that would have made the play-offs those two years to one that couldn't. We went from a team about to come into its own to one too shallow to win—but with one guy with so much potential. It showed a little bit in our standings."

The team Kevin had joined with such high hopes was dramatically changed. So many of the best players were now in Quebec. The foundation of the team, Lindros, was too young to produce immediately. The class of the team, Mark Howe, had been deemed too old by the Flyers and was now off with the Detroit Red Wings, which had signed him as a free agent. The Flyers were slow to recover from such shock. In the much-heralded Lindros's first two seasons, the Flyers failed to make the playoffs, and although it was clearly a team on the rise with the sensational young star, it could not happen fast enough for Bill Dineen. Management remained impatient, and during the 1992–93 season he, too, was fired.

"I didn't really see it coming," Bill says. "I didn't ask any questions. I didn't politic for my job."

"That's his problem," his son says. "No self-promotion. Things have to fall into his lap." His father's firing was no instant solution. The new coach, Terry Simpson, lasted less than a year and was fired at the end of the next season, when the Flyers again missed the playoffs. "If Dad had still been there," says Kevin, "we would have done a little bit better."

He was speaking then as the team captain. The incoming Simpson had wisely named Kevin Dineen the new captain. He had the respect of the players, just as his father had had their admiration. He was there, fortunately, during Eric Lindros's most difficult period of adjustment—the aftermath of a bar incident about which he was declared innocent but said to be in need of a "babysitter". Lindros himself was adamant that he was mature enough to take care of himself, but when he returned to Philadelphia after a long-drawn-out court ordeal, he went to his captain and asked if it would be all right if he moved in with Kevin and his wife, Ann. Kevin was delighted, took charge of the young superstar and helped him come to better terms with both his fame and his talent. When the Flyers named Lindros captain in the summer of 1994, Dineen agreed with the move without bitterness.

It is a family trait. The family has been split up by circumstance, its members fired, demoted and traded from various teams, and yet the Dineens express nothing but gratitude to this game. "Hockey has been great to us," says Gord. "Just look at this," Kevin says, spreading an arm out as if he had somehow painted the spectacular summer scene that is Glen Lake. "We wouldn't have any of this if it wasn't for hockey."

"You come here," says Bill, "and you look out and you can count your lucky stars every day. You can say, 'Well, you just play a game.' The truth is, it's because you work so hard to play a game that you have this."

It amazes and delights the Dineens that, as the years go on, they are all gathering together at this unlikely sight at the edge of the Adirondacks. "They're all coming back," says Bill. They say they come back for a specific reason: to put down the roots they never had.

"You always like to hope you're a good reflection of your parents," says Gord Dineen. "And we hope we are."

The man in the Mercedes on this New Year's Eve, 1992, has all the markings of success. The car, the monogrammed sleeves of an impossibly-white shirt, the expensive suit, the sure, aggressive manner in which he works the Mercedes through the traffic on Interstate 75, heading down through Detroit to the Joe Louis Arena, his white-haired father eased back in the rear seat, talking about anything that comes to mind. Including their respective abilities.

"We're completely different players," Mark Howe says. "I'm more of a finesse player." He pauses, thinking, adds, "Dad was tougher," then laughs. "And I can say *dirtier*, from playing with him."

The notion delights the father. He is headed for the rink with his son; he could not be more content. The past few years have been wonderful. Good health, he and Colleen have enjoyed their grandchildren, he had become one of the leaders of the retired players battling the NHL in court over the misuse of the players' pension funds. He and Lindsay had reconciled. He was a good and respected businessman. No one ever took advantage of him any more the way Jolly Jack Adams had for so many years.

A father and son, together on the weekend for a hockey game. Only this time the son is driving to the rink, and the pressure, if there is any, arises unspoken from within the son. Tomorrow will begin a new year. The man in the back seat will turn sixty-five. The man driving will turn thirty-eight; soon enough he would be the oldest active player in the National Hockey League—and still no Stanley Cup.

After a decade in Philadelphia, Mark Howe had left unfulfilled. Twice he had been to the finals; the last time, 1987, they had come back from a 3–1 deficit to tie the series 3–3 against the Oilers, only to lose the seventh and final game 3–1 on Edmonton's ice. Exhausted and shattered, Howe had dragged himself to the dressing room as another player, Edmonton's Marty McSorley, had reached into the crowd and dragged his father, Bill, out onto the ice where they had hugged and cried as a lifelong dream came true—the same dream that would still be driving Mark Howe at the age of forty, when his Detroit Red Wings came up short in the 1995 Stanley Cup finals.

No one understood better than the man in the back seat what that meant to a professional hockey player. Gordie Howe had won four Stanley Cups in the 1950s and, in the years since, the memories had not faded but become ever sharper. The fractured skull in 1950. The eight-game sweep in 1952. Tony Leswick's winning overtime goal in 1954. Howe's record point performance in 1955. He kept the memories in his head, for unlike today, there were no Stanley Cup rings to commemorate great feats.

He once got a cigarette case from the Red Wings, and another time a fruit bowl, but they meant nothing to him. After Ab Howe died of cancer at the age of ninety-one, the Howe children gathered in Saskatoon to clean out the old house and disperse the family treasures. One of his sisters found the fruit bowl and tried to give it to him. He said he had no need of such a thing. "Turn it over," she told him. There, on the bottom, was inscribed, "Stanley Cup champions, 1955."

Howe's old coach from those days, Tommy Ivan, who moved from the Red Wings to the Chicago Blackhawks, had once read a magazine article in which Gordie stated that he had no memento from those years and he had called Howe up and broken down in tears over the phone. At his own expense, Ivan had three Stanley Cup rings made up and presented them to Sid Abel, Howe and Lindsay. Howe considered it a lovely gesture from an old friend, not a reminder of a great hockey victory. He didn't need a ring.

Mark Howe knew in Philadelphia that his career was fast coming to an end. He had played fewer and fewer games in recent years. He was bothered by a chronic back condition that made movement difficult and skating sometimes impossible. Barely half the games in 1991–92, only nineteen in 1990–91, forty the season before. He was certainly finished with the Flyers. But was he finished with the NHL?

He thought for a while he could catch on in Chicago. A close friend, Wayne Presley, had acted as a go-between while the Blackhawks had felt out Howe. Yes, he'd love to go. He thought at one point the deal had been done. Chicago management had called his home looking for him, but Ginger Howe had told them her husband was on the road. She had called the hotel and he had sat on the edge of the bed staring at the telephone for two hours, but they never called. There was talk that Philadelphia wanted to buy him out of his contract, but his contract had a "no buy-out" clause in it. Then he heard the Flyers were going to offer him a termination contract, meaning he could try his chances on the free-agent market. He knew for certain they were trying to get rid of him.

He had come to the conclusion that this was it. He was finished. He had had a wonderful NHL career by any measure—he might even one day join his father in the Hockey Hall of Fame—but he had never won a Stanley Cup. He knew, too, that when his name came up, so too would a story that still makes grown men wince to remember. For Mark Howe had once suffered an injury so severe it ended up changing the way the game is played.

It happened in Hartford in 1980–81, the first season after Gordie Howe's retirement. He had finally left professional hockey after thirty-two years of stardom—his final NHL playoff goal, his sixty-eighth, assisted on, appropriately, by Mark the previous spring. But he had agreed to stay on in a front-office position with the Whalers. Marty and Mark were still playing in the organization and Mark was showing signs of being as dominant a player in the NHL as he had been in the now-folded WHA. But then, at the age of twenty-five—the age at which the superstars begin to emerge—he crashed into the net.

It had seemed an almost innocent, typical moment in a hard-fought hockey game. Gordie Howe had been sitting high in the press box of the Hartford Civic Center and saw what everyone saw and had seen hundreds of times before: bodies crashing into a net, the referee raising his whistle to blow down the play. Only this time it was like nothing anyone had ever imagined. The net had held. And not only had the posts held tight to the ice, but the sharp support shaft that ran from the rear of the net towards the front—a deflector plate that formed the centre of the W shape of the old nets—had pierced the first player in. Mark Howe was lying in a quickly spreading pool of blood. The shaft had gone into him like a thrust sword.

"It scraped the rectum, almost cut the sphincter muscle and missed my spine by three-quarters of an inch," Mark Howe remembers. "I lost three and a half pints of blood on the ice."

Gordie could see his son biting his hand to hold back the screams. The other players seemed in shock. Gordie began running to get down to Mark. Halfway through the press box, a man blocked his way, holding a piece of paper towards him for an autograph.

"That's my *son* down there," a stunned Howe told the man.

"It'll only take a minute," the man protested.

Fortunately, someone stepped in before the frantic father went straight through the man. He pushed through the corridors and took the stairs two at a time. By the time he arrived, Mark was already on a stretcher and headed into the trainers' room.

"I knew what was happening the whole time," says Mark. "I was really scared. I was screaming at them, 'Am I going to be all right? *Am I all right?*'"

Gordie pushed his way into the room where his son was lying, still conscious. Mark vividly remembered his father's arrival. He remembers, distinctly, the calm that came over him when his father grabbed his hand and squeezed.

"He insisted on seeing what it had done," Mark says. "He bent down to look and he almost broke my hand when he saw—that's when I knew how bad it was."

They rushed Mark off to the nearest hospital in an ambulance, the father glad that players were no longer treated as he once had been. "One time in Detroit," Gordie Howe says from the back of the Mercedes, "I had ripped cartilage all around my ribs. The pain was terrible. I could hardly move. They told me to take a taxi to the hospital."

It took five weeks to determine that Mark would suffer no paralysis. Less than an inch in another direction, and his spine would have been severed. It took him a year to recover well enough to play at his former level, and five years before he was free of painful cramps.

The stunning injury Mark Howe suffered became a convincing argument for a necessary change. With Mark lending his weight to those who fought for the change, regulations were rewritten so that the stiff posts that held hockey nets in place were banned and replaced by magnets that would give easily on contact. It caused a subtle but significant change in the way the game was played, with "crashing the goalie" becoming common practice since there was so little chance of injury; it also became a new defensive tactic, with defencemen and goaltenders deliberately knocking the net off the magnets whenever the play became too threatening around the net.

The change led to more whistles, more delays and far more fan booing. Those who boo, however, were not there the night Mark Howe was nearly killed by a hockey net. As Mark says in a quiet voice that somehow brings back that moment, even after a dozen years, "No one knows what I went through."

With Philadelphia cooling on him and age so quickly coming on—"I was always the youngest on whatever team I played on," he says a bit incredulously—Mark Howe had resigned himself to a career without one more chance at the

Stanley Cup. It was all over, he figured. The day he signed the termination contract with the Flyers, a deal in which the team would buy out the rest of his salary at a lesser rate and release him, the telephone rang with the first of two surprises.

It was Boston's Harry Sinden, wondering if Mark would consider the Boston Bruins if a trade could be arranged with the Flyers. The irony was incredible. Sinden was only a few hours too late, and yet Boston had always been a plan at the back of Howe's mind. The Bruins had been the NHL team that drafted him in 1974, hoping that they might lure the promising youngster back from the WHA, where he was playing with his father and brother. But he had not then wanted to leave Houston. Yet he had almost gone to Boston in 1977, when the Howes came within a whisker of going back to Boston as a family unit, Gordie to work for the Bruins owners, the Jacobs family, and Marty and Mark to play. He might yet make it. The termination contract would make him a free agent. If Sinden was willing to pay, then Mark Howe was more than willing to play.

But it didn't work out for the third time. The other two times he had considered himself, his brother and his parents when he had been tempted by Boston, and it hadn't worked out. This time he would base his decision entirely on his own son, Travis.

Travis Howe had been playing minor hockey in the southern New Jersey suburb in which the Howes lived while Mark played for the nearby Flyers. He had his friends and he had hockey. Like two generations before him, he was absolutely hooked on the game. He didn't want to move and leave his friends.

Then the second surprise. In an ironic twist, the very team that had just dumped Howe was now desperately in need of him. The Lindros trade had cost the Flyers two of their defence, Steve Duchesne and Kerry Huffman, and a veteran player with good speed was much in demand. The Flyers, having just terminated Howe's contract and cast him free, sheepishly offered him a fabulous deal—$1.6 million (U.S.) over two years—but he was loath to return to a team that had already given up on him. He had his pride. But did he have an option?

The call that changed everything was completely unexpected. It wasn't even from a general manager, but from a team owner, Mike Ilitch. There had been some earlier discussions with then Detroit general manager Bryan Murray, but Ilitch was now making a second Detroit offer that was, in fact, bumping up the offer his own general manager had just made. Howe had thought Murray's offer generous, but he figured he would not be leaving the Philadelphia area. The family would come first.

But now Ilitch was offering the same money the Flyers had mentioned. And for four years, not two. Ilitch thought Howe could play for two years, then coach for two. Howe thought he could play longer: "My dad once said, 'So long as you love the game, you play until nobody wants you any more.'" Ilitch thought that was great, if possible. What he wanted was a Howe back in Detroit.

The problem was still Travis Howe. Ilitch, however, had a solution. The multimillionaire pizza magnate sent his Lear jet to Philadelphia and asked Travis—as well as his father—if he'd like to come to Detroit and see what kind of hockey was available there. Mark and Ginger Howe decided to leave the decision completely in the hands of Travis. "We won't push," says Mark. "That's how I was raised."

Travis was delighted with the treatment and excited by the prospects—and, like any kid, he was fascinated with jets. Ilitch showed Travis the minor-league program that he was sponsoring through his company, Little Caesars, and Travis loved what he saw. Ilitch even had a sweater made up, Travis's name and number on the back. The kid was sold. A few more trips and a deal was signed, the Lear jet bringing in Mark Howe with a 102-degree temperature and a lingering flu for the press conference. He was almost delirious through the announcement, mostly from the fever, but partly from the obvious pressure.

He expected the question: Would the new Howe in the Red Wings uniform be wearing No. 9?

No, he would not. Mark would say nothing about a call he had already received from his father, Gordie Howe offering to let his sweater be brought out of retirement if Mark wanted it. But Mark could not do it.

"Leave it up in the rafters," he told his father, "where it belongs."

"He hates heights," the father joked. But he understood.

Mark Howe chose No. 4. He would have his own number and, if he could stay around for a few years and the Red Wings young players came along as he expected, he might have one final chance at a Stanley Cup.

It had been a good decision and, so far, a wonderful year. He was skating well and his back was fine. The family had all been together for Christmas and it had contained one wonderful surprise.

Mark had given his father a windbreaker. Brand new, red, with the Detroit Red Wings logo over the heart— forty-six years after he had been promised one by Jolly Jack Adams. Gordie had hardly taken it off all holidays.

Then there had been the fathers-sons game with Travis's team. Gordie had wanted to play and, for a while, it had felt like Houston and Hartford all over again, the old man kidding in the dressing room as he always had, playing on the ice as always.

"Thirty seconds into the game," Mark Howe says, "he kicked the skates out from under Travis."

Mark Howe had laughed, and waited, wanting to see how deep the Howe genes ran. "I wanted to see how Travis responded," Mark says as he wheels the Mercedes down towards Joe Louis Arena.

And?

"He got him back," Mark says, a smile creasing his face as he checks the rearview mirror for all that has gone before, all that has brought them here to a hockey game in Detroit on a cold Saturday night.

"He got him back."

Denis Cyr

Roy and Gord MacGregor with the Stanley Cup: It was an exhibition game being held while the Stanley Cup was on display. There was a big trunk in the dressing room. We opened it up and guess what was inside? What Canadian father and son could resist?

The Ottawa Citizen

Guy Lafleur in full flight. The relationship with Jean Béliveau was such that Lafleur would one day say of his surrogate father: "I may never be able to play like him—but I'd like to be the man he is."

Bruce Bennett Studios

Guy Lafleur and Rejean Lafleur with the Stanley Cup: His father built the rink, he built the nets, and had only one rule—anyone could play so long as little Guy was included.

The Daigles: Alexandre, Francine, Sebastien, Jean-Yves, Veronique. "Money is not the most important thing in life," says Jean-Yves. "The most important thing, être heureux—to be content. That's the big part of our life—to be heureux and close."

The Ottawa Citizen

Alexandre Daigle and Jean Béliveau set out for the Colisée. "The hopes of several million Quebecois ride with him," Béliveau would later say of this moment. "They have seen too few of their number selected high in the entry draft by NHL scouts in recent years."

Gordie Howe and grandson Travis at an NHL Legends exhibition: How did Gordie treat Travis' teammate when he came out for the annual fathers and sons game? "Grandpa flattened him."

Bruce Bennett Studios

Bruce Bennett Studios

Mark and Gordie Howe: When Ol' No. 9 offered his retired Detroit Red Wings sweater to Mark, the son told the father, "Leave it up in the rafters—where it belongs."

Bruce Bennett Studios

Bill and Kevin Dineen: How did Bill know what Gordie Howe's reaction would be when he gave him the opportunity to play with his sons? "Just instinct," says Dineen. "Just instinct."

Bruce Bennett Studios

Paul, Betty and Jack Coffey with the Norris Trophy for the best NHL defenceman. "I never got off the river," says Jack Coffey. But he could tell his son to stride like Frank Mahovlich—no matter how much it hurt.

Photo by Derek Mackesy

Bill and Marty McSorley: "McSorleys don't back down from anything," Bill once shouted at the family dog as it ran from a coyote. "Now get back in there and fight!"

Bruce Bennett Studios

Father Time in Europe: front row (left to right)—Marty McSorley, Wayne Gretzky, Paul Coffey, Mark Messier; back row—Bill McSorley, Walter Gretzky, Jack Coffey, Doug Messier.

Walter, Wayne and Phyllis Gretzky: the proudest father in the land has no memory of his son's greatest feats. "It's like I was asleep for ten years," Walter says of the aneurysm he suffered in 1991. "It's all kind of like a dream."

Bruce Bennett Studios

The Ottawa Citizen

Radek Bonk: When Jaroslav Bonk went to watch his son play his chosen game, soccer, he was so upset by what he saw he stormed out onto the field and yanked his son off. "We have to find something else," the father said.

Bruce Bennett Studios

The Florida Panthers select Ed Jovanovski first overall at the 1994 entry draft. Ed's father, Kostadin, did everything within his power to keep his kid out of hockey and in soccer. "It was boring," says the son.

Bruce Bennett Studios

Bobby and Brett Hull, the NHL's only father-son Hart Trophy winners: "Mostly genetics."

Photo by Lynda Dryden

Ken and Michael Dryden today: "He's playing to what he is," the father says of the son who suddenly shot up, "not what he was."

Photo courtesy of the Dryden Family

The Dryden Men: (from left) Ken, Dave, Murray, Greg—with little Michael in front.

Photo by Roy McGregor

Joe and Gino Odjick: When the priest sent Joe Odjick off to residential school, they took away his name and gave him a number—29. When Gino Odjick made the Vancouver Canucks, he put the number on his back.

The Ottawa Citizen

Gino Odjick and two young fans from the Kitigan Zibi reserve. "With Gino being native," says Buffalo Sabres coach Ted Nolan, "it just lights up the kids eyes. He has a presence. A wink, a pat on the back—it means a lot to those kids. It's a little more important sometimes than if Wayne Gretzky and Steve Yzerman were there."

The Ottawa Citizen

The Yashins: Alexei, Valery and Tatiana study game films at home. "If you played another sport at a high level," says Tatiana, "you understand all games. If you understand the rules of one game, if you play basketball, volleyball, hockey—it's games. You understand the rules. You know when it's beautiful, correct."

Brad Hornung as a rising young hockey star: "People out there," the radio told Terry Hornung as she listened at home, "you'd better start praying for Brad Hornung."

Larry Hornung of the Winnipeg Jets: "For the first time," Larry Hornung says of the tragic accident that paralysed his son, "it dawned on me that one of my kids might have a problem I can't fix."

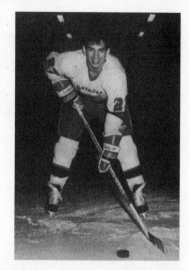

The Edwards: Ken (left) and Troy. When the Raymore Rockets hang up the Edwards sweater for the last time, will the screaming finally stop?

The Eganville Leader

WAY BACK WHEN . . . . Eganville Senior Hockey team, 1927-28. Standing, left to right, H. "Tiny" McKibbon, Howard Valliquette, Harold Costello, Dick Zadow, George Shane, Ed Freitag, Dunc McGregor, Mickey Freitag, Bob Patterson. Seated: Albert Middlestadt. In front, James Reeves, mascot. Photo courtesy of Jack Freitag, R.R. 1, Renfrew

The 1927–28 Eganville Senior Hockey team: Duncan MacGregor, third from right. "I was a bit of a ruffian."

*The MacGregors—Duncan, Roy, Gord—at the Hockey Hall of Fame:
The father on exhibit.*

Author photo

Salvation

The snow had been coming down all through the night and on into the morning: huge, feathery flakes that fell slowly, making visibility difficult and the canal impossible. The canal workers had been ploughing since midnight, the world's largest skating rink briefly emerging and quickly vanishing as the yellow floodlights guided the scrapers down towards Dow's Lake, snow swirling in their wake, snow building ahead and building again behind. By mid-morning the ploughs were beginning to win, the snow finally falling more slowly than it was being pushed to the sides, the temperature dropping and skaters starting to emerge in a calendar shot of fashionable colour and old-fashioned knits.

Just before noon, the big Caterpillar widening the canal off Lansdowne Park pulled up and shut down. A tall, thin man with skin as weathered as the emerging skating surface climbed out and dropped down, stomping to get the circulation in his feet going. He yanked his old Cumberland Ferry cap down tight to his ears, turned towards the Ottawa Civic Centre and walked away from his job with his foreman's blessing.

Joe Odjick laughed to himself as he imagined what the skaters were thinking. Had he given up? Was he going for coffee? He climbed over the soft snowbank he had been making, climbed over the retaining wall of the canal, climbed over a railing and began walking through the deep snow towards the hockey rink. His plough would be fine for a couple of hours. It had been running almost steady since Boxing Day, so it wouldn't likely freeze up. It could relax, he figured, while he went off to see what had become of the big, gangly kid who had still been playing house league by the time he reached midget, the easygoing child who had discovered there was but one way to realize his and his father's great dream and who was now known around the NHL as the Algonquin Assassin. The name alone never failed to make Joe Odjick laugh.

Inside the civic centre, the stands were already filling up with those who had come down in cars and trucks and on Russell Coté's yellow school bus. They had come from Kitigan Zibi, the Algonkin reserve from outside Maniwaki, a Quebec lumbertown two hours north of Hull. There were Algonkin families from Barrière Lake and Rapid Lake, friends and cousins and aunts and even young Patrick Odjick, going on six, who was sound asleep when the Vancouver Canucks headed out for their meaningless morning skate. He stirred when they cheered for his father, No. 29, Gino Odjick, the hulking right-winger who came out hot on the heels of the Canuck who usually hears the cheers: No. 10, Pavel Bure.

Forty-five of those who had come were children. "If I'd have advertised," Coté said, "I would've had to bring *four* buses." They had been let out of school and he had brought them here for one reason: "inspirational" instruction. So that they would see success and feel success, and know that anything and everything is possible. All they had to do was look at Gino Odjick, skating around the same ice surface as Pavel Bure. But they could have learned as much looking behind, back to the railing where Joe Odjick, still knocking wet snow off his shoulders, stood with a grin as wide as a snowplough.

To understand how Gino Odjick got here, it helps to know where Joe Odjick started out. And the beginning is known as Kitigansibiwiniwag, the People of the Garden River. This Algonkin reserve called Kitigan Zibi, or Kitigan-sibi, is at the confluence of the Desert River and the Gatineau River, which flows south to enter the mighty Ottawa almost directly across from Parliament Hill.

That there should be contradictions surrounding Gino Odjick in the 1990s—so gentle off the ice, so vicious on— is partially explained by historical context, for the Algonkin have always confused those who have tried to explain them. When Récollet lay brother Gabriel Sagard-Théodat returned from Huronia in 1624 and came down the Ottawa River on his way to the settlement at Quebec, he camped among the Algonkin and found them "good and of a kind disposition so obliging, kind and civil that I was highly pleased and edified with them." Yet another missionary called them "arrogant, given to superstition and debauchery, and very cruel." This negative description, unfortunately, became the accepted white perspective on the Algonkin, and at the turn of the twentieth century was even published as government-approved fact in the *Handbook of Indians of Canada*.

According to Peter Hessel's *The Algonkin Tribe*, the natives who hunted and trapped around the Desert River had been attached, loosely, with the Oka mission closer to Montreal. Along with the Nipissings and Iroquois of roughly the same area, these natives had long been regarded by the French as tremendous warriors, and are remembered in North American history for what became known as the Massacre of Grand-Pré, the 1747 victory over British Colonial reinforcements that had been sent from Boston to take up position in Annapolis Royal, Nova Scotia. The

French colonial government's reward for the Oka-area natives had been to offer them farms, which the Iroquois took up, but the Algonkin wished to remain hunters and trappers, moving nomadically about the northern stretches of the Ottawa Valley as they had always done. They were unhappy with the arrangements with the Oka mission and kept petitioning for a place of their own. Finally, in 1851, nearly a century after the British conquest, the Oblates set up a mission at Maniwaki and, three years later, a reserve was set aside of slightly more than forty-five thousand acres. Later, smaller reserves were established at nearby Rapid Lake and Barrière Lake.

Joe Odjick was born at Rapid Lake in 1939. His father, Basil, had been a trapper and fishing guide; his mother, Marie-Antoinette Marchand, was part French. The child's given name was Hector, which the other kids soon altered, as a joke of the times, to Hitler. It was, he remembers, a tough community, ravaged by alcohol and abuse and poor living and health conditions. His father, along with Russell Coté's father, Sam, and other able-bodied men, were soon off to war, poverty-stricken natives who enlisted in the infantry out of a sense of adventure, a persistent native sense of obligation to Mother Britain, and a strong sense that they would be better fed, clothed and paid fighting for Canada than they would be fighting the elements around Kitigan Zibi. Basil Odjick and Sam Coté found themselves in France in 1945 as part of the Allied invasion and, with Sam Coté standing beside him, Basil Odjick was killed in battle. No one ever called Joe Odjick Hitler again.

Life in Rapid Lake worsened considerably during and immediately following the war. First, the hunters were away. The women and elders and children had to hunt and trap and chop firewood and haul water. Later, when the war was over and the survivors and injured returned, the benefits that flowed to other veterans and war widows did not make it to the native communities. The struggle was almost impossible for single women with no money and several children to raise, and Marie-Antoinette Odjick had been left with three boys and two girls. If a child's parents had tuberculosis or if, as in Joe Odjick's case, a widowed mother was thought to be incapable of handling her situation, then that child would be earmarked for removal. "The priest would just round us up like cattle," Joe remembers. "They'd come in to Rapid Lake and half would be sent off to the orphanage at Amos and half would go to Spanish."

He was nine when the priest sent him off to the Indian residential school at Spanish, Ontario, on the North Channel of Lake Huron. It took him two days to get there by train. And like the other frightened, crying native children on the train, he had no idea where he was going or what would happen to him once he arrived.

"The day I got off the train," he remembers, "they took us in there and pulled our pants down and gave us such a licking. Then, when we were all crying, they told us, 'Don't let us ever catch you speaking Indian again.'"

"Spanish!" one of the older boys, Basil Johnston, wrote forty years later in his memoir of those times, *Indian School Days*. "It was a word synonymous with residential school, penitentiary, reformatory, exile, dungeon, whippings, kicks, slaps, all rolled into one."

"Those priests knew how to hit," says Joe Odjick. He had barely arrived when one of the priests struck him so hard that the blow broke his eardrum; he has been partially deaf ever since. "I swore on my father's grave that I'd like to see that priest just once before I die," he says, still finding it difficult to think about those days more than a generation later. He thinks he was lucky, being all of nine years old: "I knew how to get along. The ones who really suffered were five, six years old."

The experience profoundly affected Joe, and to this day he is reminded of Spanish every time he sits down to eat. "Groceries—they became the most important thing in my life. We used to steal food from the kitchen and trade it. Now, when I buy, I buy too much. When I cook, I over-cook. If there's no potatoes in the house, I'm not well. All that comes from residential school."

It was, in retrospect, a violation of basic human rights that would cause outrage today, yet continued all through the years before schools were finally built on the reserves themselves. The Department of Indian Affairs in Ottawa—always referred to as the Department—had complete control through the onerous Indian Act. Children could be taken away from mothers at whim—the decision usually made by the Indian agent, the local priest or the manager of the nearest Hudson's Bay Company store—and, once removed, they never returned the same. They lost their names and were given numbers. Joe Odjick was "29"—the same number his father had been given when he went off to residential school, the same number Gino now wears for the Vancouver Canucks. The Department boasted that after six months not a word of Indian was heard again in the schools. No wonder, with being beaten and having your mouth scrubbed with soap the price paid for speaking your parents' language.

The daily schedule at Spanish was gruelling. A bell would wake the children at 6:15 and mass would be at 6:45, followed by a quick breakfast and an hour of chores before classes began. Twice during each day, however, time was set aside for sports and games, for the Jesuits who ran the school were not only great believers in discipline, they believed wholeheartedly in the benefits of strenuous activity and fresh air. For many of the young boys at the school, sports became the precious moments each day when they felt they had some control, when they were free to imagine rather than forced to work.

"Every Saturday night during hockey season we were allowed special entertainment," Johnston wrote. "A radio, usually sequestered in the senior prefect's room, was unsequestered and installed in the club room on the third floor for the listening pleasure of the senior boys in grades six, seven and eight. The grade five boys were given a special dispensation to stay up a little later, not only to inspire greater efforts in their studies to attain seniorhood but also to acclimatise them to the privileges of higher rank. All the boys sat around the radio to listen to Foster Hewitt's evangelical hockey broadcasts: 'Again from coast to coast, it's hockey night in Canada...' Foster's tone and delivery were dramatic and electric. Never was there a more attentive group of grades five, six, seven and eight boys; nor a more submissive one. I think that Foster could have taught them arithmetic, geography and even grammar. No supervision was needed, except for the odd spot-check by the senior prefect in the form of a discreet opening of the door and a quick glance about for forbidden doings. It was during the hockey broadcasts that smokers used to take illicit puffs, their heads stuck out the windows and their rumps stuck inside."

Joe Odjick, so terribly lonesome when he first came to Spanish, found something in hockey that made him feel he belonged. The school played in the North Shore Hockey League against teams from Blind River, Thessalon,

Espanola, Webwood, Massey and Garnier, and with the help of such coaches as the obsessively competitive Father Hannin, the Spanish team became quite accomplished and eventually so strong that other teams would be caught bringing in "ringers" to make sure they didn't lose against the poor Indians from the residential school.

The culture of hockey, from Foster Hewitt on Saturday night to the frozen river on Sunday afternoon, permeated the school to such an extent that when Father Buck, the tough German priest who ran the work details, had something particularly unappealing to assign, like the shelling of peas, he would gather together some boys, divide them into four teams (Canadiens, Rangers, Leafs and Blackhawks) and have them race against each other to decide the Stanley Cup.

Joe Odjick found that his easy skills at hockey and baseball made him popular with the other youngsters and made getting along with the sports-loving priests much simpler. It also eased the pain of being away from his family, though his younger brother, Basil Jr., also was sent to Spanish when Joe was a teenager. By then Joe was already a star on the hockey team, a good-skating defenceman who was, by his own admission, "a little bit too small" but who dreamed, all the same, of finding work in hockey once he got out of the despised residential school.

He almost made it. He got as far as a senior team linked to the minor-league Winnipeg Maroons and he was hoping to be called up. But it never did happen. And by the time he was twenty-eight it certainly was not going to happen. He was then living in a school dormitory in St Boniface, just outside Winnipeg. The rest of his hockey team had gone home for the holidays, and he was shivering in his bed—"I could see my breath!"—when the mail arrived with a letter from his mother containing a train ticket back to Maniwaki. "I got on that train and I didn't have a cent," he remembers. "Three days without a bite to eat I sat there. But I was coming home."

He forgot about hockey and got work at the Canadian International Paper Company plant at seventy-five cents an hour." Summers were great—sixteen hours a day—and being laid off in winter was no problem. He had money to carry him over and could make even more cutting firewood and hauling pulp. He married Giselle and soon they had a family: Debbie, Steve (a foster son), Shelley and Judy. They moved to Edmonton when it seemed the entire country was moving to Edmonton, but after four months working the four-till-midnight shift for a structural steel company, he came home one night and said to Giselle, "How long will it take you to pack?" An hour later, they were on the road.

Giselle was then eight months pregnant with their fourth child. Joe was worried about how he would support such a large family, for there was no work back in Maniwaki, so when they passed through Thunder Bay he enquired at the Abitibi plant and was hired on immediately. Giselle continued on home with the children and on September 7, 1970, she delivered a nine-pound, seven-ounce baby. Her first boy.

Joe Odjick remembers how he felt when his mother-in-law told him the news over the phone: such a big baby, and already so tall at twenty-three inches. "I was real happy," he says. "There were three girls in front of him. This was our first boy." This was no crazed male obsession. Gino Odjick would never grow up to say of his father, as the son of fanatical Indiana basketball coach Bobby Knight would say of his, "I think if I had come out a girl he would have shoved me back inside." This was merely a statement of satisfaction. A boy broadened the family. A boy to help him work in the bush. As far as Joe, who had been torn away from his family, was concerned, there could never be enough children in the house. Their own children, foster children—it made no difference. The priest would never come to round anyone up. And no matter what happened, the children would find support in the Odjick home. "Every parent has the same dream for their children," Joe Odjick says. "That they be successful."

They named the boy Wayne but later changed it to Gino when they discovered there was already a Wayne Odjick growing up on the reserve. Gino would be followed by Janique, Dina and Gina, another foster child who stayed on permanently. Joe and Giselle Odjick count thirty-eight children who passed through their big farmhouse on the edge of the Kitigan Zibi reserve. Six were their own—five girls and a boy—but thirty-two would also be counted as family. Bush families were still forced to send frightened youngsters off to school, but no longer would they be headed for cold residential schools like the one Joe had been sent to in Spanish. Instead, they would find themselves being welcomed into a warm home by a man who would always be cooking more food than they could possibly eat.

To house the growing Odjick family and to provide a dormitory in the basement for all the foster children coming in from Rapid Lake and Barrière Lake, Joe Odjick built a new home on the forty-seven acres he owns just off the reserve. (He also farms three hundred acres of the reserve's land.) He cut his own lumber and fashioned his own shingles from the cedar he cut and hauled from the bush. The reason the huge building looks so odd, he says, is because he got a great deal on leftover trusses. "Only $160," he recalls

with a laugh. "But I had to build the house to fit the roof."
He put no lock on the door, deliberately.

This was the huge, rambling farmhouse in which Gino
Odjick grew up. His father, still fighting the strict, struc-
tured life he had been forced into in Spanish, indulged his
children. They were encouraged to play as much as possible. If he could help—with a rink, with a play fort—he
would. If Gino wanted hockey equipment, he got it. If the
girls needed something, he found a way. It made for a frantic life: farming all spring, summer and fall. Hauling pulp
and cutting firewood and—the best-paying job of all—
ploughing the Rideau Canal ice rink all winter. He found
he hardly needed sleep, and so he took on a late-night
weekend shift tending bar. Whatever it took. His children,
and his foster children, would never know what it was like
to lie in a bed trembling with cold or hunger, or fear that a
priest was about to thunder into the room checking for
bedwetters.

When Gino found hockey, he found what his father
had found so many years before. A place where he felt comfortable, proud. He could not stay off the little rinks his
father made or the rinks the kids cleared on the river. He
wanted constantly to go to the outdoor rink on the reserve,
even if he was there alone. "I was always happy," he says. "I
knew someone else would show up." When others came it
was always games or scrimmages. They never practised.
They didn't know how.

Joe bought the equipment and passed on what skills he
had. He became one of the coaches and organized an all-
Indian team. He was team manager, driver and financial
adviser from pee wee, when Gino joined his first real team
at age eleven, all the way through to midget.

Gino was a defenceman, just as his father had been. The

team stayed essentially intact during those years, and the highlight was when they were invited to the Quebec Peewee Tournament in Quebec City, a marvellous experience that was spoiled somewhat when a strike hit the tournament and union workers refused to clean the ice of the Québec Colisée. The tournament organizers went ahead anyway, and after every sixth game volunteers would come out and shovel away the snow. The team from Maniwaki played the sixth game—"There was four inches of snow out there!" remembers Joe—and they lost 3–2. They ended up, however, consolation finalists.

Gino Odjick laughs when he remembers those early teams and his own father as coach. "It was all right," he says. "We didn't really care about the hockey. We were just out to have fun. He didn't give any speeches and he'd only get mad when we were being lazy. He kept us honest."

Gino never dreamed about being in the NHL back then. His hero was Stan Jonathon of the Boston Bruins—one of Don Cherry's all-time favourites and a native player who played eight years with Boston and Pittsburgh, ending up with ninety-nine goals and 888 minutes in penalties—but he never thought of one day getting there himself. "The most important thing to us," he says, "was to win the Indian tournaments."

But Indian tournaments were not easy to get to, any more than Indian reserves are easy to find in Canada. It was not like playing in the next suburb or the next town; it was numbing drives and overnight billeting. And it cost a great deal of money that the native players simply did not have. To raise funds for the tournaments, Joe Odjick would have the team split firewood and sell it. He would go to a snowshoe manufacturer in Renfrew, Ontario and bring back truckloads of manganese snowshoes to assemble for the

Canadian army. For knitting a box of twelve, they would be paid thirty-seven dollars a box by the supplier. For a person whose entire life had been changed by authority, it delighted Joe to think that if the Soviet Union ever invaded Canada, the defence of the nation lay momentarily in the hands of a pee wee hockey team from Kitigan Zibi.

They enjoyed great success. They had Gino, for one thing, and Russell Coté's son, Jan, was up front to score the goals. And the determined drive of old friends Russell Coté and Joe Odjick meant there was always transportation, always a way to get the money required for equipment and sticks. They stuck mostly to the native tournaments, which were not so competitive and much more fun, and they played when they could in tournaments with all-white teams. Apart from one Rotary-sponsored tournament in Kingston, they had very little trouble with racism. The reason, Joe believes, had less to do with tolerance than with common sense: "People are really *big* here on the Algonkin reserve."

But a kid could go only so far in Maniwaki. Gino was now in midget, fifteen years old, and he was almost through with hockey. His girlfriend was pregnant, a harsh fact of life that was hardly shocking in Maniwaki. "Native kids aren't well informed about birth control," Gino once told the Vancouver *Sun*'s Mike Beamish. "You have your first kid pretty young, with your first girlfriend. When I played midget hockey, probably ten of the fifteen guys on the team had kids. Maybe it shouldn't be like that. You have to mature pretty quickly."

Joe Odjick was worried about Gino but fought hard not to show it. He knew if his son was going to go anywhere in hockey he would have to go away "to learn the plays, learn how to *think* the game." He knew that if he stayed in

Maniwaki, it would soon end, and probably not all that well. But he couldn't say so; he couldn't act like a priest rounding up a child and taking charge of a life when it was none of his business. So he waited. And hoped.

"He was okay," remembers Gino. "He never interfered when school was not good. There was never any pressure on me." Still, Joe Odjick desperately wanted his son to have the opportunities he did not. Gino was talking about becoming a welder and was accepted into a training course in Ottawa. If that didn't work out, maybe he'd become a reserve police officer. Hockey was fast slipping away as a major concern. In the fall, Gino signed up for house league but wasn't even much interested in that. When moose season opened, he headed into the bush to hunt. He could figure out what to do with his life when he got back.

One of Joe's friends in Maniwaki had a son playing for the Hawkesbury Hawks, a junior Tier II team, and word kept coming back through the youngster that the team was terrible and desperately in need of players, particularly someone big and strong. Giselle took the message out to the hunt camp, where Gino thought about it briefly and decided he would at least go to Hawkesbury and see what the team was like. Besides, the other youngster had a car, so there would at least be a ride to the games.

"I went and practised with them," Gino remembers. "I could tell they were getting pushed around. I just went in and did what I had to do to make the team."

And here is where destiny changed, as it so often does in hockey. Until that moment, Gino Odjick had been a good, dependable defenceman who could score the odd goal and loved setting up plays. He was considered as big and soft and easygoing as they came. "He never fought," says Joe. "Never." But the moment Gino hit the ice with the Hawkesbury team, he knew his skating wasn't up to the level of the other players. He also knew he didn't have their playing skills. But he did have something to offer. Size and strength. And desire.

He began fighting. And in fighting he changed the team as dramatically as if he had been a swift forward with a devastatingly accurate scoring touch. He opened up the ice to the smaller, swifter Hawkesbury players, and their fortunes began to change. The team "practised violence"—as former Boston Bruins Derek Sanderson once put it of his team—and it had the desired effect. Gino Odjick fought every game. He fought, almost invariably, until they threw him out. But by then it had had the desired effect: the opposing players intimidated, the Hawkesbury players confident. Joe realized what was happening, but he didn't do anything to stop it. At least Gino was on a team. At least it was hockey, and it was working. "The people seemed to like it," Joe says.

They loved it. Gino Odjick quickly became the most popular player on a bad team—not an unusual development in a sport where the "policemen" rank in status only slightly below the superstars. In watching games involving the pre-eminent player of the day, Wayne Gretzky, it has been debatable at times whether the darling of the crowd was the Great One or the Great One's personal on-ice bodyguards: Dave Semenko when both were with the Edmonton Oilers, or Marty McSorley who went with Gretzky to the Los Angeles Kings.

There are as many theories for this phenomenon as there are hockey policemen. Don Cherry, the popular analyst for "Hockey Night in Canada", and who has a second career selling hockey videos that feature hard hits and battles, has turned his Saturday-night CBC forum into a continuing defence of fighting as a critical and indispensable part of the game. The Cherry attitude is widely shared by many owners, most players and a large number of fans, particularly American fans. It is a belief that fighting is a necessary "spontaneous relief valve" and something that, if removed, would merely lead to more stickwork among the players. That there is not a whit of statistical proof to back this thinking up—in fact, quite the opposite, as the brief rules crack-down in the fall of 1992 showed—has not swayed those who hold strong to these beliefs.

More scientific approaches have included sociologist Michael Messner, whose 1992 book, *The Power of Play*, argued that fighting is a "symbolic catharsis" that "offers viewers a golden opportunity to purge themselves of destructive energies by vicariously participating with their sports heroes who regularly perform aggressive acts under the guise of play." The greater the violence, the greater the relief, the greater the fan enjoyment. In other words, it's part of the entertainment package.

Fighting, however, did not start out as crowd entertainment. It began as a tactic—intimidation—and its history dates from the very beginning of hockey. The Toronto Marlboros, for example, seriously considered "forfeiting the game rather than being hacked to death again" in the two-game contest for the 1904 Stanley Cup. The Ottawa Senators had so severely beaten up on the Toronto team that the final game became a formality, the cowering Marlboros desperate only to get the game over with, which they lost handily, 11–2. It was a tactic that worked.

Modern hockey policemen date from John Ferguson, a minor leaguer who was called up by the Montreal Canadiens in 1963 to protect the Canadiens' stars, Jean Béliveau and Bernie Geoffrion. Twelve seconds into his very first NHL game, Ferguson dropped the Boston Bruins' Ted Green with three unexpected punches, and five Stanley Cups later, a policeman was considered a vital part of the NHL mix. "I know my job," Ferguson said. And so has every John Ferguson since.

The debate over fighting in hockey has raged for decades, with no solution in sight. As many believe its time has come and gone—and fighting must go if the league is to expand into Europe—as believe it is necessary and must stay if the league is to remain true to the sport. What has changed, however, is the belief that fighting is spontaneous and can, by itself, affect the outcome of a game. If it is indeed spontaneous, why, then, does it affect only one or two players on each team? More significantly, why do fights happen only when said players from each side are deliberately placed on the ice at the same time by the opposing coaches? As for fighting having an effect on the outcome, no less an expert than Bobby Clarke, captain of the infamous Broad Street Bullies and current general manager of the Philadelphia Flyers, puts it: "How many times do fights ever change the momentum of a game any more?" Never.

How could they, when the other players on the ice all expect the fight, all know it is coming, all know who will be involved and are curious only as to which of the two teams' policemen will come out on top? The fight has no more direct effect on the outcome of the hockey game than a drive-in cartoon has on the plot of the main feature.

Nor, contrary to the opinion of most American fans, are hockey fights particularly dangerous. The illusion, however, accounts for the lasting popularity with American fans and a great many Canadian fans, so many of whom can never have played the game and do not, therefore, understand the difference between hockey fights and street fights. The heavy equipment, the lack of gripping friction on skates, the slippery ice and the certain interference of the linesmen mean that, in all but the rarest exception, the worst that can happen is a scrape, a small cut or rapped knuckles— usually against the other player's helmet. If as many punches were thrown in a bar fight as in a hockey fight, there would need to be an ambulance on the ice surface for each game as well as a referee. "I figure I've had a hundred and fifty, two hundred fights," Gino Odjick says. "I can only remember four or five punches that hurt."

What does matter in hockey games, however, is presence. And the Hawkesbury Hawks discovered that Gino Odjick had presence. He was already huge—soon to reach six-three and 220 pounds—and he had a mean, menacing look to him on the ice. It was not so much what he *would* do as what he *might* do. Word was out that, once the gloves dropped, Gino Odjick would go completely mad, and would fight with such a fury and desperation that one would be well advised not to offend him, or his team-mates, if possible.

Social scientists have deemed this sports dance a "face game", in that two role models engage in a dynamic exchange in which each seeks to gain or save face at the expense of the other by appearing to be tougher. If this sounds like the vocabulary of animal behaviour, it is. And Gino Odjick was winning the face games.

The effect this situation had on the mild-mannered Odjick was peculiar. His mother, Giselle, found that she could not even watch the games, so worried was she about what was going to happen. But it never seemed to affect Gino. He could be frighteningly aggressive on the ice but instantly non-aggressive as soon as the game was over. He was diametrically the opposite of American football quarterback Timm Rosenbach, who left the Phoenix Cardinals in 1992—and played briefly in Hamilton in 1994—saying that he could no longer live with what aggression was doing to his personality. "I thought I was turning into some kind of animal," Rosenbach told the *New York Times*. "You go through a week getting yourself up for a game by hating the other team, the other players. You're so mean and hateful, you want to kill somebody. Football's so aggressive. Things get done by force. And then you come home, you're supposed to turn it off? 'Oh, here's your lovin' daddy.' It's not that easy. It was like I was an idiot. I felt programmed. I had become a machine."

Gino Odjick never felt programmed. He felt, rather, that he had found his talent. And that just maybe there was a future for him in hockey.

Hawkesbury moved their new hero off defence and up onto forward, giving him the position of the boy who had invited him out. Gino had lost his ride. Joe then made a decision that would have as profound an effect on his son's hockey career as the call that came from Hawkesbury. "I went out on a Friday night and bought a brand-new Dodge Colt," he remembers. "Saturday I drove it down for the game and after the game I handed the keys to Gino. I told him, 'You'll never have to worry about a ride again.'"

For the next three years Joe and Giselle Odjick devoted themselves entirely to giving Gino a chance in hockey. Joe took on even more work in the bush and on the canal and more bartending work at Dan Murphy's Hotel. Giselle pumped gas, and the two of them put tens of thousands of dollars into their son's career. When the little Colt ran into the ground, they presented him with a brand-new Plymouth Voyager. Whatever it took to keep him on the road to hockey rinks. Headed somewhere. "It would have been impossible without them," Gino says now.

In Hawkesbury, Gino Odjick picked up the nickname the Algonquin Assassin, and his reputation spread throughout Tier II junior hockey. The scouts from the major junior leagues began checking out the big kid who seemed to fear nothing. None of them knew the story of the time Giselle found him drinking at one of the many Maniwaki hotels and, absolutely furious, had dragged him out by the ear and then thrown him into the back seat of the car she had helped buy so hard he broke the back door.

The scouting report was simple: tough but no player, poor skater, weak skills. Drummondville of the Quebec major junior league gave him a brief look, but nothing came of it. And nothing would have come had not the Laval Titan found themselves in the same desperate boat the Hawkesbury team had been in earlier. "Laval needed me," Gino says. "They were getting pushed around." Coach Pierre Creamer liked what he saw in the raw youngster from Maniwaki and in 1988 he began working with Odjick, trying to turn him into a player who could be both a presence and a contributor. Odjick also got some unexpected breaks. Two key wingers were both hurt that first year, and when those spots opened up, Odjick was given the only chance he needed. He would fight as hard to stay as he had fought to get there.

In his first season at Laval he scored nine goals and fifteen assists and had 278 minutes in penalties. In his second, his penalty total remained roughly the same, 280 minutes, but his goal production went up to twelve and he added twenty-six assists. More significant, in the playoffs that followed he was a powerful force for Laval, scoring six times in thirteen games, adding five assists and, obviously, missing a

large number of shifts while he sat for 110 minutes in penalties. His progress caught the eye of the Vancouver Canucks,
and that June they made Gino Odjick their fifth selection in
the NHL entry draft, eighty-sixth overall.

In an anecdote eerily similar to the one about the arrival
of John Ferguson nearly thirty years earlier, Gino Odjick
was called up from the Canucks' minor-league affiliate, the
Milwaukee Admirals, for a game against the tough Chicago
Blackhawks on November 21, 1990. The Canucks, many
of them small, few of them fighters, were getting pushed
around by other NHL teams and the team was struggling.
Odjick introduced himself to the NHL with an overhand
right that buckled Chicago policeman Stu "the Grim
Reaper" Grimson. He fought every tough player Chicago
had that game and, when it was over, he found out he
would be dressing again. He had made the NHL. Joe
Odjick flew out to Vancouver to see him play against the
Minnesota North Stars: "My opinion was, well, he can
come home now—he's played in the National Hockey
League."

But Gino Odjick was going to be there for a while. He
played forty-five games that first season, scored seven goals
and an assist, and ended up with 296 minutes in penalties.
The next year he had 348 minutes. The next year 370 minutes. He was, as they say in the NHL, a role player—and
he knew his role well. Someone wrote a silly song about
him and they began playing it at Canucks' home games. He
was a local hero twice—in Vancouver, where they cheered
him at the Pacific Coliseum, and in Maniwaki, where they
put up satellite dishes and where, the day after a West
Coast game, people would show up late for work and kids
wearing Vancouver Canucks T-shirts and caps would sometimes doze off in class.

Vancouver went well, and he began to change. When the young Russian star, Pavel Bure, joined the Canucks partway through the 1991 season, they put the Russian Rocket in to room with the Algonquin Assassin, and the two became inseparable. They became hockey's oddest couple, one so dark and huge, the other so fair and small, the one known for his presence, the other for how quickly he is gone.

"He's from another country," Odjick says of Bure. "He gets lonesome. He had no one at all." Odjick also had no one, also was lonesome—just as his father had been forty years earlier in Spanish. But the difference was the son wished to stay, wanted desperately for it to work out in Vancouver. He and Bure would make it together, as friends and team-mates. It was a friendship that began for obvious reasons, but it lasted even as both grew more comfortable with the city and the other players. "We can talk about anything," says Odjick. "That is hard to find nowadays. We have a one-hundred-percent trust in each other."

Bure, whose play and youthful looks have made him unbelievably popular, as well as somewhat wary, found in Odjick someone who demanded nothing of him and would always be there if needed. "I don't know," he says, unable to explain what it is that has made them such good friends. "Gino is just a really good guy."

He was also Bure's protector, the Swiss Guard to Bure's Pope. "Clearly," Richard Gruneau and David Whitson wrote in their 1993 study, *Hockey Night in Canada: Sport, Identities and Cultural Politics,* "at the top levels of hockey there are a significant number of players—including Steve Yzerman, Pavel Bure and, of course, Wayne Gretzky—who are not fighters and enjoy the systematic protection of team-mates." Get too close to Bure and an opposing player would find Odjick.

But the people of Kitigan Zibi see the friendship as running far deeper than merely that of superstar and bodyguard. "They're in the same boat," says Tony Wawatie, a young Algonquin who follows Gino's career closely. "They're both foreigners out there."

Many of the people of Kitigan Zibi have made the journey out to Vancouver to see with their own eyes what has happened to Joe Odjick's big, easygoing son. "He takes perfect care of you," says his old Maniwaki team-mate, Jan Cote, who has been out west twice. He hands over keys to his apartment and keys to his car and sometimes finds himself depending on his friend Bure for a lift, his own vehicle off somewhere on a tour of the coast.

The friendship between the big Algonquin and the slight Russian pays off in unexpected ways. When Joe Odjick and a friend headed down to Toronto for the 1994 Stanley Cup playoff series between the Canucks and the Maple Leafs, they figured they could save money by sleeping in the hotel lobby. Bure would not hear of it. He moved out of the room he was supposed to share with Gino and in with two other players who made room for him, a $6.3-million-a-year hockey player making room for an $13.85-an-hour snowplow operator.

Bure also changed his friend's attitude towards training. When Gino first went away to play professional hockey, he believed staying in shape was something that happened when you chopped wood and lifted weights. He believed diet was junk food and pop and, when it was available, wild game and fish from the reserve. Bure's fanatical training regimen—entirely directed by his father, Vladimir, a former Olympic swimmer—and the incredible results that came from this training caused Odjick to take up aerobics and cycling and specific weight training and to switch to fruits and vegetable juices instead of chocolate bars and Pepsi. His weight dropped from 220 to 209 pounds.

He found he could listen to Bure's father much as he might once have listened to his own and, in an odd way, the two fathers reminded him of each other. "Pavel has a good relationship with his dad," he says. "His dad's kind of like my dad. He won't push his nose in where he's not needed. But he is there if he is needed."

Gino Odjick set out to change his ways because a real-ization particular to all NHL policemen was slowly settling in. They discover early on that there will be but one path to the NHL for them. They take it and, often much to their surprise, they make it, and having made it they want to play regularly like their team-mates, which happens rarely. To a certain extent, they do play the regular season, which hardly matters in a league where sixteen teams qual-ify for the playoffs, but they invariably sit for the important games of the playoffs. Fighting is happily tolerated during the regular season, strictly frowned upon during the play-offs. It is the clearest and cleanest argument anyone can make against keeping fighting in the game: any time hockey matters—Canada Cups, Stanley Cup playoffs, World Championships—fighting becomes a non-player.

Frustrated with being left out of the playoff plans, Odjick altered his ambitions. He trained to get into the best shape of his life. He began working on his skating, his puck control. He began to become a threat on the ice with his stick as well as his fists. "He wasn't a fighter—never," says Jan Cote. "It's better to become a *player*." In the 1993-94 season he still led the Canucks in penalties, but by the time the team came to Ottawa for this midwinter game, he had become a regular on a line with his friend Bure and was the team's third-leading goal scorer, behind only Bure and team captain Trevor Linden.

He would end this, his third full season in the NHL, with sixteen goals, four times as many as he had scored in each of his previous two seasons. He would even score one, much to the delight of the fans from Kitigan Zibi, at the Ottawa Civic Centre. But it would be a bittersweet triumph. By the halfway point of the season he would have fourteen of those sixteen goals and score only twice in the second half. He would be dropped from Bure's line and, when the playoffs arrived, he would be dropped from the line-up most nights in favour of another strong young player, Shawn Antoski, who offered a bit more speed when speed counted far more than brute force.

Joe Odjick tried to put it down to an injury—a shoulder hurt that wouldn't heal—but his son knew the truth. He was fine for the final Stanley Cup series against the New York Rangers, which the Canucks lost, but he did not dress at all. "I have to try and develop myself into a player who can play in the playoffs someday," he said when the season was done. "I have to learn to keep my focus all year, which I haven't done."

Still, the year had paid off in other ways. In early September, before the NHL owners decided to lock out the players, he celebrated his twenty-fourth birthday with a new contract that would pay him $1.6 million over three years, a far, far cry from the $240 he used to count on for a fifty-hour week in the bush. He said he was happy with his new deal, looking forward to the coming season, and happy with how the team was treating him. As he told the Vancouver media, "I don't mind my role in hockey."

He more or less proved this immediately, leaving the

bench during a battle between the Los Angeles Kings and the Canucks and driving his stick into the midsection of Warren Rychel, an act that earned him a ten-game suspension to start the regular season, whenever it finally did start. The act also cost new Canucks coach Rick Ley a five-game suspension for failing to control his player. It was not a good start to a season that had trouble starting itself.

He could have, had he wished, played out his option year and then seen what he would be worth to NHL teams that seem forever in search of the menacing presence—especially one with some scoring skills. But in an unusual twist, the hockey player told the agent what to do. Cut a deal with the Canucks, Odjick told Gilles Lupien. He wanted to stay in Vancouver for a particular reason: "I don't feel out of place. If I ever get lonesome, there are a lot of First Nations people around."

One of those First Nations people is Ron Delorme, a Cree from Cochin, Saskatchewan, who grew up to play nine years in the NHL with the now-defunct Colorado Rockies and Vancouver Canucks between 1976 and 1985, and who now scouts for the Canucks. Like Gino Odjick, he made his way to the NHL with his fists, not his skates, and it is a story so common to the few natives who do make it to the NHL that it seems a cliché. Odjick's first hero was Boston's Stan Jonathon, a native who fought. His best friend outside the Canucks is Sandy McCarthy of the Calgary Flames, a native fighter. Another pal is Chris Simon of the Quebec Nordiques (now the Denver Avalanche), a native fighter. There have been fewer George Armstrongs, the longtime Toronto Maple Leafs captain, than there have been Gino Odjicks, but that does not suggest Odjick and the others do not take their roles seriously.

Delorme was the scout who recommended Gino Odjick to the Canucks—"I saw myself in him"—and in return Odjick has been a significant contributor to Delorme's self-assigned mission to help young natives through hockey. Delorme has vivid memories of when he first joined a white team in North Battleford, Saskatchewan: "I couldn't believe how the white kids would take off their equipment and underwear and walk around without any clothes on. Native people are shy about those things and it embarrassed me the first time I saw it."

Ted Nolan is the only native now coaching in the NHL (with the Buffalo Sabres) and is a former NHL player who built an impressive record coaching junior hockey, taking the Soo Greyhounds to victory in the 1993 Memorial Cup. Nolan grew up on the Garden River Indian reserve in northern Ontario, where he performed as a fancy dancer in the summer and built his own rink to play hockey on in winter: "I pumped a pail at a time to flood the rink. I'd run from the rink to the pump and fill the pail and run all the way back. My hands would be freezing." When he and a younger brother headed off to Sault Ste Marie to their first-ever real hockey practice, they were forced to share one helmet, one stick and a single pair of gloves, switching them back and forth between shifts as they had always done on the reserve. The other kids taunted them so cruelly it almost made him give up the game at the age of nine. He showed promise, however, and was soon off to Kenora to play for a midget team and attend high school. "I was in a fight every single day for the first month," he remembers.

Nolan never forgot the racism he faced as a native hockey player. "I would try out, be cut, but I was always good enough," he says. "They just didn't want me." Unless, of course, it was as a fighter. "I hate to think that's the only way for native kids to make it," he says, "but you have to be a pretty tough kid to grow up on a reserve.

"When I started playing, it was not the fighting but the name calling that makes you angry." Nolan came to believe that it didn't matter if a youngster's reaction was simply to let the taunts go "in one ear and out the other or you let it get to you—it keeps flashing."

When he found he could not get rid of the memories, he decided to do something about it, and more and more became involved in native politics during the summer while sticking to hockey, and coaching, in winter. He began working as a counsellor in native communities, spending more than a month each summer travelling around to reserves speaking out against alcohol and in favour of self-esteem. In 1994, Nolan was one of a dozen Canadian recipients of the prestigious Aboriginal Achievement Awards, largely because of the unique hockey school he has established with the help of other native players such as Gino Odjick.

Each off season Nolan runs his Anishnawbe Hockey School, taking players around to villages and reserves from James Bay to the west coast. They work on hockey, but they work as much, if not more, on life skills. "Hockey's only two hours a day," he says. "There's a big life out there."

And, he says, there is no better way to demonstrate this to the youngsters than to have a big, successful NHLer like Gino Odjick skate out with them. "With Gino being native," Nolan says, "it just lights up the kids' eyes. He has a presence. A wink, a pat on the back—it means a lot to those kids. It's a little more important sometimes than if Wayne Gretzky and Steve Yzerman were there."

Nolan's philosophy is shared by Ron Delorme, who says he saw dozens of talented native hockey players fail as he made his way to the NHL. He determined that if he ever got the opportunity, he would do what he could to keep them in the game past the time when, to find competition, they are forced to leave the reserve. Hockey is widely and enthusiastically played on reserves, yet only six players in professional hockey came from reserves, with another twenty or so native NHL and minor-league players having been raised and played their hockey off-reserve. The fact that, against such enormous odds, some two dozen of them are currently earning a living as professional hockey players in North America is reminiscent of Joe DiMaggio's famous line "A ball player's got to be kept hungry. That's why no boy from a nice family ever made the big leagues." If hunger is a true measure, there will be many more native players to come.

"Native kids have grown up all their lives on reserves," Delorme told Ian MacIntyre of the Vancouver *Sun*. "All of a sudden, you have to put these kids in the mixed world, the white world. Nineteen white kids and one native kid on a hockey team. That's culture shock."

Gino Odjick felt this same shock in Maniwaki and, later, in the Quebec junior leagues. "A lot of the guys I knew, when they got discouraged, would start drinking," he once said. "You've got to really learn to stay off the booze, because booze weakens you mentally. It's a real jungle out there for native kids. You feel very much like a stranger in a white man's world." Odjick takes his role model responsibilities seriously. A drinker since age twelve, he quit in the fall of 1994 after a week-long binge that he believes nearly killed him, and since then has devoted himself to warning young Natives about the dangers of alcohol and drugs.

He knows his father's stories of what it was like at the Spanish residential school. He has heard the racism coming down from high in the stands at junior hockey games. He has never forgotten when he was twelve years old and one of the Kitigan Zibi elders, a close friend of his grandfather's, lost the trap line he had worked all his life because a logging company said it had a piece of paper granting it timber rights to that same land. "I can't forget," he says.

That's why Odjick visits the reserves around Vancouver, often with Delorme, always encouraging the youngsters who play the game to reach for the top. He attends special native hockey camps across the west and makes sure he spends part of every summer back on the Maniwaki reserve where the kids can see that he is not some god on an Upper Deck card but Joe Odjick's son who still maintains that, when he is through playing hockey, he will come back to the reserve and work as a policeman. "He is a hero," Delorme says. "I stress to him to put something back in the game. Never walk by a kid who asks for an autograph. Remember where you came from."

Gino Odjick buys Ron Delorme's argument that they have "a responsibility to the next generation. They have to feel they can achieve their dreams. They sometimes think because they're Indian they won't be given a chance. It's good for our communities if the younger ones feel they can grow up to be doctors and dentists. It's a chain reaction. It's like when somebody buys a new truck, everybody starts to buy a new truck."

The chain reaction is in evidence each summer when the Gino Odjick Annual Golf Tournament is held at the Algonquin Golf Course on the outskirts of Maniwaki. It is, unlike any other celebrity golf tournament held throughout Canada, a day for the area children as much as for the paying players. The kids are everywhere—driving the carts, trying out clubs, chasing balls. One summer the organizers put paddle-boats in the ponds for the kids to play with, but it was so popular they soon ran out of caddy volunteers so it was discontinued. The kids all wear caps, all with NHL insignias, most with the Vancouver Canucks proudly displayed, half a continent from the city in which the Canucks play.

"You can't be a serious golfer here," says course owner Robert Morin. "Otherwise you won't enjoy it."

It is a golf tournament so unusual it almost defies description. The 1994 tournament, held on a hot, muggy July day, will be remembered for the cart that skipped out of control on the fifth fairway, jumped over a small hill and spread cold beer and ice across two fairways. A few years ago, when the Canadian Snowbirds were practising their Canada Day formations out of the Maniwaki airport directly across the road, the tournament shut down while the players lay down in the grass and took in the free show. To make sure everyone gets to feel like a golf pro, the par-five eighth hole is shortened each summer by two hundred yards but kept as a par five. A drivable par five, with eagle an average score.

No one is ever even sure who will turn up to play. "Gino just turns up at midnight with all these guys," says Russell Coté, laughing. "And we never know who." Some years it is Pavel Bure, and that possibility is all it takes to bring a full field of 144 golfers out. There are no prizes, no trophies, no winners. Every penny raised goes back to the kids for their hockey programs.

The golf doesn't matter. Everyone is tired from staying up half the night around Joe Odjick's big bonfire. Everyone wants to see Gino; Gino wants to talk to everyone. It is all but useless for him to try to play in his own tournament.

Players leave putts sitting on greens to come and talk to him. They shout when he swings. And everywhere there are kids. Kids for autographs. Kids with their parents for photographs of the youngster standing with his hero. Kids to talk hockey. Kids to ask if Bure is coming again this year.

Here all is forgotten. Russell Coté, whose house burned down late in the spring with no insurance, is laughing as he sits with Joe Odjick off the first tee. Joe, who has just lost three hundred bales of hay to wet rot, is laughing as they talk about all they have been through together, two fathers of two Algonquin hockey players, one of whom went on to play in the National Hockey League and one of whom stayed on the reserve. The fathers are best friends for life. The sons will be best friends forever.

What they are laughing about as they sit there in the hot sun is the irony of life and the pull of the cold hockey rink. They are still in the rinks, still watching. Gino's son, Patrick, now plays—"Hat-trick" Patrick, they call him—and Joe Odjick put in a few overtime weekends on the canal in the winter to buy a video camera so he could tape his grandson's games and send them to Vancouver where, on off nights, sometimes Gino and his friend, Pavel will put the tapes on and sit watching, two NHL stars remembering that the dream never dies, it simply begins again each winter.

"We thought we were through," Joe Odjick says. Russell Coté shakes his head, disbelieving. "But we never expected our grandchildren. Now we're right back at it."

Their fathers went to war together and only one survived. Russell and Joe fought together to build a native hockey team and both survived to see its results. The more they got involved, the more others got involved. And the more who came to watch and help, the better off everyone was in the end. The reserve school started up a skating program. To make sure everyone had the opportunity, the band council voted to pay half the registration fees for any child who joined up. Minor hockey was a blessing in disguise for Kitigan Zibi.

"The booze was very bad in our community," says Joe. "The parents used to sit all day in the pub. Now they sit in the hockey arenas."

Joe Odjick and Russell Coté are still sitting in them. They remember the time not so many years back when they repaired to the Martineau Hotel in town, ordered a couple of quarts of beer each and lifted a toast to each other. "Our careers as hockey parents are finished," Joe said to Russell. They talked about it and they felt good about it. Gino was headed for a career in professional hockey. Jan was still playing, still enjoying the game that had come to mean so much to the entire reserve.

Sitting there in the sun, reminiscing, Joe knew nothing of a letter that was in the mail to the journalist who had come to join him and Russell at their table. The letter contained one of the last thoughts of Gordon Juckes, the former head of the Canadian Amateur Hockey Association. In a few weeks, Juckes would be dead at the age of eighty, his legacy the minor hockey system he had helped to create through the 1950s, 1960s and 1970s. "I suspect," Juckes wrote, "that few fathers, really, end up able to dream their dreams through their sons."

It is unfortunate he never met Joe Odjick of Kitigan Zibi.

La Future Vedette

In a few hours it will be Saturday night at the Montreal Forum. There will be standing room only in the shrine of hockey as the fans come to check out the latest potential god in the province where this game means more than it does anywhere else in the world. The lights will be up for "Hockey Night in Canada" and "Le Soirée du Hockey". The press box will be packed. The rafters—where a twenty-fourth Stanley Cup banner has gone up this year—will swirl with the memories of Joliat, Vezina, Morenz, Richard, Béliveau and Lafleur. The roar will be that of an entire province, too long gone hungry.

High, and alone, in the famous "reds" sits a thin man with dark hair, a small moustache and horn-rimmed glasses. His name is Jean-Yves Daigle, and he is a printer from nearby Laval. He grew up dreaming of one day playing for *les glorieux*, the *bleu-blanc-rouge* of *les Canadiens*, the Habs, the Montreal Canadiens. It was an absurd dream—he was an average player—but only absurd to those who are not of this province, who did not grow up in a place of worship where the greatest of all callings was the Montreal Canadiens, and then came the priesthood. Jean-Yves Daigle's first hero was Maurice Richard, then Jean Béliveau, then Guy Lafleur; now it is his own son, Alexandre, who plays for another team, the Ottawa Senators, but who has, at times, been seen by the people of Quebec as *la future vedette*, the star of the future.

Five months earlier in Quebec City, when Alexandre

was selected first overall by the Senators in the National Hockey League entry draft, the outpouring of emotion had astonished even his father. Long before dawn on that sweltering day, when hockey should have been the furthest thing from most minds, the people of Quebec had flooded into the provincial capital for the coronation. Robert and Lynda Jobin had brought their baby, Jimmy, in from Beauport merely to have Alexandre Daigle touch the child while the parents snapped Polaroids of the laying-on of hands. The organizers had sat Daigle with Béliveau for a morning autograph session—Lafleur and Richard among the many former stars at other tables—and when the time came to close the big doors of the Mange Militaire, the line waiting to see Béliveau and *la future vedette* still stretched into the hundreds. Old men who wanted to see what was next. Teenaged girls wearing T-shirts to be signed. Quebeckers with babies, hoping for benediction.

It had taken half a dozen security guards to get the eighteen-year-old away from the crowd. They formed a phalanx around him and marched him out a side door of the Arsenal as young women shrieked and Rocket Richard and Gordie Howe and Bobby Hull and Jean Béliveau and Guy Lafleur walked off on their own—no guards, no screaming—Lafleur with a secret smile of sympathy for the dark-haired youngster being hustled out a side door.

They took Alexandre Daigle out into the streets and they loaded him into a *calèche* with the great Béliveau, Daigle in a dark suit, Béliveau in sophisticated summer grey. Daigle was sweating slightly, his mouth wide open in a smile of astonishment; Béliveau was cool and relaxed, a small, knowing smile—much like Lafleur's—as he shook the youngster's hand and the two settled down for the long march to the Colisée.

Béliveau was then sixty-one years old. He had been retired from playing nearly four years when Alexandre Daigle was born. In a few hours, Daigle would sign a $12.25-million contract, of which some $4 million would be tied to promotions and endorsements. In the first year of the five-year agreement, the youngster would receive $550,000 in salary, $675,000 in marketing revenue and $750,000 in signing bonuses, for a total of $1.975 million. When Jean Béliveau turned professional at nineteen, he made $6,000 a year from the Quebec Citadels and picked up an extra sixty dollars a week by driving around with a Laval Dairy cooler in the trunk, looking for kids to treat to ice cream on a hot summer day.

Béliveau looked across at Daigle and smiled. "He is well dressed and polite," Béliveau recorded in the biography he was already working on, "almost shy, a credit to his parents. The hopes of several million Québécois ride with him. They have seen too few of their number selected high in the entry draft by NHL scouts in recent years."

Béliveau knew better than anyone what this moment meant for Alexandre Daigle. French-speaking hockey stars, he would say in *Jean Béliveau: A Life in Hockey*, which he wrote with Chris Goyens and Allan Turkowitz, "have a particular cross to bear. The expectations of an entire province often go with them, and the pressure exerts itself in unusual ways." Béliveau knew from experience. Guy Lafleur knew from experience. Alexandre Daigle was about to know.

The pressure was already building by the time the youngster reached Quebec City. He had the front page of *Le Soleil* and *Le Journal de Québec*, the cover of *The Hockey News*, a feature in *Sports Illustrated*; TSN was running and re-running a full documentary on him called "The

Franchise Kid". And he would create his own pressures, some of them unnecessary. When asked for his reaction to being picked first overall, he would respond by telling the media, "Nobody remembers who was number two." Number two—Ontario junior star Chris Pronger, who ended up with the Hartford Whalers—would not be amused.

He was asked about Eric Lindros, who two years earlier had snubbed Quebec City by refusing to sign with the Nordiques, the team that had taken Lindros first overall in the 1991 draft. The difference, smiled the cocky Daigle, is, "I *drink* my beer"—a sharp reference to Lindros's famous court appearance in which he was charged with, but found innocent of, spitting beer on a young woman in a Whitby bar. Eric Lindros would not be amused.

He would sign a deal that week with Score hockey cards, and the first result would be a summer advertising campaign to whet the appetite for Daigle cards—only instead of a hockey uniform, Daigle would appear in an ad showing him in a number of other uniforms, including that of a nurse. His new team and the conservative hockey world would not be amused.

Down through the narrow streets of the Old City, Béliveau and Daigle paraded in the *calèche*. Women laid roses in their path, old men dabbed at tears. They were witnessing a passing parade of their hockey gods, Béliveau being shortly followed by Lafleur, then the Rocket Himself, Maurice Richard waving, his hair still thick in his seventies, his eyes forever dark. It seemed the line went all the way back to the great Howie Morenz who died in 1937 and had lain in state at centre ice of the Montreal Forum while Quebeckers by the tens of thousands filed by his casket. Morenz had not been Quebec born—he had come from southern Ontario—but he had been embraced by Quebeckers and had embraced them back. The most exciting, most beloved hockey player in the NHL had died from complications following a broken leg, but the official reason was never accepted in Quebec. He had died, they said, of a broken heart, unable to wear the *bleu-blanc-rouge* one more time that 1936–37 season.

At that same centre ice of the Forum on a cool November morning in 1993, Alexandre Daigle does figure eights with a puck, the new ice glistening beneath his skates, the sound rasping in the still air of a large, empty rink. He is out early for the morning skate before the big Saturday-night game. He has come out early to be alone. Three days earlier, his grandmother, Aline Rosseau, had died of cancer before she, too, could realize the great family dream of seeing Alexandre play at the Forum. She had tried in vain to find a Senators game on her hospital television. She had promised, when he had called, that she would make it to the Montreal game. But it was not to be. His father had called, and his son had turned again into his child; no longer a $12.25-million NHL rookie with roses falling in his path, but a child sobbing on the other end of the line.

It had been the second time in less than a year that the boy had cried when his father spoke. The first time had been in the spring, during the Quebec junior league play-offs, when Jean-Yves had taken Alexandre aside after a game and quietly told him he had taken a stupid and unnecessary penalty. He had not expected such reaction, yet in a way it pleased Jean-Yves, for it meant that what the family thought still mattered most.

Aline Rosseau had not been able to make the game, yet she had given Jean-Yves and Alexandre Daigle something that would not otherwise have been possible. Alexandre had come down to Montreal early for the funeral. The huge, extended Rosseau and Daigle families had gathered to mourn and celebrate a wonderful life. And when it was over, Jean-Yves Daigle had been given an opportunity that has perhaps never before been afforded another Canadian hockey parent: he got to drive his son to his hockey game—Saturday night, at the Montreal Forum. The first meeting of the Senators and Canadiens. Alexandre Daigle's first NHL game in the shrine. Father and son had been so excited they had forgotten to bring money, and had to borrow a ten to cover the parking fee.

"When you play in Montreal," Jean-Yves had told his son as they came along St Catherine Street, "it is your first game for me."

The first, as well, for all the Quebeckers who had been waiting to see him. Alexandre Daigle was eighteen, but they had been aware of him since he was thirteen and word began to spread of the amazingly fleet pee wee player who had scored 150 goals for his Laval team. As an all-star midget, he had, in a magnificent irony, been drafted by Béliveau's old team, the Victoriaville Tigres, and, as a sixteen-year-old rookie, had been named Quebec junior hockey's rookie of the year. At seventeen he was on his way to shattering Mario Lemieux's junior record of 282 points when, dramatically, he was suspended by the league for a vicious cross-check.

That suspension, and another that followed, cost him the chance at the record, but in some ways it did him more good than harm in National Hockey League circles. Quebec superstars, it had long been said, were too soft. But now here was a superstar with a mean streak. His stock went up even higher. When the Ottawa Senators had announced their choice it had brought down the packed Colisée as surely as if he had raced end to end and scored the Stanley Cup winner in overtime. A Quebecker going first overall in Quebec City was that important.

That he would be playing out of province was unfortunate, but not nearly as bad as it might have been. Ottawa was on the border, across from Hull, and the region was partly francophone. Montreal was two hours away, close enough for airwaves to reach, close enough for monitoring. Even so, right up to the moment of the draft it had been hoped that somehow, something might be done to get the Victoriaville star in a Quebec uniform—just as more than forty years earlier the Tigre's magnificent Béliveau had come to play for the Quebec Citadels and then the Quebec Aces. The owner of the Quebec Nordiques, Marcel Aubut, sweat pouring from his puffy face, had even run alongside the *calèche* carrying Béliveau and Daigle as it headed down into the Old City, imploring Béliveau to talk some sense into the young man. Both unable to hear, they had laughed back, waving at the frantic Aubut.

Aubut believed he had come within a single telephone call of arranging the trade that would bring Daigle here, but Ottawa had come to believe that Daigle was equally important to the future of the Senators franchise, that they might build their own $200-million rink around him. For the Daigles, an Ottawa team was almost as good, and he would be playing often in Quebec City and Montreal. It was a province's—and a father's—dream come true.

"Everyone thinks, 'My son will play in the NHL,'" says Jean-Yves Daigle as the Forum practice continues. "Every father believes that. Even when he says, 'No, no, no, it's not true.' They all think it. Believe me, I know."

Jean-Yves and Francine Daigle had three children:

Sebastian, Véronique, born two years later, and Alexandre, a year younger than his sister. They were a typical working-class family in Laval, Jean-Yves going off to work each day as a printer, Francine to an office where she worked as a clerk. The children grew up in a large circle of neighbour-hood children and cousins. Francine had no athletic ability and no interest in sports. Jean-Yves had played hockey, but then everyone played hockey—and so, too, would his children.

Like so many other fathers in Laval, Jean-Yves spent hours building a backyard rink, shovelling and pounding down the snow, levelling the surface and flooding long into the night with pails of hot water and a garden hose that would stiffen the moment he laid it down. It wasn't worth it. Sebastian and Véronique learned to skate, but were lit-tle interested. Sebastian would soon turn to cars and Véronique to softball. By the time the baby, Alexandre, was walking around and wanting to go out and play, Jean-Yves's backyard rink was a memory.

But Alexandre wanted to skate. His father and older brother took him to neighbourhood rinks, and he soon learned to push himself around the ice and was demanding to play hockey. His father laughed at the youngster's first attempts to get the stick to move the puck, yet there was something about him that set him apart from his siblings and playmates. He had what Jean-Yves calls "*la loie de con-viction*—if you want something, if you work hard enough, it's there for you."

The facts behind such determination, however, are rather intimidating. Less than one percent of the hundreds of thousands of youngsters enrolled each year in Canadian minor hockey programs will ever make a cent from profes-sional hockey, and a small fraction of that number will reach the National Hockey League. There are approximately 650 players in the NHL at any one time, fifteen or sixteen of whom are legitimate superstars. The real Quebec Lottery is *making it.*

"In Canada, hockey is a religion," says Jean-Yves. "Every parent puts skates on their child, and then it starts. It's a big job, but nobody has any experience. It's like a horse race. Ten horses start out, but only one wins. Sometimes it's a photo finish, the difference between first and second, and the difference can be just a detail.

"That's why I worked for ten years on the details. Skates just right, always new laces, the right way to lace up a skate, black tape on the stick, the right sleep. It's just the details. All the boys are the same, good parents, good boys, good skaters. What's the difference, then? I work on the details." From the time when he first signed up for hockey, Alexandre was obliged to pack up his own equipment bag before each game. "He'd say, 'Why?'" Jean-Yves remembers, then answers the boy's question: "To make him think about it."

Alexandre Daigle had decided from his first memories of playing the game that he, somehow, would make it. His father would handle the "details" outside the home—the driving, the waiting, the new equipment, tape, skate sharpening—and the mother would take care of the "details" inside the home. A snack to go, a warm meal waiting, always the long, lingering hug no matter the score. She calls Alexandre "my boy. He always does his job perfectly."

If Alexandre's team lost, Jean-Yves would say to him: "You have to think about losing. Then you go to sleep. When you wake, it's gone. When you win, when you score five or six goals, I want you to think about that very hard before you go to sleep. But tomorrow it is gone. You have to forget a bad game; you have to forget the best game."

They never pushed. No yelling. No recriminations. No despair. No bragging. They were, in fact, almost precisely the parents who would win the approval of those who have studied the minor hockey phenomenon. One such expert is University of Ottawa sports psychologist Terry Orlick, who would end up working for the Senators and, from time to time, with a struggling Alexandre Daigle. After two decades of study, Orlick knew that the minor hockey experience goes wrong when "the outcome of the game becomes more important than the outcome of the child." With the Daigles, the child was always what mattered first.

"When parents yell," says Jean-Yves Daigle, "I don't understand that. It is important to be positive all the time. He's a hockey player, but first of all he's a child."

Unable to pass on game skills, they restricted themselves to life skills. As his hockey skill soared—as, more and more, Alexandre Daigle became the talk of the province—his parents fought to keep things in perspective. "I never said to him to shoot for the top," says Jean-Yves. "It's attitude. And *attitude* is the job of the parent."

"Money is not the most important thing in life. The most important thing, *être heureux*, to be content. That's the big part of our life—to be *heureux* and close."

Alexandre Daigle would need his family that first year of professional hockey. Before every game he would call home. He would talk to Francine and then to Jean-Yves. And every time they would give him the same advice: "Do your game like you do every game, play and skate." But it rarely worked. The Ottawa Senators would once again be the worst team in the National Hockey League—only this time with no San Jose Sharks to keep them company. When fans would wonder, usually with good reason, what was wrong with the Senators, the question mark would more often than not settle over the head of the $12.25-million phenomenon. The Messiah had led them right back into the cellar. Worse, the Senators' other prize rookie—Russian Alexei Yashin, a year older than Daigle and the second selection overall in the 1992 draft—was outshining Daigle by far. Yashin scored thirty goals and had forty-nine assists for a total of seventy-nine points. He was named to the 1994 All-Star Game, which was played in New York and in which he scored two goals, one of them the winner. He was *The Hockey News* NHL rookie of the year. And he made about half what Daigle was being paid.

Daigle, on the other hand, scored twenty goals and thirty-one assists for fifty-one points. For any other rookie it would have been a most respectable result; it was not enough for the new star from Quebec. Of the top twenty-five scorers in the NHL final listings, only six had played in the NHL at the age of eighteen, as Daigle had, and only four—Wayne Gretzky, Jaromir Jagr, Ron Francis and Dale Hawerchuk—had better rookie years to their credit. But it was not enough. Not when you have a $12.25 million contract. "If Alexandre Daigle was making $700,000 or $800,000," his coach, Rick Bowness, said at one point, "everyone would be raving about his play."

It was, for the youngster from Laval, a most difficult time. His play was constantly criticized and, at times, deserving of criticism. Having come from a league where speed was the only weapon he required, he was now in a league where speed met its deterrent—brute force. Up against much older, much larger, much stronger men, he often gave the appearance of giving up, particularly in the corners. He picked up bad habits—curling as he crossed the blueline, dropping blind passes back to the point that were often intercepted, falling down even before contact was made—and the bad habits could not fail to be interpreted by those who had seen past junior superstars fade once they reached the NHL.

They began to whisper about his courage, his ice sense, his hands. And when they weren't criticizing his play, they were railing against his contract. Fans were beginning to sound like those NHL general managers who had spoken out against the contract the moment it was signed. "Absurd," Edmonton's Glen Sather had said. "There is absolutely no sanity to it." With other general managers leading the way, the Ottawa Senators were being blamed throughout the league for the extraordinary escalation in rookie salaries, as all other draft choices now measured their value against Daigle, who was not so good, instead of against Lindros, who was clearly in a class by himself. When there was talk of a coming lockout by the owners, the main point of contention was often owner outrage over the Daigle contract. It may not have been his fault, but he wore it anyway.

By late March of his rookie year, Daigle was in trouble. He opened up in an interview with respected Quebec columnist Bertrand Raymond of *Le Journal de Montréal.* "I'm often depressed," he told Raymond. "Some mornings, I'm all alone with my Rice Krispies…. I try to convince myself that I can't let the situation affect me—but, frankly, I never thought that it would be so difficult."

He admitted to Raymond that, when the season had begun, he had thought he might even win the Calder Trophy as the league's top rookie. It seemed, then, a reasonable goal. And he had started so well, scoring early and, in October, being named rookie of the month by the league. He had quickly started to fade and, by March, his name was never mentioned among those who would eventually challenge for the trophy (New Jersey goaltender Martin Brodeur, who would win, Philadelphia Flyers' Mikael Renberg and the Edmonton Oilers' Jason Arnott; Daigle's team-mate Yashin would not even be a finalist, which bewildered many who had seen him play).

"Some nights I'll play well," Daigle told Raymond, "but the next game I'll be rotten. That has to do with my preparation. It's not easy to be ready for every game." His father would have understood. The son was having trouble with the "details".

Some nights he flew. Some nights—not too many, but those who were there would remember—it seemed as if his skates never touched the ice. He would take a pass and head down the right side, always the right side, and he would simply explode past the defence, often with a chance for a shot on goal or a pass. When it happened, everyone shook their head—partly in amazement, partly in puzzlement. If it could happen here and now, why not there and then? If the Senators played the Nordiques in Quebec City, Alexandre Daigle would usually be one of the stars on the ice. If they played the Canadiens in Montreal, he would often be the story the next morning. If they played the Flyers in Philadelphia or the Rangers in New York, he would be noticed more for complaints about his play.

He knew why he performed so well against the Nordiques and the Canadiens, in front of certain fans.

"Quebec."

Guy Lafleur also knew it. At the end of Alexandre Daigle's difficult first year, Lafleur was forty-three years old and working as vice president of corporate affairs and public relations at Titrex International, a health drink company

on the outskirts of Quebec City. Lafleur had retired from
the Nordiques at the end of the 1990–91 season. He had
retired from the Canadiens after the 1984–85 season, but
three years later returned to play first for the Rangers
and, finally, for the Nordiques. He rarely, if ever, went to
hockey games any more, but he knew all about Alexandre
Daigle. And how could he not? The parallels were uncanny:
two blazing meteors streaking across Quebec a generation
apart, both so suddenly brilliant, both deemed to fizzle
almost as soon as they had come into sight.

Both Guy Lafleur and Alexandre Daigle were early on
seen as *le dauphin*, the chosen one. Lafleur was to be the
heir apparent to the great Béliveau; Daigle would be the
new Lafleur, a new Quebec god of hockey when one had
been so long overdue. Michel Bossy had gone off to star for
the New York Islanders, Denis Savard to play in Chicago,
Mario Lemieux to Pittsburgh. Lemieux had won two
Stanley Cups and his abilities were spoken of with the same
reverence reserved for Gretzky, but Lemieux was both far
away and distant, not given to letting the media in, not
open to giving himself to any public. He had not only been
aloof and in Pittsburgh, he had been struck with injury and
illness, a combination of bad back and treatment for
Hodgkin's disease taking him completely out of hockey at
the end of the 1994 season; he hoped to return, if possible,
in 1995–96. The province of Quebec had been in a long
drought.

Lafleur idolized Jean Béliveau, the captain of the
Montreal Canadiens. He even wore his number, 4, and
kept a picture of Béliveau beside his locker. Jean-Yves
Daigle idolized Lafleur, and dreamed that one day *his* son
would become like *his* player. Number One. The best. Guy
Lafleur could only smile at such thoughts. The ambition

was to be number one in the hearts of Quebeckers. He knew what it meant and what it felt like. But, as he says, "That's one thing you don't talk too much about."

Guy Lafleur had come out of Thurso, a pulp mill town on the Quebec shore of the Ottawa River downstream from Ottawa and Hull. He had been born there in 1951, when Béliveau was still playing in Quebec. Lafleur's father, Réjean, had gone to work as a welder at the age of fourteen and was determined, as all parents are, that his child would have an easier go of it than he had. When his son was five years old, he bought him his first pair of skates. He built a rink behind the house and welded pipes together to form nets, which he then covered with burlap. The kids from around the neighbourhood were invited to play as much as they wanted, and did. The only condition was that little Guy Lafleur be allowed to join in.

Chance plays a part in the development of all players. By creating such an environment, Réjean Lafleur was forcing his son to learn by trial and error, not by coaching drills. If he wanted to feel a puck on his stick, he had to get to that puck. If he wanted to keep the puck, he had to control it. If he wanted to score, he had to learn how and when to shoot. For the longest time, young Guy was oblivious to the fact that he was gifted at this game. Forced to play against all age groups, with as many as twenty players on the ice at one time, he felt he was holding his own, at best.

"All I know is that by the time I was seven or so, I was taking hockey more seriously than some of my friends," he told Chris Goyens and Allan Turowetz for their book on the Canadiens, *Lions in Winter*. "I was so bad that I used to sleep in my equipment so I could be ready to play the next morning. Quite often my dad would find me in bed fast asleep with everything on except my helmet and he'd undress me without waking me up. On weekdays, we'd start playing at seven in the morning and then we'd play the other classes at lunchtime. After school, we'd play against other teams in the area. It was hockey, hockey, hockey, and we loved it."

He began sneaking into the local rink through some loose boards, and after he was caught he struck an arrangement with the arena manager by which he could come in any time and play so long as he gave an hour of work back for every hour of ice time. By the time he was ten he was already a sensation, a youngster so obsessed with his game that, to save time, he would sometimes wear his uniform under his soutane while serving mass, racing out after the service to be first on the ice for the second round of Sunday worship.

Guy Lafleur's relationship with his father was unusual for such times. But then, Réjean Lafleur was unusual. A big, strong man, he was too nervous to drive a car and would never own one. He went to work by bicycle or on foot. He rarely went anywhere but to work or home. While other fathers became as caught up in their sons' play as the youngsters, Réjean Lafleur did not even go to watch his son play organized hockey. If he wasn't working at the factory, he was working around the house. He would not even watch regular-season NHL games on television, only the playoffs. The family enthusiast, according to Georges-Hébert Germain's *Overtime: The Legend of Guy Lafleur*, was his maternal grandfather, Léo Chartrand, an outgoing man who, unlike Réjean Lafleur, had never played the game but was a passionate fan all the same. In 1960, when Rocket Richard had retired, the grandfather had announced, "Hockey is half-dead. No one will ever take the Rocket's place. Unless Guy does something about it."

It was soon apparent that Guy Lafleur might well do something about it. He was such a sensation in Thurso that the Ontario town of Rockland, directly across the Ottawa River and connected by ferry in summer and by ice road in winter, began wooing him to join the Rockland team for tournaments. The first time he agreed there was not enough time for him to get over to Rockland to sign the right papers, so his signature was forged with the permission of Réjean and Pierrette Lafleur.

It was in Rockland where Réjean first saw what his son was becoming. They had gone across the river without telling him and he did not even know they were in the stands until he had scored for the fourth time and the rink had erupted in such long cheering that the game was delayed. When Guy saw his father in the stands he smiled. Later, when they went to dinner at a restaurant, father and son were so emotionally wound up about the game and being there together that neither could speak.

Perhaps he did not come to the games and cheer, but Réjean Lafleur helped his son in other ways. According to Georges-Hébert Germain, Réjean Lafleur used his welder's skill to add steel to a pair of old boots so his son could walk around in them and strengthen ankles that seemed, at first, too weak for hockey. He built him barbells. He lent Guy his watch so the boy could practise holding his breath—working himself up to two minutes at one point—convinced in his naive way that somehow this would make him a better hockey player.

Guy was barely twelve when the first requests began coming in to persuade Réjean and Pierrette Lafleur to send their son off to a city where there would be better competition. The youngster wanted to go, but his father refused. A year later, with the pressure building, Réjean relented, and, at thirteen, Guy was off for Quebec City. It was a difficult decision, but it made some odd sense to Réjean Lafleur. His son was obviously much too good to continue playing in Thurso and Rockland; besides, he was nearly as old as Réjean had been when he struck out to make his own way in the world. It was 1964.

Guy Lafleur was fourteen years old and playing far, far away from home. He cried every night. He called his father and begged to come home. "But my dad wasn't having any of it," he told Goyens and Turowetz. "He told me, 'You cried for a year to go there, you are going to stick it out. You're not coming back.'"

There could be no turning back. It had been apparent by now for years that Guy Lafleur was headed to the NHL. His coaches had seen it and given him all the ice time he could handle. Even his teachers had seen it, Brother Léo Jacques exempting him from homework when it might interfere with away games. From that remarkable day—February 5, 1962—when he had scored an unheard-of seven goals in a single game at the Quebec Peewee Invitational, the junior scouts had started the chase, with the NHL scouts not far behind.

He was by then convinced himself that he would follow his hero to the Canadiens. He had met Béliveau at one of the three Quebec Peewee Tournaments he had played in when the great Canadiens star, out of NHL action with a broken leg, had come to Quebec City to present the trophy named in his honour. Young Lafleur had bought a poster of Béliveau and put it up on the wall beside his bed back in Thurso, the last thing he would see before going to sleep, the first thing he would see on rising.

Guy Lafleur had chosen his role model well. Jean Béliveau would turn forty the summer twenty-year-old Lafleur became the number-one draft choice in the National Hockey League. That Lafleur would go first was not much in doubt—though another junior player, Marcel Dionne, was threatening—but that he would go to the Canadiens was unlikely. The first choice overall would go either to the Los Angeles Kings or to the California Golden Seals, whichever finished last in the 1970–71 season. Canadiens general manager Sam Pollack, in a series of deals that are now part of hockey legend, engineered it so that Montreal ended up with the Seals' first choice and the Kings would come second-last instead of last, meaning the Canadiens, fresh off another Stanley Cup win, ended up with the player their fans were demanding: Lafleur.

Béliveau had just announced his retirement. It was time for a new god. The quote from World War I poet John McCrae that graces the wall of the Canadiens dressing-room—"To you from failing/ hands we throw/ The torch; be yours to/ hold it high…"—said perfectly what was happening, what was expected. The Canadiens brought Lafleur to Montreal for his very first professional training camp, and wisely boarded him with Béliveau. He could watch, and he could learn.

They had so much in common and yet were so different. Lafleur was given to impulse, Béliveau to consideration. Lafleur would make mistakes, Béliveau none. But Lafleur had the ability that no one since Richard had—not even Béliveau, who freely admitted it—and that was to electrify a hockey crowd with a combination of speed and skill that had been the Rocket's signature and would now be the signature of the one they were calling "The Flower". The Canadiens knew what his capabilities were; they needed the steadying Béliveau to protect the young man and bring them out.

Béliveau had been born in Trois-Rivières in 1931, the eldest of five boys and two girls for Arthur Béliveau, a lineman with Shawinigan Water & Power, and his wife, Laurette. The young family had moved to Victoriaville when Jean was three, and, soon after, Arthur built the traditional backyard rink for his growing family. Jean and his brother Guy, four years younger, took to it so fanatically that Arthur had to find industrial-strength linoleum that he then laid under the kitchen table so the boys could keep their skates on while eating meals, so keen were they to skate and play as much as time would permit.

Béliveau was tall and graceful and gifted. He stood out from the very first, and he was soon noticed. There were no drafts in those days, merely persuasions, and Arthur Béliveau soon found that he was spending much of his time fending off those who had other designs for his oldest boy. "One after another," Béliveau later wrote, "he had stared them down, waiting out their promises and ploys, until he received what was right for his son, and his son's future."

The local junior team, the Victoriaville Tigres, were most persistent. They presumed that the youngster was their property by right of address, which would usually be the case, but Arthur Béliveau had other ideas. As Jean would later write, his father told Roland Hébert, the team owner, "Jean will sign to play for you for one season only. But after that, his rights revert to me."

"That's not how it works," Hébert countered. "Players become the property of the team they sign with, unless they are traded or released."

"Not Jean Béliveau."

The Tigres had no choice. They had to have the local superstar. Any other father would have handed his son over happily, as if the bishop himself had asked, but the likes of

Arthur Béliveau had never been seen in hockey. Before agents, before the first meddling fathers of modern hockey would come along, he had understood that hockey had a desperate need for his son. This was not the priesthood calling; this was a congregation in search of a new god. And that put power in the hands of the player, not the game.

"My dad was looking out for my interests," Béliveau wrote. "He knew that I could go far in hockey and that if I committed to one team, one management, that it might not do me any good. He was right, of course, the Victoriaville team lasted one year in the league and then folded."

But what a year it was for the youngster. Jean Béliveau had played brilliantly, even better than expected, and though the team had been terrible, its best player had been awarded the trophy as the best pro prospect—the same trophy Alexandre Daigle would win more than four decades later while playing for the same city. With the team out and Béliveau's rights now back with his father, the youngster was considered fair game, and Quebec City and Montreal began what would be years of competing for his services. Quebec City would win the first round for the best of family reasons: it was closer to home.

In Quebec, Béliveau became the definition for what is today called a "franchise player". He arrived the season after the original Quebec Colisée burned to the ground. The new one was built, and filled, largely on his promise. He was, as expected, the rookie sensation of the Quebec Citadels; on December 8, 1949, the day the new Colisée opened, he packed the place even though construction workers had yet to install the seats. When the ten thousand seats were finally in, he once brought 16,806 fans into the new rink. If he did not play because of injury, the rink might be half full. His pay for this was a gift from the fans: a new Nash and what may have been the first vanity licence plate—9B—for his number and name. He had not yet switched to No. 4; but then, No. 9 was already famous throughout Quebec as the sweater of the great Richard, playing two hours up the St Lawrence River in Montreal.

The Canadiens were desperate to add Béliveau to the line-up. It was necessary not to fill the Forum—Richard and the other stars were doing a fine job of that—but to appease the tough, demanding fans of the Canadiens. They felt it obligatory that the province's NHL team have the best the province had to offer. An island of francophone culture in an anglophone North America, the Canadiens image was the francophone image. Flair, attention, success, all were considered vital. It put Béliveau in a remarkable bargaining position. He moved from the Citadels to the old Quebec Aces, a professional team that may well have been the equal to NHL teams but did not compete in that league. He was well paid—then $15,000 a year by the team owners, the Anglo-Canadian Pulp and Paper Company— and content to stay in the city where he had friends, family and a new love, Elise Couture.

Béliveau's reluctance caused the Canadiens to make increasingly attractive offers. On his father's advice, he turned down a three-year deal for more than $50,000 knowing that the only Montreal player making similar money was the long-established star, Maurice Richard. He finally agreed in October 1953, and signed for $110,000 over five years. Montreal general manager Frank Selke said signing him was a simple matter: "All I did was open the Forum vault and say, 'Help yourself, Jean.'"

Béliveau would often say that he was, in fact, glad to have delayed his arrival in the NHL. Alexandre Daigle would struggle as an eighteen-year-old. Guy Lafleur would struggle as a twenty-year-old. Beliveau was twenty-two in October of 1953, the age at which Wayne Gretzky had already set his single-season scoring records in Edmonton and was dominating hockey as no one before and no one since ever has. Béliveau felt his long wait gave him time to grow up. Unlike the others, he had not lost his youth to publicity and pressure. In Elise, he had met a strong woman and they had married the previous June in Quebec City. He was a man, sure of himself and of his abilities and, as he would later write, "as a result, the Jean Béliveau who finally did sign with Montreal in 1953 was much better prepared for the demands of NHL stardom."

He never forgot what his father had said when the Aces and Canadiens were battling over him: "Loyalty is another form of responsibility. If you feel that you owe something to someone, no matter what the debt, it behooves you to pay it. Sometimes these very people will do or say something to indicate that they are discharging the debt, but only you will know what the best policy will be. Your good name is your greatest asset."

It was a wonderful name, Béliveau, one so untainted by scandal, so revered throughout Canada that, in 1994, he would be offered the office of governor-general of Canada, only to turn it down because he felt a larger obligation to his only daughter, Hélène, and his and Elise's two grand-daughters, Mylene and Magalie. The two girls had been left fatherless at the ages of five and three when their father, a Quebec policeman, had taken his own life.

Béliveau's NHL hockey career had been everything the Montreal Canadiens had hoped for and more. He scored only thirteen goals that first season in Montreal and came fourth in the rookie race—right behind the shifty little

Detroit forward Bill Dineen—but his eight assists in the playoffs that first year was the highest total in the league, astonishing for a rookie in his first Stanley Cup appearance. The following season he moved up to thirty-seven goals and thirty-six assists, and the following year to forty-seven goals and eighty-eight points, both league-leading. He won the Art Ross Trophy as the NHL's top scorer and the Hart Trophy as the league's most valuable player.

Béliveau's twelve playoff goals in the 1955–56 season—in which the Canadiens won the first of ten Cups with him—stood for fourteen years. All told, Jean Béliveau played 1,125 regular-season games, scored 507 goals and had 1,219 points, as well as 162 Stanley Cup playoff games with 79 goals and 176 points. He won the Hart Trophy twice and ten times was on the Stanley Cup winning team. His total of 176 points in playoff action survived sixteen years until it was surpassed by Wayne Gretzky, who was then playing in a playoff structure twice as long as what Béliveau had played in through all but his final three playoff seasons.

It was one of hockey's most charmed careers, and yet Jean Béliveau was fully aware of the pressures any hockey star feels, but particularly the chosen star of Quebec. When injuries slowed him in the 1960s, the media became, he felt, obsessed with "Will he retire?" stories. "I was continually being analysed by the press pundits," he later wrote in *Jean Béliveau: My Life in Hockey,* "who didn't like what they saw, or made up what they wanted to. My mental stability was called into question. Was I strong enough to handle all this adversity?" Never having felt it before, he found he was sensitive to criticism, and the experience made him suspicious of the media. "Fan reaction is always blown out of proportion," he wrote. "The press hears four or five guys boo and its a headline."

He knew when to retire and did so in 1971. He turned forty later that summer. His size and strength, his abilities and NHL expansion would have permitted him to play on, but his pride argued against it. He had gone out with a Stanley Cup, which seemed appropriate. Perhaps just as appropriately, Guy Lafleur was now a Canadien. "To you from failing/ hands we throw…"

"After Richard," Béliveau wrote in his autobiography, "other French stars came and went—J.C. Tremblay, Yvan Cournoyer, Jacques Lemaire, Guy Lapointe, Serge Savard—but none stirred the emotions as did Guy Lafleur, who followed me down the highway from Quebec City. We both discovered that when you garner more than your share of publicity during your junior days, the fans have dramatically heightened expectations right from the start."

The province had every reason to be excited about Lafleur. He had scored 130 goals in his last year of junior and taken the Quebec Remparts to the Memorial Cup. He had been treated like a star—making $20,000 a year as a junior, driving a free car and dressing in the finest free clothes—and he had handled himself with *élan*. The spotlight loved him. It seemed then so easy; but, of course, it would turn out to be not quite as easy as it looked.

Lafleur was lucky to have Béliveau there when he arrived. Not only did he live with the Béliveaus while attending his first Canadiens training camp, he had Béliveau to talk to at the rink and after practices. Béliveau was moving off the ice into a corporate job with the Canadiens, and he was able to watch the difficult development of the team's next star. He was also able to play a pivotal role when it was necessary.

"He came to me and asked me what I thought about him taking my sweater number," Béliveau remembered in an interview years later. "'If you want it, take it,' I told him. 'But don't you think you already have enough on you? Why don't you pick another number and make it famous yourself?'" Lafleur decided to pass on wearing his old junior number and the number made famous by Béliveau, 4, and went instead with No. 10. He hoped to make it his own.

In his first season, he would score a respectable twenty-nine goals, but it would not be enough for those who expected so much more. The Calder Trophy for rookie of the year went to his team-mate goaltender Ken Dryden, and Lafleur was not even named runner-up, an honour that would go to Buffalo's Richard Martin. Martin, not Lafleur, was the best young francophone in the National Hockey League. And if not Martin, it would be Marcel Dionne, who was playing his first year in Detroit. In his second year, Lafleur scored twenty-eight goals; in his third, twenty-one goals. In six playoff games that 1973–74 season he would count only a single assist. The province would turn its back on him.

Lafleur considered himself a failure. He heard the boos in the Forum and he heard the anger and disappointment on the radio talk shows until he could listen no more. He stopped reading the papers. He became almost reclusive in his apartment, watching television endlessly and finding joy only in the meaningless pratfalls of Three Stooges reruns. His love life was a mess. "My legs were in Montreal," he says, "but my heart was in Quebec City. My mind wasn't on hockey." The new Nordiques of the competing World Hockey Association tried to lure him back to Quebec City with a three-year $465,000 offer, but the Canadiens kept him for a figure that sounded better but was considerably less: $1 million over ten years. In fact, he didn't know what he wanted to do, with his hockey or his life.

He wrote melancholy poetry to himself, often about suicide and the meaninglessness of life. He was so tightly wound—"like a coil," team-mate Steve Shutt would later say—that he began to do more harm to himself than good. He drank too much beer. He smoked constantly, sometimes between periods. He took to arriving at the rink hours before anyone else, dressing completely—even his skates tied tight—and drinking endless cups of coffee until the others arrived and began preparing. At times he was so drained from waiting that he could hardly play. Others worried about him, including Béliveau. Yet Béliveau saw something in Lafleur's character that held out enormous hope: "When you see an athlete worry so much, it is a good sign."

"It was difficult," Lafleur recalled more than twenty years later. "I came just as Jean Béliveau left. The team was very, very strong. The mentality around the Canadiens was 'You have to wait.' It had been my dream to play with the Canadiens. I get there and 'Whoops, what's wrong?'"

Everything was wrong. Fortunately, Lafleur had Béliveau to turn to as a surrogate father, and Béliveau was more than willing to offer comfort. Béliveau had his own office in the executive portion of the Forum, and often Lafleur would climb the stairs, knock and go in. Béliveau would sit him on the large *bleu-blanc-rouge*-coloured chesterfield to the side of his desk, Lafleur would put his face in his hands, and Béliveau would simply wait until the crying stopped. "He kept saying, 'Be patient,'" Lafleur remembers. "'Be patient.'"

Béliveau often thought of his own first year, when he had scored only thirteen goals. "I had two different injuries," he said. "I played forty-four games and had thirteen goals. It was very rough. I knew what he was going through. When you are preceded by the publicity, people expect so much. Sports fans are so demanding.... I told him, 'You have a heavy load on your shoulders. I remember some nights I would score three goals and on the way out people would say I could have scored four or five. Whatever you do, people expect more. And it makes you press when you're on the ice. You want to do so well to get rid of this anxiety.'"

But the anxiety only kept rising. The fans and the media were beginning to say Lafleur was *jaune*—yellow— just as, many years later, they would say that Alexandre Daigle was afraid to take a hit, afraid to go into the corners to make a play. Lafleur's agent, Jerry Petrie, said later that there was "probably more pressure on him to perform from the people of this province than there is on (then separatist leader) René Lévesque." Petrie was not necessarily exaggerating.

In the spring of 1974, with Lafleur coming off what would be his worst season, Béliveau took a gamble. He let it be known that he was less than pleased with the performance of his heir. He castigated Lafleur for his work ethic. Lafleur was shattered, but Béliveau's public criticism became just the "wake-up call" he needed. He sulked a while and then he told his few close friends: "I'll show the bastards."

And he did just that. Lafleur went from a bust to the first all-star team, from twenty-one goals to fifty-three—a record for the Canadiens—and from one whose courage was challenged to one whose courage soon became a trademark. He threw away his helmet after a practice and soon the familiar image had become a hockey icon: Lafleur in full flight down the right wing, his hair flying, Lafleur dancing around the attacking defence, Lafleur shooting hard and true and high into the enemy net.

The next season it was fifty-six goals and 125 points, good enough for his first Art Ross Trophy as the NHL's leading scorer. He would score fifty or more goals six years in a row, reaching a high of sixty in 1977–78, and his record would show three Art Ross Trophies, two Harts as the league's most valuable player, six first-team all-star selections and the Conn Smythe Trophy as the MVP of the 1977 Stanley Cup playoffs. The five additional Stanley Cups his teams brought to Montreal would place his number, 10, forever with Béliveau's 4 and Richard's 9 in the hearts of a demanding province.

Lafleur never forgot what it was that Jean Béliveau had done for him. "I may never be able to play like him," he once said of his hero. "But I'd like to be the man he is."

At the peak of Lafleur's fame, Jean Béliveau sat in his Forum office and talked about the young protégé who had become the heir apparent who was now the true *vedette*. "I've been his number-one supporter," said Béliveau. "I've always been there when he needed somebody, and he knows I'll always be there."

Béliveau understood, just as Lafleur came to understand, just as Alexandre Daigle is beginning to understand, that the pressures of being a francophone hockey player in, or even on the border of, Quebec are unlike the pressures known by any other Canadian athlete. To compare it to religion, as Jean-Yves Daigle has, is not so far fetched. Since he began travelling away from home to play, Montreal Canadiens defenceman Patrice Brisbois has said a prayer at a precise moment before every game, knowing that his mother, no matter where she might be, will be saying the exact same prayer at the same time. The Bordeleau brothers—Christian (eleven years, Montreal,

St Louis, Chicago of NHL; Winnipeg and Quebec of WHA), Jean-Pierre (nine years with Chicago) and Paulin (three years with Vancouver)—all recite the same prayer that had been given to them by the family priest back in Noranda for precisely this purpose: "Thank you, Lord, for using me to sow beauty in the world…"

Marcel Dionne, on the other hand, used to pray that he could somehow escape Quebec and the terrible pressures that come from being a hockey star in that province. Dionne was Lafleur's greatest rival in Quebec minor hockey when Lafleur starred for Quebec City and Dionne for Drummondville. He had been expected to make the NHL from the moment he first wore skates at the age of two. He could remember falling asleep in his bed above the kitchen behind the grocery store his family ran in Drummondville and the sounds of his father and many of his thirteen uncles below as they watched the Montreal game on television and drank beer out of quart bottles. He could even remember the sound of dropping change as the men slid quarters across the kitchen table to buy a new stick for *Le p'tit Marcel.*

When Dionne was only a pee wee player, a letter arrived with the logo of the Montreal Canadiens. His parents read it aloud so he would understand that he was to take special care with his hockey because Senator Molson and the Canadiens were already watching and waiting. He could remember the way, after a game, the fans would reach down to touch his gloves for good luck and how, when he undressed, he would find dollar bills had been stuffed in— an official of the church, taking collection.

It was Lafleur-Dionne, Dionne-Lafleur for a genera- tion. Lafleur handled the pressures, Dionne wanted away from them. The fans, the coaches, the other players, his

father, his uncles, his five sisters, all of them at him to succeed as no one ever had before. Friends of his father's took
to following Marcel's team almost as if he were their own
son, long cavalcades of Drummondville cars heading out to
the other towns where, when they played, the stands would
be as packed with Drummondville supporters as with the
home team fans.

"Hockey, hockey, hockey, hockey," he said one day in
1980, long after he had left the province. "I was going
nuts." To escape the pressures, Dionne and his parents,
Gilbert and Laurette, went through one of hockey's most
elaborate ruses: they faked a separation, and Laurette
Dionne, Marcel and three of the girls and a brother left
Quebec for St Catharines, Ontario, where young Marcel
was then able to play for a junior team that was not
Quebec-based. Lawsuits were threatened in Quebec. His
family was attacked. "You would not believe what my dad,
my mom, my family, my relatives went through," he said.

Away from the provincial pressures, Dionne flourished.
He won two successive Ontario junior scoring championships and, as irony would have it, his team then met the
Quebec Remparts in the 1971 Memorial Cup. Once again
it was Lafleur-Dionne, Dionne-Lafleur. It would turn out
to be the most miserable experience of Dionne's life.

When the youngster from Drummondville returned to
Quebec for the Memorial Cup series, he was branded a
"traitor" in the Quebec press. His mother and father were
abused in their seats by the Quebec fans. "I had forty
tickets, all for the family," remembers Dionne. "I could see
where they were sitting and that people were throwing
garbage at them. My dad was standing up challenging
everyone. I'm playing the game and I can *hear* him yelling
at them." The fans attacked the bus that he was supposedly

on, so terrifying his aunt Denise that she miscarried shortly after. St Catharines refused to complete the series and Quebec was awarded the Memorial Cup by default.

Such experiences had a profound effect on Marcel Dionne's entire career. He had wanted to go number one in the draft, and many felt he should have, but when Montreal engineered the number-one choice away from the California Golden Seals it was certain that the Canadiens would pick the adored provincial hero over the "traitor". Dionne went instead to Detroit, where he was billed as "the next Gordie Howe". Just as Béliveau departed upon Lafleur's arrival, so too did Howe leave—only to return again for several more years with other teams—on the arrival of Dionne. Detroit did not work out—again, a case of too much impatience, too much immaturity—and Dionne was soon off to Los Angeles, where he played the majority of his long career with the Kings, eventually ending up in New York with the Rangers before retiring.

Dionne was hardly the only francophone star whose career would be played out far away from Quebec. Mike Bossy played ten years and scored 573 goals for the New York Islanders, Gilbert Perrault played seventeen years and scored 512 goals in Buffalo, Luc Robitaille has more than 400 goals in Los Angeles and now Pittsburgh and, of course, the Magnificent One, Mario Lemieux, had 494 goals for Pittsburgh before taking the 1994–95 season off for health reasons. But Marcel Dionne's may well be hockey's most curious superstar career. Dionne played eighteen years. He scored 731 goals and 1,040 points for a total of 1,771 points. In eighteen years he played in only 49 playoff games, scoring a respectable twenty-one goals and twenty-four assists, but never won a Stanley Cup. The one scoring championship he did win, 1979–80, is remembered because he had tied with the young Wayne Gretzky, then in his first NHL season with the Edmonton Oilers, but the trophy had gone to Dionne, who had more goals. The next season Gretzky took over the scoring race semi-permanently. Dionne's 1,771 points place him third on the all-time scoring race, behind Gretzky and Howe but well ahead of Lafleur, who stands eighth, yet Lafleur's career shines while Dionne's struggles through the shadows. Had he ever played in Quebec, people have wondered, what might he have accomplished?

In 1979–80, the season Dionne finally won an NHL scoring championship—Lafleur stood third—he felt the pressure building all the way from Drummondville to his palatial home in the exclusive Rolling Hills Estates of Los Angeles. "They want me to win the scoring title so badly," he said as the race wound down. "*More* than I want it.

"If I was not Marcel Dionne and he was not Guy Lafleur, maybe then it wouldn't matter so much. But…"

"Alexandre," Guy Lafleur said in late 1994, "is going to have a rough time. He's going to have to work twice as hard. But it doesn't matter how much talent you have, he must have the tools to work with—he can't carry the team on his back."

Lafleur understood the easy similarities between himself as a player and Alexandre Daigle. Both the Quebec junior sensations of their day, both six foot tall, 180 pounds, both with lightning speed down the right side; the centre, Daigle, becoming a left shot on an off wing, the winger, Lafleur, a right shot deadly to the far side. Both had been labelled "can't miss" at sixteen. Both were called "franchise players" in the year they were drafted, both going number one overall, twenty-one years apart.

The draft, however, had changed by the time Alexandre Daigle came along. The threat of the World Hockey Association and of legal action had seen the draft age drop from twenty to eighteen, and Lafleur had long been an out-spoken critic of the "devastating" effect being drafted too early was having on so many players. He himself had been twenty and not ready. It would take a rare and mature talent to be ready at eighteen. Perhaps Bobby Orr and Denis Potvin and Wayne Gretzky and Mario Lemieux had all stepped right up at eighteen, but it was not an automatic step from stardom in junior hockey.

Both had fair first years in the National Hockey League—Lafleur scored twenty-nine goals, Daigle twenty—and both came short on the rookie-of-the-year award, which went, in both incidents, to surprising young goal-tenders, Dryden in Lafleur's first year and, in Daigle's, the New Jersey Devils' fine young netminder, Martin Brodeur. And both heard the grumbling begin at the start of their second season. "They were patient for a while, not the whole year," Lafleur remembers of his own first season. "Then they started saying the Canadiens had made a mistake." If Montreal fans were looking longingly at Dionne or Martin, Ottawa fans were wondering about Hartford's Chris Pronger or Edmonton's Jason Arnott.

So many similarities, yet so many crucial differences. Lafleur had gone to a strong, established team. Lafleur had a strong sense of waiting his turn. Yvan Cournoyer would carry the torch for a while, and Henri Richard was still capable of playing well. The Mahovlich brothers, Frank and Peter, were there, as was Jacques Lemaire. Lafleur was not expected to carry a power play. Lafleur was not even a first-liner. Daigle, on the other hand, was expected to star immediately. The Senators had Daigle and Yashin and precious little else. The teenagers would play the power play. They would kill penalties. They would be on the first and second lines. They would be expected to produce.

Lafleur also had Jean Béliveau. Daigle had no one. The last Ottawa Senator to star in the NHL had been King Clancy, the last time the Senators had won a Stanley Cup was 1927. The most established francophone player on the team, Sylvain Turgeon, was also struggling. With Daigle in the line-up, the Senators had not even been able to rise out of last place, and would remain the worst club in the National Hockey League. Lafleur thought the situation for young Daigle would be even worse than for him, and at the beginning of Daigle's second season he spoke out: "Alexandre is going to be great, he's got everything. But the organization has to wake up. And they have to surround Alexandre with the right tools."

The organization brought in no one who could be described as "the right tool" for Alexandre Daigle. They brought in a new goaltender, Don Beaupré, for the shortened 1994–95 season, and they signed their most recent top draft choice, Czech sensation Radek Bonk, to a $6.125-million five-year contract. Bonk, however, was another centre and playmaker. The Senators now had three young centres—Daigle, Yashin and Bonk—and none of them had proven goal scorers to work with. By the quarter mark of the forty-eight-game season, Daigle had become an experiment, playing right wing to Yashin's centre. When the Senators' veterans spoke up in outrage over Daigle's refusal to play tough on the road, Senators coach Rick Bowness took the extraordinary step of benching both Daigle and Yashin. The radio hot lines began sizzling with rumours that one of them would have to be traded, and what better trade to look for than Daigle to the Montreal Canadiens or the Quebec Nordiques.

There was another extraordinary difference in the two experiences: money. When Lafleur began with the Canadiens, he was paid $25,000 and he fully expected to be paid less than such proven veterans as Henri Richard and Frank Mahovlich. "The more money you make," he says, "the more demanding the fans are." At the age Guy Lafleur finally came true, twenty-three, Alexandre Daigle's first five-year $12.25-million contract will already have expired. Lafleur himself feels the impatience that this profligate spending has brought on. "People are getting fed up with it," he says. Fed up and angry, they lash out at Alexandre Daigle for something beyond his control. And sometimes it showed. At one point in his frustrating first year Daigle turned the pockets of his jeans out and shouted, "I have *no* money! Nothing! I never think about my contract—*never*!"

Had Guy Lafleur been in Ottawa during some of the Senators' home stands, he would have seen the frustration in the face of Jean-Yves Daigle and it would have reminded him of his own father, who finally began attending his son's games when Guy became a Canadien and who felt on his own enormous back the pressures that were coming down on his son from the Forum seats. "They gave him a rough time," Lafleur remembers. "They did it on purpose, to crank him up. He would get mad, but he would not fight."

Gradually, the pressures lifted off both father and son. Guy Lafleur gave Réjean his first Stanley Cup ring from 1972–73, and the father never took it off. He came to games and he took to watching them on the television that Guy bought his parents. He put together massive scrapbooks of his son's accomplishments—thirteen bulging albums—and he set his son's trophies on special shelves in the basement. His son rarely came to visit—in the end, the most expensive price of fame—and, after Réjean Lafleur died in 1992, his son threw most of the trophies in a box and forgot where they were. The albums he would sometimes look through, always with the same reaction: "It's like a dream."

A dream that could sometimes flex into a harrowing nightmare. Lafleur survived his early troubles and rose to Hall of Fame greatness, but it was never totally dreamlike. In the spring of 1976, with Lafleur in full flower, Montreal police investigating a Brinks robbery stumbled upon a plot to kidnap the Canadiens star and hold him for a $250,000 ransom. Police turned first to Béliveau, who then went to Lafleur's house and told him. Béliveau told him there were two possibilities: Lafleur could go into hiding in Miami and the team would invent some injury excuse for him, or he could play while his family was under police protection. Béliveau was delighted when his young friend told him he would stay, and he would play.

The Canadiens went on to another Stanley Cup and Lafleur's play was understandably affected. He slept with detectives sitting in chairs outside his bedroom door. His wife, Lise, and eight-month-old son, Martin, were moved first to a hotel and then to stay with her parents in Quebec City. His nerves nearly cracked. At one point he cowered, shaking, under the windowsill as he watched a black car pull up the driveway of the old farmhouse the Lafleurs had renovated and sit there idling, four cigarettes glowing through the windows. The car later left, with no explanation. The fans booed him on the ice, unaware what he was going through off the ice.

At the age of three, Martin Lafleur was already talking of being a hockey player like his father. He had seen the glory on the ice, heard the cheers, but he had also seen the impossibilities of fame: the crushes at the shopping malls, the endless crowds that waited on the streets outside the Forum. "I tell him to sit down and relax," Lafleur said at the time. "I know he'd have even more pressure on him than I had."

Martin was born the same year as Alexandre Daigle. By the time he was nineteen, he no longer played the game that had made his father a god. "I don't put any pressure on him as long as he does sports," says the father. "He skis a lot." His second son, Marc, born in 1985, decided to play later than most Quebec hockey players, and the father, like any other Canadian father, signed him up for house league. "When Marc asked to play hockey, I was surprised," says Lafleur. He suddenly found himself going back into arenas, the same smells, the old thoughts, the old memories and, to his small surprise, the old lessons.

"My father followed me all through minor hockey," he says. "He'd never talk to me about the game. He never said I should have played better. He was a spectator. That's why I'm doing the same thing with my kid."

He thought about coaching but dropped the idea when he found out he would first have to take a coaching course to do so. Instead, he began sometimes renting ice and conducting private lessons, just the two of them on the ice and no pressure. He wanted to help, but he did not want to interfere. "I won't tell him to do this, do that," he says. "I'll be there."

They were almost the same words used sixteen years earlier by Jean Béliveau: "I've always been there when he needed somebody, and he knows I'll always be there."

Jean-Yves Daigle was there for Alexandre in Tampa. He and Francine flew down to Boston for the final regular-season game that would ever be played in Boston Garden—the Bruins barely surviving the Senators with a 5–4 victory— and then on to Tampa Bay for the Senators' final game of the 1995 season against the Lightning. Alexandre set up two third-period goals, including the winner, in a 4–3 win by the Senators, their fifth victory in the final seven games of the shortened 1995 season.

In his sophomore year he was once again second in scoring behind Alexei Yashin, Yashin finishing with twenty-one goals and twenty-three assists for forty-four points and Daigle with sixteen goals and twenty-one assists for thirty-seven points. Both had recovered from the mid-season dressing-down from the veteran players. The Senators might once again be the worst team in hockey, but Daigle was at least feeling better about himself. He was no longer "alone with his Rice Krispies". He had friends—all of them out of hockey, many of them academically inclined—and both his English and his spirits had vastly improved. He now spent his mornings watching himself on videotape instead of "Beavis and Butthead" reruns, and he was con- vinced he was "playing better" because of it. In the final months, there had been periodic bursts of speed that had left the crowds shorter of breath than him. There had also, of course, been some more lost pucks and panic passes. He was learning, he said, how not to "rush my play."

He had rushed nothing in Tampa Bay, and it had paid off, one on a nifty pass out to Steve Larouche from behind the Lightning net, one on a perfect pass, again to Larouche, of a puck Daigle had used his speed to trap along the boards. It had been a meaningless game—the Senators long since out of the playoffs, the Lightning listless having just missed the playoffs—but Jean-Yves Daigle, searching for his rented car in the parking lot after, thought he had seen something that made the trip worthwhile.

"It's coming," he kept saying. "It's coming."

But, of course, there were still a few details to work on.

To Each His Own Story

Toronto, February 1989

Not long ago, they agreed to stop talking at these
moments. It is one thing to have a brilliant, highly
analytical mind, to see and understand things as few others
do and to be able to articulate matters concerning this
game and the way it is played as well as—perhaps better
than—anyone who has ever come before; but it is quite
another thing to be a father with a son in the back seat,
headed for a hockey game.

The small Japanese import heads west along Lakeshore
Boulevard away from the Toronto downtown. The man in
the front seat does not quite seem to fit—but then, Ken
Dryden has not quite fit most places he has been. He
seemed, when he arrived on the national scene back in
1971, too large for the net. At six foot four inches and well
over 200 pounds, he had a reach that exceeded that of
Muhammad Ali by seven inches. The best shooters of the
day—Boston's Bobby Orr and Phil Esposito, Chicago's
Bobby Hull and Stan Mikita—found he left no room
whatsoever for pucks, that remarkable spring as he came
out of nowhere plugged the Montreal net solid and took
the Canadiens to an unexpected Stanley Cup.

Ken Dryden was instantly larger than life and stayed
that way: the Conn Smythe Trophy as the most valuable
player in that first playoff season, the Calder Trophy the
next year when junior sensations Guy Lafleur and Marcel
Dionne were supposed to be battling for NHL rookie-of-
the-year honours; the goaltender whose third-period saves

gave Paul Henderson that last-minute chance to win the final game of the 1972 Team Canada–Soviet series; five more times a Stanley Cup winner—six Cups in a career that ran only eight seasons; then retirement at age thirty-one. He left, as so few ever do, still at the very peak of his game. He left with 258 wins, 74 ties and only 57 losses, with 46 shutouts and a lifetime 2.24 goals-against average.

But those are only statistics. His scope, as well, had seemed at times too great for the game. He was not only a player they wrote about but a player who wrote himself. He put himself through school with his hockey and kept up his studies even after he became an NHL star. He took a year off hockey to study and work. He became a lawyer and a goaltender at the same time, knowing that law, like hockey, would not be enough in the long run. That the long run, the life after hockey, was something to look forward to rather than dread.

He never played goal again after May 21, 1979. The Montreal Canadiens were ahead of the New York Rangers 4–1 in the fifth and final game of the Stanley Cup playoffs; the Forum crowd was on its feet in the final minute, and he announced his retirement to a single person, his wife, Lynda. He had raised his arm and waved and she had waved back, no one else noticing, and when the puck came caroming around the boards and he scooped it up as the siren sounded, it was all over. Forever. He knew there would be no more hockey. He was pretty sure, even then, that he would never practise law.

But he never knew until he got there what it would be like to be a father. There were never any drills to prepare him for this, no books to read or courses to take. There was a time when he might have said the true test of mettle was facing Orr or Hull or Kharlamov or Yakushev, or trying to concentrate on tort law during a rambunctious team flight back from a victory, but no more. "It's the toughest thing in the world," he would eventually come to believe, "watching your own kid play."

His own kid, Michael, sits quietly in the back seat. Michael has his mother's colouring and his father's cool analytical bent. He is only eleven years old in 1989 and has been playing for only four years, deciding later than most of his friends to take up the game most would have thought he had taken up at birth. He plays novice major, defence, and has only once tried goal, which did not feel right for a great many reasons. He plays a quiet style, staying back, staying in position, avoiding both complications and possibilities. He likes to think of himself as he is both off and on the ice: dependable. He is not a star and has no vision of himself becoming one. He just likes to play, and doesn't much care to talk about it before it happens.

It took a while for father and son to discover a dynamic that would work for them as they travelled together to and from these Metropolitan Toronto Hockey League games. The father knows far too much about the game and can talk about it endlessly, effortlessly, enlarging the small parts like a microscope, shrinking the large ones so they, too, come into a fresh and sharper focus. He is a man acutely aware of his surroundings, and has long been sensitive to the fact that Michael's wilfulness is both reality and necessity. When you are last-born in a family that includes a famous father, an energetic, extroverted mother and a high-achieving older sister, the fight for your own space is life's first battle, and the stubbornness it requires sticks. Michael wants to do his own thinking.

The father in the front seat, like other fathers throughout the country, had often thought of the fun to be had coaching his own children. He had helped out with his daughter Sarah's team when she played minor-league hockey, and the experience had been wonderful. He had coached and been assistant coach for Michael, and although it, too, had been wonderful, he was beginning to see that it could not go on much longer. No wave, no final game. He would withdraw slowly.

It was not that he didn't enjoy coaching. Quite the contrary. "I would get really excited," he remembers. "A kid would do something that was really smart or selfless, I couldn't wait for them to come to the bench so I could say something to them."

But in time, as Michael moved into pee wee and then bantam, this thinking and caring father would realize that he was better off in the stands, watching. He would never say that was the way it should be for all fathers and sons involved in hockey, but it was the right place for this particular father and this particular son. Ken in the stands, Michael on the ice. "It wasn't the right combination," Ken would eventually come to say. "I wasn't overly harsh or anything, but I was getting in the way of his experience. This was his game, his friends. I was intruding on his experience."

He had sensed this from novice, when they changed the manner in which they would drive to the games. The father feared he would say too much; the son worried that he would hear too much. In working so hard to share the experience, they put the experience itself in jeopardy. Hockey is a game that happens, its unpredictability its wonder, and they had to learn to just let it happen. So they stopped talking. And while they drove together to games, they began a ritual that had nothing to do with talking, but much to do with communication.

They made a game of their little ritual. They would put in the same tape—the late Stan Rogers singing "Flyin'"—and, in silence, they would continue on to the arena with one goal seemingly in mind: to arrive at the exact moment that the tape came to an end. They both loved Rogers' chorus:

And every kid over the boards listens for the sound;
The roar of the crowd is their ticket for finally leaving
     this town
To be just one more hopeful in the Junior A
Dreaming of that miracle play,
And going up flying, going home dying.

"Flyin'," Stan Rogers, 1984

It was a harmless game that had the enormous benefit of freeing each other. Since Michael played at such a variety of Toronto-area arenas, they would get so caught up in the calculations concerning their arrival and Rogers' dying chorus that all thoughts of hockey would vanish. Ken would speed up, slow down, sometimes deliberately pass by the arena in order to land on the final line of "Flyin'". They could always talk about the game after, if both felt like it.

At the arena, Michael Dryden goes to the dressing-room, Ken Dryden to the stands, where he stands and chats easily with strangers who recognize him as the former great, as well as with other parents from Michael's team, people who are coming to see him as Michael's father, another parent though one who, clearly, knows the game very well. He watches the game just finishing with the relaxed, happy smile of one who has no vested interest. These are simply children on the ice, playing a game that can be as exciting as the observer wishes. He does not know the team and, therefore, has no idea that the tall defenceman's father may be a jerk, the little centre's mother may be a single parent uncertain whether she can afford to have her son play much longer, the goaltender might be in net because his father is the manager and controls the pads. He watches this game as games are best watched: each team composed of players with different numbers, their skills and short-comings on display, their parents invisible and beyond consideration.

When Michael's team comes onto the ice, Ken Dryden outwardly remains the same. He would prefer to watch in silence but is far too polite to move off on his own. He enjoys the other parents, knows each of their youngsters and has a knack of saying exactly the right thing to those who will read any comment from him in every conceivable way. He jokes, he smiles, he watches—and the only dis-cernible difference lies in the watching. When Michael is on the ice, so, too, is Ken. It is, however, an out-of-body experience: the man still standing along the back row, still chatting, still fitting in. But the father is the son's shadow.

He was surprised by the intensity of emotion when he became a parent watching instead of a fan watching or a player playing, but the more he thought about it the more he came to understand why the feelings might be so strong. "So long as there are stands for parents," he says, "that's the way it will be. You just can't help yourself.

"Just imagine for a moment that this is all taking place outside your home and you're standing at your living-room window looking out and you see another kid come up and be unfair to your kid. You race out, you can't help yourself."

This fascination with the parent in the stands was a main intrigue for Dryden and this author in *Home Game: Hockey and Life in Canada*. "A parent must split the brain to watch his or her own child. The social side, the mature side, the acceptable side, must keep track of the game and watch it as a whole, alert and supportive of the *team*. The self side, the parent side, is aware of the baby out there. It is like sitting through a one-man play, all eyes on the only player on stage, all ears aware of what is being said. The parent soars and dies with each awkward step of the plot....

"For parents watching their child play for the very first time, it is a shock. The child, it seems, is suddenly on his own as he has never been before. Elevated and distant, the parents look down with rare and dangerous perspective. The child, in the midst of the uncontrolled, uncontrollable play of life, lies exposed. Is he a puck hog? Is he useless? Does he keep trying even when the game is lost? Does he quit? In the comfortable, controllable climate of the home, none of this is clear. Here, it is on display for all to see. The cliché has a corollary: sports may *build* character, but more often it *reveals* it. To everyone."

In Dryden's view, the parent is as much on display at a typical minor hockey league game as the child playing. It is not just the parent watching the child and being acutely aware, but the child being equally aware of the parent in the stands. "He can see a father who at home is always calm and reasonable," he wrote, "a mother warm and loving, now out of the parental habitat. His shock is no less."

Today's hockey has been changed as much by new parenting as by new equipment and theory. Parents attend the games now, and often both will appear at a practice, always in the stands, ever on guard. And this dynamic affects the dynamic of coaching—the coach working under surveillance, always feeling the need to explain, too often being asked to explain. It is what had to happen once modern parents took a look at their investment in minor hockey—

their time, their money, their child—and began to look for a return on that investment. Hockey as career, not game.

What else could happen, the authors asked in *Home Game*, when parents came "to apply the attitude and ambitions of the workplace to everything in their lives? They have committed more to their child's activities and so expect more from them. Kids and parents relate differently, too. The passion, pride and disappointments stored up from the game don't recede very quickly when it ends, so their journey home has little of the easy, breezy feel that other rides do. Sometimes the closeness of such an intensely shared experience will cement parent–child bonds like few other things can. Sometimes it will destroy them."

This, in part, explains the Stan Rogers tape and the silent, smarter rides of Ken and Michael Dryden. But only in part. It is in Ken Dryden's character to remain calm under pressure, to observe, analyse and only then, perhaps, comment after much consideration. His demeanour at games, in fact, is not even distantly related to that of his own father, Murray, who would gleefully let himself go when he would travel to Ithaca, New York, to watch Ken play for Cornell Big Red.

"I used to go through a striptease watching," says Murray Dryden, now eighty-four and a frequent, but much calmer, spectator at Michael Dryden's games. "I got absolutely carried away."

He had never imagined that he would be this way. One of Murray's most prized possessions is a photograph taken in 1953 by Nat Turofsky, the well-known sports photographer, who happened to be in Maple Leaf Gardens when the Humber Valley Hornets came to play on the big ice surface. Turofsky picked out the Hornets' six-year-old goaltender, Kenny Dryden, and took some pictures. One of them appeared with the caption "Future great". At the time it had seemed cute, not prophetic.

While delighted with the thought, Murray Dryden never for a moment saw his child as an NHL goaltender. And yet, as the six-year-old became a ten-year-old, a sixteen-year-old and a twenty-year-old, Turofsky's caption began to fall more and more into the realm of possibility. The more intense the competition, the better Ken played; the more intense the experience, the more Murray Dryden felt himself being carried away with it.

He would often go to the Cornell games with his wife, Margaret, though they would usually separate before the game began, she to sit quietly watching and cheering her son, he to go to the very top and back of the stands where he would have room to *play*. There is no other description for it, for he would kick out every one of his son's saves. He would keep on his winter mitts and use them as if they were blocker and glove. And as the game heated up, so, too, would the strange man at the back of the stands. He would remove his topcoat, kick out more saves, block more shots, then loosen his tie, kneel down for a screen shot, take off his sports jacket, then the tie, then his toe rubbers, his shoes, until there he was, a balding, middle-aged man high in the stands along the back wall, his winter clothes in a stack beside him, his shirtsleeves rolled up and hopping in his sock feet. All the better, he believed, for handling the pucks that he imagined were flying towards him.

"I'd get so excited," he says, "I couldn't live with myself. I'd yell so much people would think I was a mad person. I was very vociferous. I was not getting on individuals—I was merely cheering. I wasn't calling anyone by name. But there was nothing I could do about it. I'm just made that way. The body English was wild. I was just moving all the time. I had the leg action. I had a stick in my hand. I had a mitt on. It was quite an exhibition."

He could not act the same way at crowded NHL games, but he would still re-enact everything as much as possible in his cramped seat, usually with Margaret beside him, shaking her head. They began attending professional games in the early 1960s, when Dave—six years older than Ken— was playing junior for St Michael's College in Toronto and would sometimes be asked to come down to Maple Leaf Gardens and just sit in the stands in case something happened to the visiting NHL team's goaltender. This was before the league required a back-up goaltender to be dressed and ready on the bench, and it was common for teams to give a local junior goalie $10 to be there in case, though it was rare one would ever play. Dave Dryden played his first game for the New York Rangers during the 1961–62 season on a night when Gump Worsley was hurt. He played senior hockey after junior and was eventually a regular goaltender in the top league. After Ken was called up from the Canadiens minor-league team, the Montreal Voyageurs, in the spring of 1971, the Drydens had two sons in the NHL, and attending games became regular exercise for Murray.

"I remember asking myself a question," Murray says about these early NHL experiences. "If I'm doing this at a game Ken's playing—and doing it also at games Dave played—what would I be like if I had to play the shots at both ends of the rink?

"One night the boys did play against each other. One of them came up to me at the end, I forget which one of the boys, and said, 'I'm exhausted.' I said, 'You shouldn't be exhausted—you only played the shots at one end. Your mother and I had to play both ends!'"

In time, he grew calmer. He retired, his sons both retired from professional hockey, and the game became once again something to be watched and enjoyed and not taken particularly seriously. He began going to see grandsons and granddaughters play, and remembers vividly driving with Ken and Michael to one of Michael's games—in the days before the Stan Rogers tape—and how they played this little word-game on the way back.

"It was this thing with ratio. How well did he play compared to how he might have played. Was it a six? Maybe a three? It was kind of cute, I thought. You could see that the new generation certainly attacked the topic differently than the previous one had."

Murray Dryden is the eldest of eight children raised on a farm outside Domain, Manitoba. He went as far as grade eleven, by his own account faring poorly in school, and quit at seventeen to make his way in the world. He felt he had a knack for selling: he liked people, he liked talking, and a lifetime of farm chores had made him unafraid of hard work. He had no idea when he set out from the family farm how he would be tested, and how hard work would not necessarily pay off. The Great Depression began less than a year later.

He tried selling everything from silk stockings to ten-cent can-openers. He kept a diary from those years, entries scribbled in his slanting hand and the journal—which he later published as part of a small memoir, *For the Love of His Children*—survives as a telling reminder of how tough the 1930s were for him:

> June 23–28: Put in terrible week. Made less than $10. Slept on the office floor the last couple of

nights and ate only when in dire need. Looks like a tough Dominion Day for me, but there is always a better day coming.

July 8–12: Very poor week. No business. Still slept in office and ate one meal a day.

July 13: Sunday. Starved. Spent day at office. Sad outlook.

July 14: Still fasted, but finally got a break and ate.

July 21–26: Spent whole week recruiting men as I couldn't go outside due to carbuncle (an infection on face—due, probably, to improper food—like raw sugar by the spoonful from the landlady's sugar bowl to save on food).

July 27–August 2: Eventful week with the Elections (Mackenzie King defeated). Made rigid preparations for next week. Ate two meals in 5 1/2 days. Outlook brighter.

August 3–9: Worked like the dickens to put production over. Hired and bonded one representative for the week. Ron Graver and I decided to go to Moose Jaw. Started walking. Such an experience...something to talk about! Worked hard but only made enough to take us back to Regina by train, arriving 11:40 p.m.

I have tried to sleep for a couple of nights in Wascana Park, but each time the police moved in on me and I'd spend the nights walking around the streets. I had to find somewhere to get some rest. I discovered that the Westman Chambers office building wasn't locked at night so I sneaked inside about midnight when no one was about, climbed up five flights of stairs to the top floor and got to the very back of the hallway. There I lay down on the terrazzo floor and tried to sleep. It was very hard but I managed to sleep fitfully and always afraid of someone coming in and finding me.

Murray Dryden wandered and sold and slept fitfully for more than two years, covering most of the prairies and then heading east down into Ontario. He had little luck as a salesman and took whatever work he could, though there was rarely any to be had.

He had what might be described as his first epiphany on the roadside leading to the northern Ontario village of Callander, which four years later would become familiar to the world as the birthplace of the Dionne quintuplets. He could not get a ride. He had been standing for hours, hoping one of the few passing cars would stop for him, but they would not. Given his appearance, he could not blame them.

It grew dark, darker than he had ever before experienced as he stood under huge overhanging trees unlike any he had known on the open prairies. It was cold, and a wind had picked up. He began thinking of home and, almost spontaneously, familiar words came to him: "Lead kindly light, lead thou me on. The night is dark and I am far from home. Lead thou me on." He began to cry.

In desperation, he all but threw himself in front of the next car, forcing the driver to stop. He explained his predicament, and the man offered to take him as far as the outskirts of the village. It was snowing when he was let out. He looked for a haystack to sleep on, then happened upon a small home where, through the window, he could make out two elderly women knitting by lamplight. He knocked in the hopes of finding a place to curl up, was invited in and ended up with a sale of silk and wool hose. Their seventy-five-cent deposit would be his commission.

He took a room at the Callander Hotel for $1.50 a night. "While I hated to cough up that kind of money, I was so doggone dirty and tired—remember, I had slept in a bed in Nipigon on Monday night and then not until Thursday night in Chapleau—that I felt desperate. Then the friendly lady made me an offer. She would provide bed and breakfast for $1.50 and be happy to take me as far as Powassan in the morning on her way to mass.

"After a shave and a bath and as I lay in that comfortable, clean bed, I spent considerable time in reflection. How was I ever able to sell three orders of merchandise totalling over thirty dollars in a one-eyed village on a late Saturday night—particularly when I was so filthy and repulsive in nature?"

He kept wandering and selling and sleeping where he could. He hopped freights, skipped meals and almost froze to death ("April 2, 1932: Arrived in White River at 7:30 a.m. Quite stormy. They pulled a corpse out of the locomotive tool box"). And he never forgot the people who helped him out along his incredible, forlorn journey. Years later he found the man who helped him hop a freight in Nemogas, Ontario, and gave him an electric blanket. He visited and sent flowers to a kind woman who gave him a free hot meal in Chelmsford, Ontario. He swore he would never, ever forget what it meant to be desperate and what it felt like to find someone who truly cared.

The Great Depression came to an end with the beginning of the war, but by then Murray Dryden was already well on his way to success. He had become a superb salesman, a friendly, outgoing man who made people instinctively trust him. He moved from socks to can-openers to blueing paddles to concrete blocks to full entrepreneurship, dealing in everything from construction supplies to Christmas trees. He married a young kindergarten teacher, and soon Murray and Margaret Dryden were settled into a comfortable bungalow on Pinehurst Crescent in Islington, a classic postwar suburb of growing Toronto. Their three children—Dave, Ken and Judy, the youngest—soon became familiar fixtures around the neighbourhood.

The most familiar landmark of that neighbourhood, however, was eventually "Drydens' Backyard". Murray Dryden, having grown up at a time when children too quickly ran out of time to play, having lived in an era when dreams were too often shattered, was determined that his children would have time to play and to dream. He saw how the youngsters on Pinehurst were taking to street hockey, a year-round endeavour, but they faced the problems and dangers of traffic. Murray solved this in one astonishing stroke. He was a building contractor. He had a big backyard. So he paved it over for a permanent hockey rink: Drydens' Backyard.

"It was more than seventy feet long," Ken Dryden wrote in his magnificent 1983 book, *The Game*, "paved curiously in red asphalt, forty-five feet wide at 'the big end', gradually narrowing to thirty-five feet at the flower bed, to twenty-five feet at our porch—our centre line—to fifteen feet at 'the small end'.... It was an extraordinary place, like the first swimming pool on the block, except that there were no others like it anywhere. Kids would come from many blocks away to play, mostly 'the big guys', friends of my brother, a year or two older than him, seven or eight years older than me. But that was never a problem. It was the first rule of the backyard that they had to let me play. To a friend who complained one day, Dave said simply, 'If Ken doesn't play, you don't play.'"

The children of the neighbourhood turned Drydens' Backyard into their own Memorial Arena that seems, in the memories of those who partook, to have lasted forever but in fact lasted only a few precious years in the late 1950s and early 1960s. They once tried to freeze ice over it for a real rink, but it didn't work out very well, so after that they played only ball hockey on hot pavement or ground-down snow, every day of the year. Here, as much as anywhere, Ken Dryden became a superstar, playing and practising alone under the floodlights, his head filled with the imaginary broadcasts of Foster Hewitt.

"When I think of the backyard, I think of my childhood; and when I think of my childhood, I think of the backyard. It is the central image I have of that time, linking as it does all of its parts: father, mother, sister, friends; hockey, baseball and Dave—big brother, idol, mentor, defender and best friend."

Both Ken and Dave were multi-talented in sports, both fine baseball players as well as hockey players, both good at basketball and later, tennis.

This was just before hockey became a year-round activity for so many aspiring Canadian players—a trend that all the Drydens, even Michael, oppose—and, at times, it led to scheduling impossibilities. "I had to have a rule with the coaches," says Murray. "If there was a conflict, then Ken had to honour the sport he had first started.

"I remember one time when he was playing Junior 'B' hockey and was also in the city baseball championships. He had to play every single night for two weeks. He came up to me near the end and said, 'You know, Dad, I can't get up for this game.' Little wonder. You pull, pull—and finally, this night there's nothing left to pull. It's too bad when that happens."

By their late teens, both Dryden boys had settled on hockey, and seventeen years from the first Drydens' Backyard game, Ken and Dave faced each other for the first time in an NHL match. Neither began the game, but when Montreal goaltender Rogatien Vachon was injured in the second period and replaced with the tall youngster from Cornell and the Voyageurs, Sabres coach Punch Imlach yanked his starting goaltender, Joe Daley, and sent out Dave.

"I didn't enjoy that game very much," Ken later wrote about the experience. "I had played only two previous NHL games, and seeing Dave at the other end was a distraction I didn't want or need. And while I became more comfortable as the game went on, I was surprised and disappointed that I didn't feel more. All those hours we had spent in our back-yard, all our childhood fantasies, the different routes we had taken, the different careers we had seemed destined for; then, years later, the Forum, our father in the stands—the unexpected climax. Yet try as I did, I couldn't feel that way. I could sense the curious excitement of the crowd, I could feel its huge vicarious pleasure, but my own excitement was vague, it had no edge to it, as if somehow it wasn't new; as if in fact we *had* done it before.

"When the game was over, proud and relieved we shook hands at centre ice. A few hours later, I began to feel differently. What had surprised and disappointed me earlier, I found exciting and reassuring. It *really* had been no different. Those backyard games, the times we stood at opposite ends of the yard, the times we dreamed we were Sawchuk and Hall, we *were* Sawchuk and Hall, there *had been* a connection, we just never knew it."

But a big, grinning man in the crowd knew. Murray Dryden had taken the train to Montreal on a hunch, hoping his boys would finally have the chance he had been dreaming of since he would stand at the kitchen window staring out over the backyard. He couldn't have joined them at centre ice for the handshake. He was too drained from blocking shots for them.

Murray Dryden took more out of the Great Depression than a desire to see his children achieve. All three did, and he was grateful for the chance to help them, yet he never felt he was doing enough. What he learned in the thirties— the struggle for survival, the importance of compassion and sharing—gave him huge satisfaction when his children graduated and excelled at sports, but he wanted to do more. He could not forget all the people who hadn't even known him who had offered a meal, a bed, some work.

Murray was in many ways a typical father of his times, hopelessly sentimental, endlessly hopeful. He had the habit of going to bed later than anyone else in the Pinehurst Crescent house, and he would often stand at the bedroom doors staring at his sleeping children in the faint glow of the city's lights. One night in 1961, when Judy was nine, he stood at her bedroom door and began laughing softly to himself. She had twisted into a most unusual sleeping position. She seemed so childlike, so innocent, so *safe* in the comfort of a warm bed, warm room, warm family. He got his camera and took several photographs, careful not to awaken her. When the photos came back from the developer, they gave off the same sense of security, of happiness, of childhood—what Murray Dryden wished for everyone.

His artistic approach was so ingenuous and sincere that he was soon taking pictures of other children as well. Neighbours and business acquaintances were as delighted with the photographs as the photographer. He said he was catching their children "in limbo", and some had never looked carefully at their own children in this precious state. Often he would be invited to the homes of virtual strangers, where he would spend the evening photographing and getting to know the children, then shooting them again while they were sleeping.

It struck him early on that there was something universal about a sleeping child. It did not seem to matter what sort of personality a child had; asleep they all seemed calm and sweet and happy. In the late sixties, Murray and Margaret set off on a European vacation, and he decided to test his growing theories there, often walking up to houses out of the blue and asking if he might set up in the child's bedroom and then photograph their sleeping babies. Quite often he was turned down—"My sales background helped me to accept the rebuffs," he jokes—but more often than he would be today, he was invited in, the parents as curious as he was.

He had no idea what to do with his growing collection of pictures. He continued travelling and soon had a portfolio of 132 shots from twenty-eight countries. He thought perhaps it would make a book and went to New York to talk to publishers, but only one publisher seemed interested and, even then, wanted him to almost double his travel by bringing it to a round fifty countries. The figure seemed impossible, even though Murray and Margaret continued to travel and continued collecting. In Pakistan, he came across his most profound image of a sleeping child, and was not even carrying his camera at the time. Walking back to the hotel, he stumbled through what he took to be a pile of rags, only to find that, buried inside for protection from the cold, was a very young child, alone and afraid, living in the streets.

In December 1969 Murray Dryden had what might be called his second epiphany—nearly forty years had passed since he stood in the pitch dark and beginning snow outside Callander, Ontario, weeping over how cold and miserable he was with no bed that night. Now it was snowing again—a blinding snowstorm—but he was in a warm, comfortable car. He was successful beyond all his imaginings from those years when he set out to sell nylons and can-openers. He had a thriving business, and even his Christmas tree farms were beginning to pay off. He had been driving home from one of them as the snowstorm struck and, as the traffic slowed, his mind began racing.

He wanted to do something for children. Something to do with the comfort of a warm bed and safety. Something to help children like the child he had stumbled upon that late evening in Pakistan. He was hit by the question that would change his life: "Why not beds for children in the developing countries?"

He took his idea to the Salvation Army, and with the Army's help he approached ten needy countries with the notion of supplying bedkits—each containing a groundsheet, a mattress, sheets, pyjamas, a blanket or mosquito netting and some personal-care items—to poor children. Six of the countries readily accepted, and Murray Dryden's great idea, Sleeping Children Around the World, was born.

The first distribution was to India—fifty bedkits—and today, a quarter of a century later, SCAW is active in at least thirty other countries, with nearly two hundred volunteers distributing bedkits each year. Some 400,000 of the poorest children in the world have benefitted directly from Murray Dryden's crazy idea that he could give them a little comfort through the night.

Murray and Margaret turned their house on Pinecrest into a permanent office/warehouse/headquarters for SCAW and the many volunteers who have been attracted to the project. No one gets paid a cent for their efforts, and volunteers even pay for their own trips to the designated countries.

After Margaret died of a weakened heart in 1985, Murray continued. He sold off the tree farms they had started in the 1950s and put the money from the sales, some $3.5 million, right back into the bedkits project. He knew what he was giving; he also knew what Sleeping Children Around the World was giving him.

SCAW continued to be the perfect project for Murray. He was retired, but still had boundless energy and still possessed his incurable salesman's drive. He was alone, but SCAW had grown into a second family for him. The Kiwanis Club gave him its World Service Medal and the Governor General awarded him the Order of Canada, but SCAW gave him a reason for being. And he needed that as much as SCAW needed him.

This sense of contribution passed on to his sons. When Dave was playing goal for the Edmonton Oilers in the old WHA, Edmonton *Sun* columnist Terry Jones wrote that, "David Murray Dryden, I've said it before and I say it again, may be the classiest person ever to perspire in public in Edmonton." Having just been selected the top goaltender in the league, Dave had given the $4,000 to the Glenrose School Hospital for the physically and mentally handicapped. Traditionally, such an award would have meant a team party. But not this time, and Dave Dryden knew his team-mates would understand. When Canada's world-class cyclist Jocelyn Lovell became a quadriplegic following a training accident in which he was struck by a truck, Ken put together a charity hockey game between the Flying Fathers and NHL oldtimers that raised some $30,000 towards the refurbishing of Lovell's home. The Drydens are adamant that there is nothing special in acting in this manner, and that nothing special be made of it.

Murray Dryden does not consider himself the perfect father. He got far too wound up at one point, he says, over hair length, convincing Dave to get rid of his beloved ducktail because coaches frowned on anything but crew cuts. His long arguments eventually worked, but the experience upset Dave and, Murray later wrote, "Looking back, I wonder why I made a big thing of it." The then-long-haired sons got him back when he retired, poking fun at a toupee that was, mercifully, a temporary vanity for a man lucky enough to be able to laugh at himself.

Though he might get carried away at games, Murray was never destructive in his enthusiasms. He cheered: all the children, all the good plays, win or lose. But he was often deeply bothered by the behaviour of other fathers at games. As he says, "There's as big a difference in fathers and their relations with their children as there is between coaches and the players on a team."

At one point, Murray became so disgusted with the performance of certain other fathers in a hockey rink that he rigged a tape recorder into the pocket of his topcoat and ran a cord down his sleeve to a small microphone. While he bounced around the upper row, he was able to capture the sounds of other parents watching their children, supposedly at play. What he ended up with was a tape filled with "obnoxious, obscene language", and though he had planned to make copies so these parents could hear themselves, he could never bring himself to do it. He knew it would upset them. He also knew, from his own experiences in the stands, that in many cases the only difference between the parents watching silently and the parents screaming is that the silent ones merely know enough to keep their mouths shut. It does not necessarily mean that they do not feel the same naked emotions.

But few parents would ever, even silently, feel as one parent Murray encountered one day outside the dressing room. The team had lost and the father was screaming, "You'll be walking home!" at the youngster. "It was terrible," he remembers. He said nothing, and regretted it. Another time he did speak up. He happened to overhear a youngster excitedly telling his team-mates that his father would be at the next game. When the father didn't show, Murray and the coach went together to the missing father's place of business, which happened to be a popular local restaurant. "We met and I presented the case," he says. "We thought he should be there. We thought his youngster needed him there. But he told us, 'I can't do anything about it. Business is here, not the arena.' We struck out." Business, Murray Dryden would have argued, is to be there when your children need you.

They were always different, the Dryden boys. Not only in skill level but in manner. They did not swear. They did not drink. They never spent foolishly. And they always looked to the future. Dave wanted to teach and eventually became a school principal in Mississauga, Ontario. Ken studied law, even sitting out the 1973–74 season to make $6,968

with the Toronto law firm of Osler, Hoskin and Harcourt
instead of playing goal for the Canadiens for $80,000 a
year. He played hockey that year for Vulcan Industrial
Packaging, a big, lumbering defenceman who threw his
two bucks into the ice-time kitty the same as every other
player.

When Ken retired after the 1978–79 season, he moved
to Ottawa for a year, where he played defence for the
Whiskey Jacks, a local lawyers' team in the old-timers
leagues, and completed his bar course, though he knew
that he would never practise law. He was curious by nature,
and he had developed a habit of taking notes whenever
anything came along of great interest. When Team Canada
had headed off for Moscow in 1972, he had stood apart
from the other players, as interested in the ballet as in
Soviet minor hockey, as impressed by the extraordinary
skill of European players as he was by the determination of
his own team-mates.

One of the most difficult things to do on a hockey
team, he once said, is "to spend your time constructively."
The lure of the hotel, the nap, afternoon television, the
rink almost invariably take precedence over walks, muse-
ums, historic sites, bookstores. Throughout his career, Ken
probably made as good use of the vast quantities of down
time a hockey player has as anyone ever has.

He wanted to write and tried his hand at a couple of
magazine articles before Douglas Gibson, then an editor at
Macmillan, talked him into trying a book. It took years,
but when *The Game* appeared in 1983 it rose immediately
to the top of the best-seller lists and was a stunning critical
success as well. Dryden's book was nominated for the
Governor General's Award, an unheard-of honour for a
"sports" book.

Throughout the eighties he became involved in a variety of projects—a study of education, a stint as Ontario Youth Commissioner—and also completed *Home Game*, a social and cultural look at hockey that became a six-part television series and, again, a number-one Canadian best seller. With *Home Game* he decided that his examinations of hockey had come to an end, and he moved on to establish his writing credentials on other topics. In 1993, he published *The Moved and the Shaken*, a non-fiction effort that marked a daring step in his career: here was a hockey hero forsaking the easy route by switching topics. The book was an investigation into the life of Frank Bloye, an average suburban family man whose life, Dryden hoped, might help explain to a country exactly what was meant by the increasingly popular phrase "ordinary Canadian".

His approach was the one he usually takes: total immersion, total committment. And the result was a fascinating look at what makes Canadians Canadian. It also proved, if there was any doubt, that there is much more to Ken Dryden than hockey—the game plays no part in the book.

Now as much an author as a hockey player, Dryden decided to apply his new talents to a topic that had formed as much of his life as hockey: education. In 1993, at age forty-six—and again the tallest student in grade nine—he began classes at T. L. Kennedy Secondary School in Mississauga, Ontario. It had been thirty-three years since he had started grade nine the first time around, and yet he was still worried about the same thing that had bothered him the first time: what the other kids would think about what he was wearing. But he had nothing to worry about: "The acceptance was almost instant. They just thought I was a teacher."

Ever inquisitive, Ken Dryden had a notion to write a book, not just about education, but about those most directly affected. "If *The Moved and the Shaken* is looking at Frank Bloye and the average guy," he said, "this one is looking at kids and how they live." He found, from the first day, that he was entering a world apart from what he had come to know. He had trouble at first adapting to the incredible pace of a huge, vibrant school. "You know what a living-room is like with three kids in it?" he says. "Imagine a school with fifteen hundred kids in it. The frenzy is amazing. Each day I'd come in and still be shocked by it." The demographics were dramatically different from what he experienced in the early sixties, the curriculum was different, the expectations different and the world students will be heading out into more different each day.

When Ken Dryden went to school the first time, professional athletes were forever advising young athletes to make sure they got a good education to fall back on, and he was one of the rare ones who listened. Today, however, the basis of that argument has been undermined by the enormous sums of money young players are paid. Professional contracts often appear to make an education unnecessary. Dryden would argue, though, that the true reward of learning is not financial, but personal.

"The way I look at education," he says, "is that we learn in countless different ways and in different places. We learn from books, from textbooks, adults, other people, the classroom, television, friends, parents, experiences, travel, sport, computers.... I think probably what we as adults were saying without saying it is that we hope they will be comfortable in all of those areas because, if they are, they will have a chance to learn forever."

This, of course, was exactly the philosophy of the "well-rounded" preached by Murray Dryden when his two boys were beginning to rise in hockey. Ken considers himself fortunate to have had such a father, fortunate, as well, to have come under the spell of coaches and managers in the Humber Valley organization—Ross Johnstone and Ray Picard were two of his favourites—who taught their teams that hockey "was just *part* of a life." He took that attitude with him to Cornell, where not only the hockey was superior to what he had imagined but so, too, were the possibilities beyond hockey. The team played only a maximum of twenty-nine games each season, leaving "a chance for a life as well. There were classes before practice, the library after—it wasn't hard to fit hockey in."

When it was no longer his own hockey he was wrapped up in, he saw the need again for "a chance for a life" with his own children. Certainly there were bad sides to minor hockey—anyone with a video camera at any game can gather evidence for that—but there are also the wonderful sides to it that so rarely get aired. Being a parent involved with a child in minor hockey, he believes, "is also a recipe for all the most wonderful feelings in the world. You see not just the selfish act, but the unselfish act, the unbelievable heroic act, and you feel so proud."

It took Ken Dryden years to understand that sometimes the best thing a hockey parent can do for a child is to turn around and walk out of the arena. "I'm not sure parents should be at every game," he says. "The kids need to come home and have their stories, instead of that other voice that is always saying how it went. He should be able to tell his own story and judge himself."

It was naturally expected that Michael Dryden would become a goaltender, perhaps even anticipated at first by his father. Talking to Peter Gzowski on "Morningside" in 1983, the retired goaltender turned author said that he himself had loved the nets from the beginning. As a child, he said, he had a love of "sprawling around", a preference that he now believed lent itself to the position of goaltender. He said he could already see this same love of sprawling in Michael, who was then only five.

But Michael Dryden already had a determination to make his own way. He was, the family remembers, a stubborn kid, with good reason: as the youngest he was at the bottom of the house flow chart. "We knew it was necessary," the father now says with a laugh, "but sometimes tough to take." If the rest of the family got caught up in a Toronto Blue Jays run for the pennant, Michael would cheer for the New York Yankees. He knew, instinctively, what would get to them.

When Michael began playing minor hockey, he was equally determined to stay his own course. He would not play goal. He would do it once, as the other youngsters did throughout that first season, and even though he sort of liked the position, he would not play it again. Because his father was Ken Dryden. "People expect you to be the same and play the same position and be up to the same level," he later explained. "But I wanted to be a different person instead of the 'junior'."

He became a defenceman and, unlike his father and uncle, was never instantly a star. But he was what he wanted to be—Michael Dryden, steady, dependable, popular. He never resented his father's presence; rather, he loved having him come to the games, loved talking to him afterwards about the game, and was never bothered when one of his team-mates or another minor leaguer would come up to him with an old hockey card and ask if he would mind getting his father to sign it. He even signed up for goaltenders' school one summer just to see what it would feel like to play the position, but abandoned it as soon as the real season started. He just wanted to know, for himself.

Michael can remember the first time they put the Stan Rogers tape on in the car and how the ride changed that day forever. In time, they would stop playing the song, but they would never again return to dissecting games before they had even taken place. Michael would happily "stare out the window, and think." Or else they would "talk about regular things—life in general."

When they talked hockey it would more likely be about the NHL, the son discovering that he had much the same analytical bent as his father but—much to his delight—one that went in a somewhat different direction. "It's really strange," he says. "My dad could tell you which way every player in the NHL shoots and where they were born. But I can tell you their stats and what were their best years." They found they enjoyed each other's company as well as anyone else they knew.

"It might be," says Michael, "because I think of my dad first as my father, then as the player, even though everybody expects it to be the other way. But even for my friends my dad's Mr Dryden now, not the goalie. Everything's gone past that. It's important, but not to my career. I'm Michael Dryden, not Ken Junior."

For whatever reasons, fathers who once played professional hockey rarely have foolish dreams about their sons following their paths to the NHL. Perhaps it is because, in rising themselves through that increasingly tightening collar that leads from minor hockey to professional hockey, they have seen so much bitter disappointment. Perhaps it is because they have found, without exception, that for every one of them who makes the NHL there were two, three or four along the way with equal or even superior skills who did not make it for reasons that range from desire to drink. Perhaps it is because, having been there, they know there is much more to life and success than having "made it", that "making it" is far more complicated than pulling a sweater over the head and checking a scoreboard at the end of the night. Ken Dryden had no such illusions, no such expectations: he hoped Michael would find, in hockey, a game to enjoy for life. Player, coach, fan, spectator—forever.

Michael Dryden, however, was becoming that increasing rarity in hockey, a late bloomer. Whereas for most it would be already too late—they would have quit long ago, they would have fallen behind for lack of ice time and coaching—in Michael's case, sheer determination and wilfulness had kept him on the edge of excellence. Something happened as he began moving into his mid-teens. He shot up to well over six feet. He changed first in basketball, where he suddenly seemed to become aware of the new advantages of size and reach and began crashing the boards and blocking shots and realized that this, too, was him. As his father put it, "He's playing to what he is, not what he was."

It happened again in hockey. "He used to start out the fourteenth player on the team," his father says, "and by the end he'd be maybe the eighth. Next season, he'd be fourteenth again. Now it's different. He was captain last year." Michael was beginning to be a star at the midget "AA" level, a most unusual star in that, unlike others, he knew perfectly well what it was like not to be a star, and it gave him a wonderful perspective on the game. He took the standard dream and gave it his own twist.

He was not only quickly improving as a hockey player but he was doing better and better at school and began to relish a growing reputation as "the smart jock". He was a good hockey player, a fine baseball pitcher, and a top student. He had, of course, once dreamed about playing in the NHL—"Everybody has," he says—but that dream couldn't last long when he applied his increasingly analytical mind to it. He was a good player, steady, but he didn't even play at the highest levels. He began to form another dream: that he would study hard and get even better marks, and then, "I'll get into a school on my marks—and I'll surprise them with hockey and baseball."

He began to think about chasing an academic scholarship to Harvard University, where his sister, Sarah, is a student. Sarah, he says, "has a lot of my grandfather in her." She spends her out-of-class time working at a shelter for the homeless in the Boston area. She spent the summer of 1995 in Ecuador teaching children, just as a few years ago Dave's son, Gregory, spent his summer vacation in South America, distributing hundreds of bedkits for Sleeping Children Around the World.

Michael thought he would like to play hockey and study medicine. Hockey because he loves the game and because, in thinking about it so much, he has come to believe playing has given him "a better knowledge of how the world works. I like the team. I like the competition. But it's not life or death. If you lose, you lose, but you have to get over it."

Medicine, on the other hand, is life and death. And like his father and his grandfather, Michael Dryden wants to contribute off the ice as well.

Bloodlines

Freiburg, Germany, December 14, 1994

Sometimes he is hard to take seriously. He calls himself, proudly, "the laziest man alive." When he stands in the dressing-room, a blond, pudgy body surrounded by scrub-board stomachs and rope backs, he likes to think of himself as the only hockey superstar "who comes complete with love handles." He once described his teenage years this way: "At seventeen, Wayne Gretzky and Mario Lemieux were already headed for greatness. At seventeen, I was headed for a doughnut shop." At eighteen, he quit the game, certain beyond a doubt that there was nothing in it for him but more frustration.

He is thirty now, and for fifteen days he has been travelling around Europe with Wayne Gretzky and friends; he has played seven games since this ageing National Hockey League all-star group gathered in Detroit to catch their charter over the Atlantic, and he—the greatest goal scorer in modern NHL history—has yet to score a single goal. He thinks it's funny. He thought it was funny when he went out for a walk one evening in Malmö, Sweden, turned too many corners without thinking—"Maybe I'm *too* easygoing?" he sometimes wonders—and then could not remember the way back or the name of the hotel where the Gretzky team was staying.

And he loved it in Tampere, Finland, when two young boys wearing jackets and caps with NHL logos stopped him for an autograph and asked, in perfect English, "Who are you?"

"I'm *Brett Hull*!" he announced, the rasping voice almost as familiar to hockey fans as the famous shot, the even more famous last name.

But now, on a day when the thin winter light has turned this thousand-year-old city on the Rhine into a fantasy, Brett Hull has suddenly turned serious, determined to stick to reality. He wants to talk about divorce. He wants to speak about what it is like to have the most famous father in hockey—and not have him at all, at the same time.

"My folks wasted ten years of their lives staying together because of the kids," he says. "I would rather have my folks divorced than stay together and fight every day. They fought like cats and dogs *every single day*."

He is speaking, of course, of Bobby, his father, and Joanne, his mother. Bobby Hull, who played professional hockey for twenty-three years, who scored 1,018 goals in the NHL and the World Hockey Association, second only to Gordie Howe's 1,071 in both leagues. Bobby Hull, hockey's first millionaire, the single player who made an entire league, the player whose shot alone changed the game, twelve times an all-star, fifty goals or more in nine seasons. And Joanne Hull, mother of five, abused wife, divorcee, single mother raising Brett Hull and his younger brother and sister, remarried now—"to a terrific guy," says her son—and, finally, happy.

But it certainly wasn't a happy time when Brett Hull was twelve years old and his parents' divorce was the talk of Winnipeg, where they then lived, and the hockey world, where his father's name was certain to live forever. "It was all over the press," the son remembers. "It was ugly stuff. I wouldn't read it. But I came home one day and I saw something in the paper—'estranged'—and I asked my mom, 'Why are they calling you strange?'" Strange was what was happening to them. Strange was the father who was leaving them.

Ten years later, when pudgy Brett was about to play in his first NHL game as a member of the Calgary Flames, he was asked about his famous father's contribution to his hockey career.

"Mostly genetic," the son answered truthfully.

Brett Hull was the only one of Bobby and Joanne Hull's five children to be born in Canada. The Hulls spent their summers in the Bay of Quinte region of Ontario, where Bobby and Dennis Hull had grown up on the family farm before heading off to junior hockey and then the Chicago Blackhawks. Brett was born in Belleville in 1964 and grew up, he likes to say, in Chicago Stadium and the Winnipeg Arena. His father was at the peak of his career, one of the best-known and most charismatic of all players. His mother had been a professional figure skater. There were five children—Bobby Jr., Blake, Brett, Bart and Michelle— and for each of them skating was merely the next stage of walking, holding a hockey stick and puck as natural as feeding yourself.

Brett's memories do not come into sharp focus until he is an eight-year-old and sitting beside his famous father as the family is paraded into Winnipeg, Bobby Hull having left the NHL to join the Jets of the new World Hockey Association. There is a photograph of the youngster leaning on the huge cheque the Jets presented his father in a civil ceremony that afternoon, an eight-year-old staring wide-eyed at all the zeros required to write "$1,000,000.00."

But others remember him from before Winnipeg. John Robertson—"Mr R." to Blackhawks players since the

1950s—is the custodian of the Chicago home dressing-room and can remember how he would sometimes sit behind the glass during Blackhawks game with one or two of the Hull boys on his big knees. "That Brett," he recalls, "was a terror. He used to take the saws the players had for working on their sticks and go in and cut off all the chair legs and table legs. We had to declare this place off limits to him." Brett thinks Mr R. is confusing him with his older brothers but he does not deny he was a handful as a youngster.

When the family first arrived in Winnipeg, Brett Hull remembers it as a magical time. His father was the star of the team and the league. "My dad ran the show," he says, "and whatever he said, goes." That meant the kids had the run of the rink.

He remembers the joy of the rink because he prefers not to remember the fights at home, but it does not mean the memories of his father in those days are all bad. Far from it: at the rink his father was perhaps the most accommodating of all professional hockey players, always with time for people, especially kids, always willing to sign autographs until everyone was satisfied. The best day of his life may well have been the evening Bobby and his Swedish linemate, Ulf Nilsson, took three of the Hull boys and their equipment to an outdoor rink. When they arrived, however, the floodlights had been turned off and no one was there. Bobby and Ulf pulled several of the boards off the sides and Bobby pulled the car up so the headlights shone out over the ice, and they all played shinny for two hours, three young boys and two of the most skilled players ever to play the game professionally. "Awesome," remembers the son.

Bobby Hull says Brett could shoot like an NHLer when he was only ten years old. Like the Jets players during practice, the youngsters used to try to hit the huge portrait of Queen Elizabeth, high in the Winnipeg Arena rafters. Brett could do it more often than some of the pros. "I never saw any youngster with better action in his hands than Brett," Bobby once said. "He had better hand-and-wrist action than 98 percent of the Jets." The boys were essentially left on their own to learn the game, and they were taught far more by the two Swedish stars, Nilsson and Anders Hedberg, who brought to the Winnipeg Arena a European joy of practice that was shared by very few North American players.

"Dad wouldn't teach," remembers Brett. "He would show you. And he only did it a couple of times, max. You watch and *learn*." Only once can the son remember the father getting technical with him, and that was over Brett's skating, by far the weakest part of his game and that part most unlike his father. Bobby told Brett to "get down" when he skated, and stay down. "He'd say, 'Look, there's Anders Hedberg and Ulf Nilsson. Watch what they do.'"

"I always figured that if one of my boys was going to make it, it would be Brett," Bobby Hull wrote in a special feature on the two Hulls carried by *The Hockey News* in 1991. "Bobby Jr., the oldest, had the most heart, but just didn't know how to put the finishing touch on it. Blake, the second oldest, had the most talent but didn't have the drive to match it. Brett just had the overall ability to execute the basic fundamentals. He skated, passed and shot so well. He was so smart.

"I remember watching him play a game when he was a kid. He was floating out by the redline or blueline and his two linemates were mucking in the corner to get him the puck. They would get it to him, he'd break down the ice and score. So after the game, I was giving him hell. I said,

'Brett, you gotta get back in there and help your linemates.' He said, 'My coach said to stay out around the blueline and redline.' I said, 'Yeah, but your coach never played a game in his life. He's an annuity salesman. He can hardly skate and I make a living at the game. Who are you going to listen to?' He said, 'My coach.'"

The father's memories of those years are, as he told *The Hockey News*, of "a little, snotty-nosed kid. His sneaker laces were always undone, his fly was undone and he didn't care whether the cow calved or whatever. He'd come in from playing outside for his dinner and he'd sit down, mix all his meat and potatoes and vegetables all together and pour Heinz ketchup all over it. It was like a dog's breakfast.

"That's just the way he was. He didn't have a care in the world, that kid. He just loved to go out and have a good time."

"My relationship with Dad isn't Ward Cleaver and the Beaver," Brett wrote in his 1991 autobiography, *Shootin' and Smilin'*. "It also was never as strained as portrayed by the media." The marriage between Bobby and Joanne fell apart completely in Winnipeg, and the divorce proceedings that followed were carried—every dollar, every slap—in the Canadian media, which merely shifted its fascination with this hockey superstar from the sports pages to the front page. When Joanne moved to Vancouver to begin a new life, the two older boys, Bobby Jr. and Blake, stayed on with Bobby in Winnipeg while the three youngest Hulls, Brett, Bart and Michelle, moved to the West Coast. "It was distance and circumstance that kept Dad and me apart," Brett wrote, "nothing more and nothing less."

"It's tough to have a relationship when your parents are divorced and live on other sides of the country," Brett says this sunny day in Freiburg. "The mother-father relationship has nothing to do with how the kid turns out."

How this particular kid turned out, he says, has more to do with "luck" and "breaks" than anything else. He played minor hockey in Vancouver but was never the top player even on his own team. He could score, but even in scoring he did not dominate. He was merely one of the team. "At sixteen," he says, "I looked at myself one day and said, 'You are Brett Hull. You will never be Bobby Hull. You will never live up to what he has done. You will not live in his generation so don't worry about it. You are Brett Hull. Just go out there and do the best you can.'"

Perfectly satisfied with his lot in life, he gradually lost interest in the game. After midget he quit, and began playing pick-up hockey once a week, fooling around with friends. He was eighteen and, as far as he was concerned, finished for good with hockey. He had never, ever considered it a career possibility. At the 1982 NHL entry draft—the year he was eligible to be picked—he wasn't a name on a single list, nor did he even think twice about the fact that his draft year was upon him and no one had the slightest interest in him. Why should they? He hadn't the slightest interest in hockey, and wasn't very good at it, anyway.

A friend tried to get him to help a struggling area junior team, but Brett said no, he wasn't interested. A few days later he called the friend back and said maybe he would go out. It was just something to do. Looking back, he has no idea what happened, but he began to improve markedly in junior. Playing for Penticton of the British Columbia Junior Hockey League in 1983–84, the year he was nineteen, Brett Hull scored a remarkable 105 goals. It got him scholarship offers—only major Junior players are ineligible—and, in June, it made him a very late draft choice, both in age and number. The Calgary Flames took him in the sixth round, 117th overall. They were intrigued by the number of goals; they were taken by the name.

Brett went off on a full scholarship to the University of Minnesota in Duluth and played two seasons, scoring an impressive eighty-four goals in only ninety games. He made the WCHA all-star team his second year and decided to give professional hockey a chance. He played five games for the Flames, was unimpressive, and spent most of the year in Moncton, playing for Calgary's American Hockey League affiliate. The following year, with the NHL club, he scored twenty-six goals, a promising figure, but on the 1988 trading deadline was shipped off to St Louis with Steve Bozak for goaltender Rick Wamsley and defenceman Rob Ramage. It seemed a brilliant trade at the time: a year later the Flames were the Stanley Cup champions.

But very quickly Brett Hull came into his own with the Blues. "I just got the opportunity" is the way he puts it. But he also got pushed, and it helped. After his first season of forty-one goals, his coach at the time, Brian Sutter, "tore a strip up and down me. He said, 'You can be so much better.'" Sutter was right: Hull followed that first season with seasons of 72, 86, 70, 54 and, 1993–94, 57 goals. It had reached the point where, when he scored in the fifties, he was considered to be "slumping". Hull won the Lady Byng Trophy as the league's most gentlemanly player in 1990, and in 1991, the year he scored eighty-six goals, the Hart Trophy as the league's most valuable player and the Lester B. Pearson Award, voted by his peers as the top player in the NHL. "If they have a definition of a 'goal scorer' in the dictionary," says Bob Berry, who coached Hull in St Louis, "they should just put his picture right there."

"The better I do," he told the *Toronto Star* after his eighty-six-goal year, "and the more recognition I get, the more I look back and think about what my father did. Just to get anywhere near the greatness he had and have someone say that I was even close to my dad would make me happy. To me, he was the greatest player ever. I'm lucky in that I think I've inherited some of his personality in that I can take the pressure and turn it into something [positive] and go out and have fun.

"I'm starting to come into my own, but I'll always be in his shadow, I'll always be Bobby Hull's son, and I have no problem with that at all," said Hull. "I think it's great. If I can do anything to make a name for myself then it's great and if people still say that I'm Bobby Hull's son, I'm not going to worry about it. To be able to live up to the name is not something I felt I had to do, but now that I'm doing it, it's neat."

But he didn't always think it was neat. At first there was distance and, though he will not come out and say it, the natural bitterness a youngster will feel when a family goes two separate ways, especially when the siblings are also split up. Even so, he believes he handled the situation as well as possible.

"I had two older brothers I watched react to my family situation," Brett told CBC's "Inside Track" in a revealing 1991 radio interview, "and I got to learn a lot. I tried to use myself as a role model for my younger brother and sister in the way I dealt with the situation. Sometimes there was good and sometimes there was bad. I mean, I was just a kid and you react to different situations. My folks were divorced and they were really divorced a long time before they were ever divorced. There was constant fighting. It happens to families like my father's. It happens to families all over. It just was a case where mine was so exposed because my dad was a Hall of Fame hockey player. I had a chance to learn that you can't really do anything about it. He didn't divorce me. He divorced my mother."

Father and son kept in touch, but sporadically. "I'm sure he called and my mother told him I wasn't there. I'm not bitter about that. I'm sure there were times when she called and he told her the same about my brothers."

Once Brett moved back east to Duluth for college, contact between the two increased. Bobby Hull was retired from hockey by then and had moved with his new wife, Debbie, to a small village by the Bay of Quinte. Father and son even played together on a line during a Minnesota–Duluth reunion game and, with his father's help, Brett scored. To the youngster, the goal was absolutely "meaningless". He could not understand, then, his father's delight. Bobby Hull had scored more than a thousand goals in front of millions of paying fans, so how could this one, which he hadn't even scored, matter? He did not fully understand until last year, when he and Alison, his long-time companion, became parents. Jude Hull is now walking. Soon he will be on skates.

Bobby Hull played twenty-three years of professional hockey and left unsatisfied. He had what the statistics and headlines would call one of the finest dozen or so careers in the game, and yet he could not let go of the disappointments. He wanted to play in the 1972 Summit Series, Canada against the Soviet Union, but was stopped by an NHL grown vindictive over the rise of the World Hockey Association, which Hull had just legitimized by joining. Even the intervention of Prime Minister Pierre Trudeau had been unable to change the selection committee's ruling. Hull had played until 1980, the year after the merger between the NHL and the WHA, but when his playing days were over so, too, was his connection with hockey. As he told *Newsday* in 1988: "I've been blackballed since '72."

It has been an awkward relationship at best. Three years after he retired he was elected to the Hockey Hall of Fame, but he threw his sticks and memorabilia in a basement closet rather than hand them over to an organization that dared charge hockey fans yet again for their pleasure. He has often criticized the sport just as, during his playing days, he sometimes dramatically spoke out against the violence and interference that he believed were harming the game. He has not had an easy time of retirement. When a proposal to rename the Winnipeg Arena in his name was made in the late 1980s, it was quickly dropped when opposition grew over honouring a man who had abused women. Hull's second marriage had also ended disastrously, with assault charges later dropped but the former star fined for assaulting the officer who came to arrest him. The third marriage finally worked out for him.

"He's mellowed a lot," Brett Hull now says of his father. "I always thought he thought the world was out to get him. He's learned to go with the flow." Even so, his father's experiences have had a profound effect on the son's attitudes. "I've learned a lot," Brett says. "It scared me off marriage. I am deathly afraid of it." He and Alison have been together for years, but even the birth of their first child could not change his opinion.

Looking back, Bobby Hull was eventually able to see more clearly what had become of his first marriage and his family. His priorities were, first, the fans, second, the guys and third—if there was any time left—marriage and family. "To me," he told *Newsday*'s Jim Smith, "they were always first—the people that paid good money to watch us. There was no way I was going to give a 'part' of myself. If I do something, I do it full out. If I have a glass of wine, it's a bottle. Like the way I played hockey. It wasn't going to be one rush. It was going to be every time I got the puck. If I went out with the guys, it wasn't going to be for an hour."

Bobby Hull threw himself into being a professional hockey player, and, so long as only his game was examined, it was an exemplary performance. He thrived on work: the more ice time he received, the harder he played; the more his coaches and team-mates expected of him, the more he delivered; neither injury nor shadows could slow him down. He would often sign autographs throughout a complete warm-up, kids and adults hanging over their boards and the glass with their programs and cards stretched towards him, Hull with a pen in his hand while his team-mates held sticks and chased pucks. He would delay team buses while he signed. He always had time for a photograph, the big Bobby Hull smile its own flash.

A generation later, it is Brett Hull who is known around the NHL for always making time for kids. "I learned that from him," says Brett. "It's sometimes a bit difficult. You're leaving the rink and suddenly you're forty-five minutes late." But it is also different now. There are the kids, as always, but there are usually just as many, if not more, grown men with multiple cards laid out in binders for mass signing. Brett Hull will usually refuse these autograph seekers, convinced that their purpose is not fan support but profit.

"He yells at me today," Brett says of his father's reaction to the refusal to sign for the binder holders. "I tell him, 'Look, when you were playing they had little pieces of paper and match tops.' I see when kids are done, I'm through. I couldn't care less about those assholes who sell."

And yet it is the trading card market that has helped ease Bobby Hull's retirement, making him a regular on the trade show circuit, the main draw at big card shows and the price of admission including an autograph. As the memorabilia market took off, the Hulls—the only father-son combination to win Hart Trophies—were offered a large amount of money to sign seven thousand colour photographs of them together, which would then be marketed by the dealers. Bobby agreed; Brett refused. "He wants me to do shows with him," says Brett. "I say, 'No. I won't do it. I won't charge for my autograph.' Maybe when I'm done, but not now."

They are a most unusual father-son combination. Both so talented, both so similar in some ways, so different in others. If Bobby Hull always seemed driven to succeed, Brett Hull has always appeared as a player who needs to be driven. "I don't have an aggressive bone in my body," he has said. Ron Caron, the former general manager of the Blues, has called Hull a "floater," something that would never have been said about his father. All his life, even by himself, he has been called "lazy".

"I'm not saying he's lazy," his father said in *The Hockey News*, "but he gets more things done with less work than anyone I've ever seen. I'm saying he's a lot smarter than the rest of us. ...Some people say Brett isn't competitive, that he tends to be lackadaisical, but that's not really true. I knew players who were the greatest cheerleaders in the world, but when they got out on the ice, they didn't do anything. Brett leads by example and you can always count on him. Don't ever think he doesn't come to play. People may think his attitude lacks a little bit as far as being gung-ho, but he gets it done. You don't score eighty-six goals by not coming to play every game."

But the criticism went deeper than merely style, or appearance, of play. There were squabbles on the bench, criticisms in the St Louis press. "A lot of people are sick of his whining," one sportswriter wrote, "his attitude is really bad. He has no leadership qualities whatsoever."

Brett, however, says he was only voicing what he felt. He hated the trades the Blues were making—particularly the one that sent his best friend and centre, Adam Oates, to Boston—and, unlike almost any other player in the league, he had no compunction about speaking out. "They make those trades," he says, "and then they blame me."

"I hate it when people give me hell about it," Brett says of his outspokenness. "I get sick of hearing about great effort and that the team played better than the score indicated. I heard that all my life. Good God, can't we have the truth? The people deserve more than that. I give a real interview." Just like his father a generation earlier.

When Bobby Hull thought about what he had done for his famous son, he told *The Hockey News* the truth. "I have raised cattle and I know a thing or two about genetics," he said. "And I can tell you the biggest contribution I've made to Brett's success is providing him with the genes to do what he does so well."

"One of the strangest relationships in the world is that between father and son," the great American novelist Sherwood Anderson wrote. "I know it now from having sons of my own. A boy wants something very special from his father. You hear it said that fathers want their sons to be what they feel they cannot themselves be, but I tell you it also works the other way. I know that as a small boy I wanted my father to be a certain thing he was not. I wanted him to be a proud, silent, dignified father. When

I was with other boys and he passed along the street, I wanted to feel a glow of pride: 'There he is. That is my father.' But he wasn't such a one. He couldn't be."

When the Canadian writer Guy Vanderhaeghe talks about the game he loves—and still plays as an old-timer in Saskatoon—and how it affected his relationship with his father, the words are warm and humorous.

"My father, who grew up on an isolated farm, did not have a love for the *expensive* national sport. As he says, the closest he came to playing the game was when he and his brother, Dan, used to club a frozen horse turd around with poplar sticks they picked out of the bush. This early experience strongly conditioned his sense of what equipment was needed to fully enjoy the sport. Being of a frugal bent, he couldn't understand why one hockey stick couldn't last a careful youngster a lifetime. After I had needlessly broken one or two, he decided to counter with space-age technology and bought me a stick encased in so much hideously blue fibre-glass tape I could hardly lift the blade. As my father had thought, the stick proved indestructible, and for several seasons made me the most notoriously conspicuous player on the ice. In desperation, I once laid this albatross between two benches and jumped on it off a window ledge, hoping to destroy it and end my shame. But the stick didn't break, it simply catapulted me into an open door on which I chipped a tooth.

"As bad as the unusual and distinctive stick was, it wasn't nearly as humiliating as my hockey pants. My father was no more willing to invest hard-earned cash in hockey pants than he was in hockey lumber.

With each year that passed, they shrunk alarmingly. By the time I was twelve, they had dwindled to the size of bathing trunks, earning me my hockey nickname 'Frankie'—a reference to movie surfer-singer Frankie Avalon of 'Beach Blanket Bingo' fame. Which only goes to prove that to have a successful hockey career you ought to have a father who has played and failed at the game, who will push and prod and destructively drive you to fulfil his broken dreams, rather than some disinterested spectator who constricts you in tourniquet-tight hockey pants and buys you repulsively blue sticks which have the specific gravity of petrified redwood."

Vanderhaeghe and others are fortunate to be able to laugh at their experiences and to keep them in perspective. It doesn't always work out that way. As much as sports are based on sentimentality as statistics, it would be foolish to presume that all father-son relationships in sports are as Norman Rockwell would sketch them. There are fathers who do damage by their absence, fathers who do damage by their presence.

Part of the confusion surrounding men and games— where there is value and where danger—abides in the rise of popular sports itself. Games, especially professional games, are a phenomenon of the past century. (The first professional baseball team was the Cincinnati Red Stockings, established in 1869.) The very notion of sport, especially in Western societies, has been to "make boys into men." As Richard Gruneau and David Whitson wrote in *Hockey Night in Canada: Sport, Identities and Cultural Politics*, "Even Pierre de Coubertin's dedicated promotion of the modern Olympics was very much tied to his belief that young French men of his class were becoming effete."

"Masculinity is a socially constructed set of meanings, values and practices," Gruneau and Whitson wrote. "It is something boys *work at* and try to stake their own claim to, rather than something they grow into simply by virtue of being male. Sports and other ways of demonstrating bodily prowess are particularly important among adolescent males, for whom other sources of adult male identity (fatherhood, family authority, earning power and career) are not yet readily available. Masculine identity is pursued as an urgent task by most boys, and sports, especially sports involving strength and aggression, are among the surest ways of staking a claim to masculine status."

Sometimes the relationship is misinterpreted by pop psychologists. Shere Hite, for example, in *The Hite Report on the Family: Growing Up Under Patriarchy*, took a look at males and sports interest and came to the following conclusion: "It seems that by bonding together against the opposing 'team' or 'dangerous animal', men achieve the maximum emotional contact that they are able to have under the male 'family system'. Here, they are allowed to feel excitement together (but not directly towards each other); sharing emotions in a 'team' makes emotional sharing 'legitimate', since the emotions are directed (ostensibly) at something other than each other. Thus, the two have an emotional interchange, an emotional climax, that is sanctioned by the society because it is channelled through a third party." Interesting words, but their logic shatters the moment one remembers that one of the great joys of being a father and a son—or brothers, mothers and sons, brothers and sisters, or sisters, for that matter—is cheering for opposing teams. It is part of the fun of sports.

A more astute, if very tough, view of the relationship is offered by Mariah Burton Nelson in *The Stronger Women*

Get, the More Men Love Football: Sexism and the American Culture of Sports. "Men's interest in sports begins, usually, with Daddy. A father may not bathe his son, or read stories to him, or prepare meals for him, or hold him when he cries, or listen to his concerns, or tie his shoelaces, but he will probably at one time or another play catch with his son, take him to a ball game, or quiz him about the current or past feats of male sports heroes." Sports become the bond between many fathers and sons, with games becoming the way in which the male child wins approval from the father. "To earn male privilege," Burton Nelson argues, "one must enter the sporting arena."

And, she adds, "While sports connect boys to Daddy, they disconnect boys from Mommy. They reinforce the illusion—common to many social institutions but nowhere near as prevalent as in sports—that men are not only separate from but exist on a level above women."

There are, of course, many exceptions. It would be hard, for example, to describe Tatiana Yashin as "disconnected" from her son, Alexei, as she sits on the hard seats of a Kanata hockey rink, watching an Ottawa Senators practice wind down. When Alexei, the Senators' only star and *The Hockey News* Rookie of the Year for 1993–94, scores in a meaningless one-on-one with the goaltender, he looks up at his mother, arms raised in victory, and she waves but does not smile. She has seen something she does not like.

When Alexei later emerges from the dressing-room, his thick hair damp under a high toque, he hugs his mother as always, and once Tatiana Yashin has a good grip on her son's arms, she does not let go until her point is made. She does not like the positioning of the Senators forwards when the defence has the puck on the power play. Alexei listens

to her point, then has his own to make. He does not like
things he sees, either—who could, beginning his playing
career with the weakest team in hockey?—but he does not
necessarily agree with her. He insists on making his own
points, with equal time and force.

Valery Yashin, husband and father, stands off to the
side, smiling and shaking his head. "Who will win?" he asks
with the amusement of one used to this scene. "I don't
know. We will have to wait and see. It could go on all day."

Just as there are profound differences in the style of game
played between Russian and Canadian players, there are
enormous differences in the relationships between parents
and players. In some cases, the parents have hardly been a
feature, as in the case of Buffalo's Alexander Mogilny, who at
fifteen refused to return to his home in Khabarovsk, a city on
the Chinese border, and showed up instead at a Moscow Red
Army practice and talked them into giving him a look. Five
years later he was off again on his own, having defected at the
1989 World Championships in Stockholm. He was headed
for the NHL, never to look back.

Alexei Yashin, on the other hand, would agree to come
to the NHL only if his parents and younger brother,
Dimitry, could accompany him and live with him. And he
wanted his parents for more than company and comfort—
he felt he needed them for advice. Alexei is surely the only
player ever to play in the National Hockey League who
leaves each home game with his mother and his father, his
mother with a videotape of the game stuffed in her purse.
They then drive together to their suburban home where the
family will often stay up until two or three going over and
over the game on their VCR, the mother more often than
the father stopping, backing up and going through in slow
motion plays where her son might have done better.

"We speak with him about his good and bad position," Valery says. "We tell him when he does his job well. Sometimes he argues, 'No, you're not correct.'"

"After the game," says Tatiana, "we are all so tired we can't sleep half the night.

"Hockey is all our life."

It is difficult for North American players and their parents to appreciate the rigours of Russian hockey training. The great goaltender Vladislav Tretiak remembers an early discussion with the legendary Soviet coach Anatole Tarasov:

"'Do you think playing hockey is difficult?' asked Tarasov in the early days of my career.

"'Of course,' I answered, 'especially if you play with the best.'

"'You are mistaken!' he said. 'Remember, it is easy to play. To practise is difficult! Vladik, can you practise 1,350 hours per year?' His voice was rising. 'Can you practise to such an extent that you may end up physically sick? If you can, then you will achieve something!'

"'1,350 hours!' I couldn't believe it.

"'Yes,' said Tarasov sharply."

Better than most Russian parents, Valery and Tatiana Yashin understood what it would take. Both had been élite athletes themselves—Valery in handball and Tatiana in volleyball—and both competed at the national level in the old Soviet Union. As parents, they were determined to be directly involved in whatever games their children elected to pursue. "If you played another sport at a high level," says Tatiana, "you understand all games. If you understand the rules of one game, if you play basketball, volleyball, hockey—it's games. You understand the rules. You know when it's beautiful, correct."

Unlike so many Canadian parents who become deeply involved with their child's hockey pursuits, however, the Yashins did not believe hockey stood above all other extracurricular pursuits. It was but one opportunity shown to Alexei and Dimitry, who is seven years younger. With the parents advising, correcting, the children played volleyball, tennis, soccer and basketball, as well as hockey, with none considered *the* sport. The various games, Tatiana believed, all fed together into a clearer understanding of any game. "He understands his position in sports," she says.

The boys were also raised to love live theatre and opera and ballet and to excel in school. Back in their home city of Sverdlovsk, Valery Yashin had been a university professor and Tatiana an electrical engineer; Alexei, the family expected, would become an engineer working in environmental concerns. Hockey would be a hobby.

But the Yashins eventually came to accept that hockey would never be a mere hobby for their son. When they began to see it as a potential career, the family focus became as strong as if he were studying engineering and they were both putting him through university and helping him with his studies. It paid off in June 1992, when Alexei became the highest-drafted Russian ever, the Senators' first choice and second overall. He would be coming to North America, and the rest of the family would be coming with him.

"Many young players like Alexei come to North America and get their own apartment, a car," says Valery. "They have no family. Some have many problems. They come here and they have no science for language, no science for life, no understanding for what it is to live in these countries. When we landed in Toronto we know nothing about living in Canada. We don't know the money. We don't know how to use a bank. How to get a car."

The Yashins were fortunate. The day they arrived in Ottawa they were adopted by Judy Bowness, the wife of Senators coach Rick Bowness. Judy Bowness was willing to spend as much time going over the payment of house bills and the operation of appliances as her husband did over Alexei's role on the power play and killing penalties. She even dressed and made up Dimitry as a clown for his first North American Hallowe'en.

For whatever reasons, Alexei Yashin adapted to the National Hockey League quicker than any Russian player who had ever come over to play. He played well from the beginning, and his maturity astonished both his coaches and his team-mates. "We tried to teach Alexei that it is necessary to have his own position not only in sport but in life," says his father. "He must be understanding to his friends. He must be caring to his grandmothers, his brother. We speak to him about these things. Alexei, you have hockey, but you also have a family."

In Yashin's case, the family became both comfort and, eventually, confusion. His successful first season in the NHL was followed by an acrimonious contract dispute with the Ottawa Senators in which Yashin and his parents maintained that Senators general manager Randy Sexton had promised a renegotiation if Yashin turned out to be the team's best player, which he clearly was. Yashin, however, was making approximately half what another rookie, Alexandre Daigle, was being paid on a five-year, $12.25-million contract. Sexton denied any such promise had been made and was able to produce legal documents in his favour. The Yashins and their agent, Mark Gandler, maintained that the promise was verbal, but still legally binding. Sexton maintained nothing had been said.

In a matter of months, the young player identified as the mature "franchise" player of the struggling young club was being identified as a "problem". He went off to play for the Las Vegas Thunder of the International Hockey League during the NHL owners' lockout and returned to the Senators only after a last-minute deal was worked out that would pay the young Russian bonus money for performance and promised, in writing, a renegotiation if he reached certain set goals.

Yashin remained the best player on the Senators—twenty-one goals and twenty-three assists in forty-seven games—but little else remained the same. His disenchantment grew in direct ratio to the number of losses Ottawa suffered. The part of Sexton's alleged promise that annoyed him the most, he said, was a commitment to build a real hockey team around him. The only players he had enjoyed as linemates, Bob Kudelski and Dan Quinn, were gone: Kudelski dealt away by Sexton, Quinn let go over a dispute about whether he should be paid in American or Canadian dollars.

With the third year of the Senators looking like their worst year of all, Yashin gradually withdrew from his teammates, which only caused resentment to grow. Days after his father was seriously injured in an automobile accident, Yashin was astonished to find the veteran players on the team screaming at him for what they thought was selfish play. They also attacked Daigle, whom the veterans thought lacked courage on the road, and both were subsequently benched for a game. Hurt and angered by the action, Yashin became even more upset with the slow progress of the Ottawa organization. Privately, he told friends, "I can't wait until I'm forty-five to win," and it became increasingly clear that he wanted out.

It seemed an improbable souring. A year earlier, the Senators had glorified Yashin for his skill, his maturity, and his character, much of which was based on the family values he held. A year later, the Senators were privately wishing he would move out of his parents' home and "grow up". The dramatic maturing of Tampa Bay Lightning defenceman Roman Hamrlik—drafted first overall the year Yashin went second—had come about, word had it, as a result of Hamrlik moving into his own place and his parents returning to the Czech Republic. The Senators hoped for the same from Yashin.

In fact, he may well have been growing up—just not quite the way the club wanted. The more the young superstar learned of the NHL, the more confident he had become of his own opinions. He became convinced that Senators management knew nothing about putting together a winning club and, in fact, that there was little commitment to do so. He questioned the trades and even questioned the coaching, despite the happy relationship between Bowness family and the Yashins. No matter how often they showed him videotapes of mistakes, no matter how many times they sat down to discuss matters with him, the stubborn young man had his own opinions. Senators staff began to refer to him as "Yes, but…" A year before delighted that he had his parents to turn to, a year later the Senators were praying he would turn from them.

But they refused. Valery—when he had recovered from his injuries—and Tatiana continued to come out to every game, continued to leave each game with a fresh videotape to go over with their son.

Mario Lemieux would probably say he and his hockey fell far more under the influence of his mother, Pierrette, than his father, Jean-Guy. She was the one to take him to the arena; his father, prevented from ever playing by allergies and a lung ailment, would watch the three Lemieux boys play, but seemed distinctly uninvolved. "He'd sit in the arena like a frozen fish," Lawrence Martin wrote of Jean-Guy Lemieux in his 1993 book, *Mario*. It was Pierrette who, on winter days when the snow was too deep for them to clear the rink or road, would sometimes shovel snow into her own house, spread it about the carpet and pound it down to a smooth surface so her boys could still practise.

Ray Sheppard, the extraordinary goal scorer for the Detroit Red Wings—"His hands should be in the Smithsonian," says team-mate Paul Coffey—would give all credit to his mother, Vera. Sheppard's father was in the Canadian Armed Forces, young Ray played his minor hockey in Pembroke, near the Ontario base of Petawawa. But the family soon split and, today, Sheppard is not even interested in where his father might be living. It was Vera who stood behind him all through minor hockey and his junior career in Cornwall, Vera who kept him going when coaches told him he was lazy and couldn't skate, who believed in him after the Buffalo Sabres had given up on him, and who cheered loudest when he became a fifty-goal scorer. "I knew my time would come," he says. So did Vera Sheppard.

Marg Cater, the mother of New York Rangers general manager Neil Smith, may have the most lasting mother-son relationship in hockey. After her husband, a professional piano player, died when Neil was only ten, she set out to raise her only son in the sport she considered her own, having once played defence for the Winnipeg

Olympics of the old Canadian Ladies Hockey League. She taught him the game; she encouraged the game by watching televised games with him; and she has remained a part of her son's hockey career long after he gave up playing the game and moved into management. In her Toronto home she has a fax machine to maintain a constant link for newspaper clippings and advice, and has even been known to send information directly to the Rangers coaching staff at their Rye, New York, practice facility.

"My mother is what you would call a real student of the game," Smith once told the *New York Times*. "I just remember conversing about it all my life. I remember when I was a scout, she used to call me and tell me about all these different players on different teams in the league."

Toronto Maple Leafs coach Pat Burns has yet another experience that differs from the sentimental cliché. Burns's story begins like a hockey storybook—big Albert Burns carving two miniature hockey sticks, hanging them over baby Pat's crib and announcing to his wife, Louise, "This will be my hockey player"—but it quickly changed. Albert Burns died when Pat, the youngest boy of six children, was only four years old.

The story from this point on is neither simple nor happy. Louise Burns remarried and took Pat to northern Quebec, and then to the Gatineau, where a sister, Diane, joined them. It was a distraught time filled with poverty and alcohol, and to this day Burns does not discuss his stepfather. His sister, Diane, however, told the *Toronto Star* that it was precisely this experience that moulded Burns's character: the intensity, "the attitude that he would make it on his own." But not entirely on his own. It was Louise, his mother, who made sure he had skates during those years, who would tie them up and send him off to play on the neighbourhood rinks, his mother who would ask the parish priest to look out for her son and make sure he came home at the end of a long day spent at the rink avoiding the harsh realities of home life.

Everything cannot always work out perfectly. Hockey is also filled with stories of youngsters who could not escape the game or the parents' expectations soon enough. A young man from a small town near Montreal tells of how he turned to steroids to gain size and strength and satisfy his father's ambitions for him to make the NHL, only to have the dream fall short. For the father, it was shattering. For the son, releasing. The boy's happiest moment, he says, was when no team elected to draft him and he was free, finally, to get on with his own life.

"He has his illusions," the American poet John Morris wrote about fathers, "and you are one of them./ Every day he brings you/ Himself for your approbation./ Though his belief in you is unbounded,/ Tutor him in disappointment./ Like you he will have to learn/ To live with your limitations."

Vladimir Bure decided that neither he nor his son, Pavel, would live with the limitations others might accept. Most hockey fans know the rudiments of the Pavel story, how the Vancouver Canucks superstar had once been pegged to join with Mogilny and Sergei Fedorov as the great Russian hockey line of the future, one that was expected to be equal to the famous Krutov-Larionov-Makarov line of the 1980s. How Mogilny had defected in Stockholm in 1989; how Fedorov had walked away from the Russian team during the 1990 Goodwill Games in Seattle; how the Russian authorities had so feared losing the third member, Bure, that they had refused to bring the youngster to North

America to play in the 1991 Canada Cup. How a month later, the young player, his father and his younger brother, Valeri, were on a flight to Los Angeles, leaving the Central Red Army hockey team and the crumbling republic behind them. How he joined the Canucks for the 1991–92 NHL season late but still won the rookie-of-the-year award, how he went on to have two straight sixty-goal seasons and sign a new four-year contract for $31.5 million. But only those close to the team know the role Vladimir Bure plays in his son's story.

It is written into Bure's new contract that his father will serve as his personal trainer for the years in which Bure plays for the Canucks. Vladimir Bure holds a rare Order of Lenin and is an élite athlete in his own right—a swimmer who won four Olympic medals, twice finishing just behind Mark Spitz in the 1972 Games—and he cheerfully admits he has driven his son virtually since birth. At three months, he forced Pavel to swim in the bathtub. Vladimir's dream, not surprisingly, was to raise an Olympic gold-medallist swimmer. He had no idea then that his son would prefer his water frozen.

"When I started Pavel in swimming," Vladimir told Vancouver *Sun* columnist Mike Beamish, "it was with only one thought: Making the national team and winning gold medals. He learned to swim before he could walk."

Unfortunately, Pavel found swimming "boring". He wanted to play the game he saw other, older Moscow youngsters playing, and, perhaps to cure him of this passion, his father took him, at age six, to the Red Army sports school. He didn't have the right equipment—no equipment, really, apart from a pair of figure skates—and the first experience was disastrous. "There were about 120 kids there and he was the worst," Vladimir told Beamish. "I told him, 'If you're not one of the best in two months, I'll take you out.' That was a critical point. Pavel pushed himself. He was very competitive and very mature for his age. In the evening, he would put himself to bed early, because he wanted to be at his best the next morning. He loved to practise. At the end of his first season, he was the best."

Nothing less would do. The father's training concepts verged on the fanatical: weights, cross-country running, soccer, gymnastics and, of course, swimming. Vladimir pushed him as a child and as a teenager and continues to push him as an NHL superstar. In Vladimir Bure's mind, Pavel must not only be the best, he must get better.

Pavel's own team-mates have, at times, been astonished by some of the rigours Vladimir Bure will run his son through. With a stopwatch and permitting only a ten-second rest in between each session, Vladimir will have Pavel do twenty hundred-yard dashes in a row. He will do as many as 250 push-ups in a single session. His father trains him so hard in the summer that his friends on the team believe Pavel must view the start-up of the NHL season as a welcome break.

Pavel, on the other hand, holds no such feelings. "I'm appreciative of him," he has said. "I wanted to be like this, what I am now. I think he was right."

Some would say that, in this case, the father has held almost Svengalian control over the son. Not just in training, but in lifestyle, as well. In one memorable moment when the Vancouver papers hurried to Los Angeles to interview the newly arrived franchise hope, young Bure grew bored and restless at the photo session, only to suffer a humiliating slap from his father. Vladimir later denied he had slapped his son's face, saying he had been careful to hit him on the back of the head.

"Sure, I am a little bit crazy," he said, "like every father who dream that his son the best. Pavel, he is my son. I have lots of work with my kids. Now, when he scores goal, I know it is my score. Pavel's work is my work."

Vladimir Bure knows from experience. His great-grandfather, Pavel's namesake, was a renowned watchmaker, and the family's obsession with precision and sports has continued down through the generations. Vladimir's father coached him as a swimmer and was, according to Vladimir, "tougher than I am with Pavel."

In one of his rare revealing interviews, Pavel displayed a perfect understanding of how the expectations of his family ended up on his shoulders. "Dad always came second," Pavel said. "He wanted me to win over everybody. It's true, he couldn't beat Mark Spitz. He really work hard but he still couldn't beat him. Maybe he dream about how his son going to beat everybody. He just remind me all the time I must work hard. Even if I win MVP, win trophy, I must work harder.

"I can't drink. I can't smoke. I can't do these things even though sometimes, maybe I like to. I have to be in shape. I am held up as an example to young kids. It is price you have to pay."

"I know you are thinking," Vladimir Bure said to one puzzled interviewer, "not too many young guys live under their father. He's free. When I disagree, I say, 'Pavel, it's my opinion.' He's not like a kid. He's a man. He has to have his opinion. We have a normal relationship."

Fathers and sons and hockey is a decidedly different dynamic south of the U.S.–Canada border. It may well be that Canadian parents, and perhaps even European parents in the 1990s, might rather have their child make the

National Hockey League than excel at any other game, but Americans would rank their games of national importance as football, baseball, then basketball. Hockey would not likely register even though, increasingly, many of the best players in the game are being produced by the United States.

The most talked-about American-born player in the NHL in 1995 was Washington's sensational rookie goaltender, Jim Carey, who compiled an 18-6-3 record after being called up from the minors and, single-handedly, turned the Capitals into a playoff contender when it seemed they would not even make the playoffs. Carey's lifetime record from high school on is a stunning 152-44; at the age of twenty he had never had a losing season, he had been named rookie of the year in the American Hockey League, named to the AHL all-star team and was a candidate for NHL rookie of the year. And yet he wasn't even the all-star of the Carey family, that honour falling to his brother, Paul, a first baseman with the Baltimore Orioles organization.

"My brother always kind of stole the spotlight," Carey says. "Even to this day, he's the star of the family."

He grew up in Weymouth, Massachusetts, in a world where, he exaggerates, "people didn't even know what hockey is." His father, Paul Sr., had been an athlete, but his first love had been baseball, then softball and basketball. "He can't even skate," Jim says. Paul Sr. and Beverly—herself once the shortstop on a state champion softball team—saw their children turn readily to sports and, not surprisingly, to the sports they themselves loved. Paul was a junior sensation as a ball player. Ellen, the second oldest, was a star basketball player at college. Then came Jim. Had Jim Carey not become a hockey goaltender, he might have ended up a football star—he turned down more football scholarships than he received offers for hockey. But, as he puts it, "I wanted to go my own way."

Kevin Stevens, former Pittsburgh Penguin now a Boston Bruin, grew up in the village of Pembroke, halfway between Boston and Cape Cod. His father, Arthur, had been an exceptional baseball player, a catcher who made it to "AA" level with the Cincinnati Reds organization; he'd grown up in Florida and Massachusetts and never learned to skate. Hockey meant nothing to him, but he was determined not to force his son into a sport just because it was something he knew.

"I'm not a believer in coaching your own children at a young age," Arthur Stevens says. "I think you tend to lean on your own without even realizing it. I can remember my wife used to say to me, 'Honey, you're all over him.' And we'd be just fooling around."

Patricia Stevens had been a cheerleader, knew and loved most sports, and had an intensity that she passed on to her son. Kevin had such extraordinary ability in all sports—a high-school quarterback, good enough to be offered a football scholarship, a terrific catcher in baseball—but so gifted in hockey, as well, that the speed and emotion of that game appealed to his intensity even more than the others.

Hockey was fine with the father. Arthur had been coaching in the Babe Ruth leagues for fifteen- and sixteen-year-olds for more than a decade, and he found one of the appeals of hockey was that it held far more parental common sense. "It gets pretty wicked," he says. "I've had fathers around where I had to tell him if he didn't get in his car right now by himself, I'd *put* him in. I've coached teams where they're leading 20–0 by the third inning and still the parents are standing along the sidelines hollering and screaming for more."

It was, in effect, the opposite experience from the usual Canadian one. When the game is perceived as potential career, as hockey is in Canada and baseball is in the United States, irrational behaviour is sure to follow. When the game is seen as a game, it is much more fun for both parent and child—and if something comes of it all, it is accepted as bonus, not payoff.

"I only ever had one rule," says Arthur. "I didn't believe in the twelve-month hockey deal. Once Kevin got into the sport, we kept running into parents who were making their kids play summer hockey. I'd say, 'Why not try ball or football? Why not play the sports in their season?' A year later I'd run into them and they'd tell me their kid was no longer in hockey. You know why? Burned out, that's why."

Some of the American players' experiences are unlike anything that can be found in Canada. The Mullen brothers—Joe, who plays for the Pittsburgh Penguins, and Brian, who retired in 1995 from the New York Islanders—learned to play on roller-skates on the hot pavement of the poor, tough New York neighbourhood of Hell's Kitchen. The New York Rangers star defenceman, Brian Leetch, grew up in Connecticut and was taught to skate backwards by his father, Jack, who had played for Boston College. He deliberately aimed his son at playing defence for the simple reason that "you get more ice time." Mike Grier, a young player with Boston University and a 1993 St Louis Blues draft pick, is a bit of a pioneer: when, and if, he reaches the NHL it will be as the first American-born and trained black player. His athletic ability he got from his father's side—Bobby Grier was a running back at Iowa State, Uncle Roosevelt was a National Football League great—but his attitude he took from his mother. "Parents would yell things like, 'Hey, kid, you're in the wrong sport; you should be playing basketball,'" he told *Sports Illustrated*. "But my mom always told me the best way to shut them up was to score a goal."

Jeremy Roenick, the fine young centre of the Chicago Blackhawks, was born in Boston and ended up going to Hull, Quebec, to play in the Quebec junior league to improve his game. So intense are his parents, Wally and Jo, about the game that, a few years ago, he had to tell them he could no longer take their telephone calls if the subject was going to be hockey.

"My parents are intense people," he told Mike Kiley of the *Chicago Tribune*. "But they are also winners. There were times I'd play hard when I was young and my dad still wouldn't talk to me. They drove it into my head—you need drive to succeed."

Brett Hull always wondered where his own drive was. He was never pushed by anyone; he never pushed himself. He called himself lazy. The Calgary Flames rid themselves of him because he seemed to lack enough drive even to keep his weight down. It seemed a short career until the St Louis Blues got him and coach Brian Sutter changed him into recent hockey's most prolific goal scorer by telling him, "You can be so much better."

He lacked drive again in 1994, but it was neither his fault nor anyone else's. He had come to Europe with the Ninety-nine All-Stars in terrible shape and had played terribly. By the time the team reached Freiburg, he and the goaltenders were the only ones yet to score in a game and, when he finally scored in Freiburg, the bench had erupted in laughter, not cheers. As he said himself, "I've been brutal, absolutely brutal."

He had told no one that he had not even been on skates

since the previous season. They didn't know that he had been falling asleep all summer long by 8 p.m., often going to bed before the new baby, Jude, was ready to go down for the night. It hadn't been until the false training camp of September that doctors had diagnosed a mononucleosis-type blood disorder known as CMV. His liver was enlarged. They also measured his spleen and found that it was more than twice normal size. Surgeons examined him and didn't want to operate, but they warned him not to play, either, for fear of rupture.

He skated at training camp but took part in no contact. He was, in fact, saved by the October first lockout; his health and conditioning were such that he would not have been permitted to start play. Either way, the lockout or his health were certain to prevent the most anticipated event of the coming season: the clash of wills between the St Louis Blues' tyrannical new coach, Mike Keenan, and the Blues' outspoken, easygoing captain and top scorer, Brett Hull.

Keenan, after all, was the antithesis of Hull, a self-confessed fanatic who would one day tell *Sports Illustrated*, "I gave up sanity to chase the dream" of winning a Stanley Cup. The coming clash between the driven Keenan and the easygoing Hull was one of the most anticipated NHL stories delayed by the lockout. But everyone knew it was coming. Hull had already predicted they wouldn't get along.

But the expected clash never happened. With Keenan as coach and Hull as captain, the Blues took off early and ended with a 28-15-5 record for the forty-eight game season, good enough for second place in the Western Conference and tied with the Pittsburgh Penguins for the third-best record behind the Detroit Red Wings and the Quebec Nordiques. Hull himself scored twenty-nine goals and twenty-one assists for a respectable fifty points—fourteenth best in the league—but, for once, it was not Brett Hull's scoring they were talking about. He had become a defensive player under Keenan. He had even scored a remarkable goal when the Blues were two men short one night. He played the power play, regular shifts and killed penalties. He logged more ice time than any member of the Blues.

Mike Keenan never said publicly how he managed this unexpected transformation, but he did tell friends. He played a hunch, he said to them. He remembered how, many years ago, another player of similar talents had thrived under ever-increasing workloads. And he remembered how successful the strategy had been, both for the player and for his team, the Chicago Blackhawks.

He worked Brett Hull, Keenan told them, the way they used to work Bobby Hull.

Keenan, too, knew "a thing or two about genetics."

Game Misconduct

It would be nice, but hopelessly naive, to think that every time a father and son enter a hockey rink only good things will happen. No one ever expected, however, that in the summer of 2000 the very worst could also happen: two fathers getting into a fight over—of all things—the level of *violence* in a Pee Wee practice, leaving one father dead, one father charged with murder and, before it was all over, the hockey-playing sons with no fathers at all to take them to the place they once believed was all about having fun.

The story, somewhat surprisingly, came out of a small town in Massachusetts rather than, as might be more expected, some northern small town or city; but it involved the Canadian game, and while the location might have been unexpected, the psychology was not. Many longtime hockey observers were only surprised that such a disaster had not taken place years earlier.

It became known in the North American press as "Hockey Rage," and it involved a 270-pound truck driver named Thomas Junta pummelling a 156-pound assistant coach named Michael Costin to death over a heated debate that, in retrospect, seems rather impossible to comprehend. The fight began, according to testimony that involved even their own children, over whether or not the practice had been too physical. Costin, who had been on the ice with the youngsters, believed it had not been. Junta, who had watched from the stands, believed it had been, and decided to settle the debate with his own physical logic.

The attack took place in the hockey rink and in full view of the young Pee Wee players. Junta, who returned to the scene to finish the scrap that seemed, at one point, to have dissipated, pleaded not guilty to the charge of murder, claiming his fists were raised only in self-defence, as the smaller man had started the fight. There was certainly evidence that Costin was hardly innocent in the altercation, but nothing to justify the end result of the disagreement. The jury deliberated two days before finding Junta guilty of the lesser charge of involuntary manslaughter, for which, in early 2002, he was sentenced to six to ten years in prison.

The trial stunned minor hockey coaches and parents everywhere. They knew, many by firsthand experience, that what had happened in a suburban American rink that summer day was not all that much different from what takes place many times a year in Canadian rinks—only without the ambulance, the death certificate, the charges and the two ruined families that believed, at one point, they had a love of hockey in common.

The story coming out of Cambridge, Mass., reminded me of something the Canadian novelist Hugh MacLennan had written nearly a half-century earlier when he was asked by *Holiday* magazine to explain the Canadian game to American readers. "To spectator and players alike," MacLennan wrote, "hockey gives the release that strong liquor gives a repressed man." It is a fascinating metaphor—one we would not likely see in print today, when drunken acts have lost all connection to amusement—but it is, all the same, apt for its sense of barely contained violence.

MacLennan was talking about the professional game, his beloved Montreal Canadiens playing the Detroit Red Wings, and he merely wished to point out that the national game of America's northern neighbour represented "the counterpoint of the Canadian self-restraint." And he did so with enormous pride, tying the ice game to both "the fiery blood of Gallic and Celtic ancestors" and the harsh northern environment—where staying heated can sometimes be critical to survival.

In certain specific ways, not all that much has changed since MacLennan's piece was published. The game is still played on the same surface, has the same dimensions and enjoys the same passionate following, particularly during the spring playoffs. Protective equipment and the demographic makeup of the players have changed, but the essential equipment, the puck, remains one inch thick and three inches in diameter and weighs between five-and-one-half and six ounces—just as it did when MacLennan headed off to the fabled Forum that night in 1954.

The NHL game could often turn violent, MacLennan acknowledged, but he argued that Canadians "take the ferocity of their national game so much for granted that when an American visitor makes polite mention of it, they look at him in astonishment. Hockey—violent? Well, perhaps it is a little. But hockey was always like that and it doesn't mean that we're a violent people."

He was, of course, speaking of on-ice violence, which is quite apart from violence in the stands, of player violence, which is a world apart from parental violence. That is not to suggest, however, that on-ice violence has never had its own raging controversies. As far back as 1904 the president of the Ontario Hockey Association, John Ross Robertson, was warning that "we must call a halt to slashing and slugging, and insist upon clean hockey in Ontario, before we have to call in a coroner to visit our rinks." The coroner was indeed called only three years later, in Cornwall, Ontario, when a player, Owen "Bud" McCourt, was killed by "a blow from a hockey stick."

Nearly a full century later, on-ice violence remains an issue in hockey. And there are still annual demands to clean it up. After Dallas Stars' forward Mike Modano was severely injured by a check from behind by Mighty Ducks of Anaheim defenceman Ruslan Salei in the fall of 1999, Modano asked, "Do we have to wait for someone to be killed or paralysed" before something is done about the way the game is being played?

Not long after the Modano concussion, Colorado Avalanche star Peter Forsberg was injured by an illegal check. Kent Forsberg, Peter's father and the coach of the 1994 Swedish Olympic team that took the gold medal, angrily suggested that a situation had now been reached where, "you put your life in danger to play in the NHL." It turned out to be a remarkably prescient comment, for in the spring of 2001 Peter was again so badly injured that he lost his spleen and, unable to recover fully that summer, decided not to play the 2001-2002 season until he felt once again fit enough for the rigours of NHL hockey.

The most famous on-ice incident of hockey's modern era—perhaps the most examined since the Richard Riots that rocked Montreal in 1955—was the February 2000 slash to the helmet and head of Vancouver's Donald Brashear by Boston Bruins defenceman Marty McSorley, a slash that resulted in Brashear suffering a serious concussion and McSorley being charged with assault and found guilty in a court of law, proof to many that society's values had changed regarding professional hockey and that professional hockey cannot be trusted to police itself, as the NHL had always maintained was its right.

"Everyone must understand this type of violence will not be tolerated," Judge William Kitchen said as he gave

McSorley an eighteen-month conditional discharge, "either on the street or in the hockey arenas."

Judge Kitchen, a fan of hockey, also spoke of the hockey world beyond this singular incident in Vancouver.

"There is work to be done," he said.

"The game deserves it."

There is also work to be done in the stands. The old MacLennan piece makes some intriguing observations about the evolution of merely *watching* the game. He even attributes some of the spirited action in the stands to the bitter cold of the old outdoor arenas, just as many have connected the game itself to climate. If the American passion for baseball—a leisurely game with sporadic movement and built-in pauses—can be tied to summer afternoons and sun-baked fields, then surely the exertion and constant movement of hockey have something to do with keeping the blood flowing. The same applies, on a limited basis, to those watching the winter game.

Perhaps it was the cold, perhaps the excitement of the game, perhaps the caffeine from the coffee they drank to keep warm—whatever, the fans could be as pumped up and boisterous as the players. But there was another connection, vital, that MacLennan pointed out: "Players and spectators were close in body and spirit then because every spectator was a player himself."

And now we come to what has changed so dramatically about the game of hockey, not so much on the ice surface as in the stands.

Rinks today are, if not warm, bearable. And spectators are not at all automatically former players. For one thing, today's stands hold large numbers of women, especially mothers in minor hockey games, and while some may indeed play, most others will not have. Perhaps even more significantly, the demographic make-up of North America has changed so dramatically since MacLennan was writing that it is not uncommon for half those in the stands, men as well as women, to have grown up without the slightest connection to hockey. Their game of choice might have been soccer; their child's, however, is hockey.

But the greatest difference, by far, is in what today's spectator *sees* from those changing stands. It is not just a familiar game that he or she is staring down at, but a culture and—in the case of minor hockey—a possible career.

This is what has gone so sadly out of whack in hockey. The early spectators watched young amateurs, the finances of hockey going no further than the cost of equipment, including a few wide-mouth shovels to clean the snow off the ice. Even at the game Hugh MacLennan strode off to in the early Fifties, the economic situation of those in the seats compared far more favourably to those on the bench. Many good players, in fact, used to say they could not *afford* to play professional hockey, opting instead for a steady job with security and annual raises, while those who did turn professional had to have summer employment to supplement their winter earnings. The greatest currency the players had was fame, and while it certainly caused those watching to dream, it did not have at all the same effect on the relationship between stands and ice that today's inflated hockey currency has.

Something else was happening to hockey in Canada as MacLennan was writing, though he could not possibly have foreseen what it would turn into. The postwar "Baby Boom" was on, a population bulge the likes of which history had never known. Prosperity not only encouraged North American families to have more children, but it attracted families from all over the world, particularly war-torn Europe, to emigrate here to take up these new opportunities. New arrivals and growing families caused a building boom, and as towns expanded so, too, did facilities, with community after community building new indoor and artificial ice surfaces, invariably called "Memorial Arenas" in honour of those who had sacrificed so much.

The numbers of new people and new facilities required organization, and the Canadian Amateur Hockey Association (CAHA) was prompt to realize this need and address it. Hockey registration, insurance, leagues, officials, coaches, tournaments—all had to be organized in some manner, and more and more volunteers were needed each year to handle the rapidly increasing enrollment in minor hockey. In particular, more and more minor hockey players required rides to and from their games and practices, usually from a parent, or the parent of a teammate.

At the peak of the Baby Boom, in the early 1960s, someone at the CAHA suggested a brilliant idea. Why not a campaign that would involve the parents, that would make them a key part of the minor hockey experience? Eventually the association came up with an advertising plan pressing parents not to *send* their child off to the local rink, but to *take* that child. Be there with him—for it was all boys back then—and stay there with him and share in the experience.

It was, in many ways, a self-serving campaign. The CAHA was always desperately in need of volunteers. Perhaps if more parents felt more involved, they would become more involved.

For the most part, it worked wonderfully. Many parents, men and women, had much to offer. They supplied the coaches, the managers, the timekeepers; they organized the schedules, the officials and the tournaments; they ran the tuck shops and held tag days and came up with new ideas for fundraising that allowed travelling teams to get to tournaments all over the country.

But in some other ways, it was also a disaster in the making. The Sixties turned into the Seventies, expansion came to hockey, and soon a financial gap began to widen between those attending professional games and those watching. Bobby Hull was handed a huge cheque for $1 million by the Winnipeg Jets, and soon players of only moderate skills were millionaires. Free agency came along and gave the players even more money until, by the turn of the century, the total payroll of the National Hockey League had passed $1 *billion* (U.S.) and the *average* salary of an NHL player reached $1.5 million (U.S.) a year.

As well, any eighteen-year-old child who happened to be gifted enough in the game to be drafted in the first round of the annual June entry draft—any one of the thirty best eighteen-year-olds in hockey—would become an instant millionaire the moment he signed his name to a contract. That million dollars got him in the door; after that, the team and the player's agent could talk about bonus clauses that were making a farce of the National Hockey League rookie salary cap and could, in some instances, more than triple that million-dollar "starter" fee in the first year alone. The old phrase so often heard in earlier hockey days—"You better have an education to fall back on"—gradually lost most of its well-intentioned meaning.

Hockey is not a cheap game to play. The equipment costs can run to the outrageous—$400 skates for a twelve-year-old—but beyond the cost of basic equipment lies the cost of gasoline and wear-and-tear on the family vehicle, often a second vehicle, to make those games and practices. Single parents often find the game impossible to handle, both in terms of cost and commitment. Once parents found they were spending so much money and time on their child's hockey playing, it is hardly surprising that so many of them began looking for a return on that investment.

Ken Dryden, the president of the Toronto Maple Leafs, who has been both a hockey professional and a minor-hockey parent, once summed up the insidious effect huge hockey salaries were having on so many parents. He told the "Open Ice" Hockey Summit, which was held in Toronto in the summer of 1999, that, as time went on, "Parents dreamed harder for their kid, committed more; in turn, demanded more from them and their coaches."

All parents, of course, are blind when it comes to their own offspring. Caught up in an overwhelming hockey culture where a child's on-ice exploits tend to accrue to the family, and where the possibilities of instant financial security seem on daily display, it is hardly surprising that many ambitious parents would come to consider the NHL draft a higher goal than medical school.

There can, of course, be parental madness in all sports. Any given year seems to produce its own list of shocks: fathers in Baltimore demanding a 10-year-old soccer player pull down her pants to prove she was a girl; the Texas mother willing to commit murder to ensure her daughter made the cheerleader team; the parents in California who got a Little League baseball team disqualified for daring to play a non-sanctioned game—a benefit game for a recently deceased teammate.

But the game we are talking about here is hockey, and there is ample evidence of parents going over the top every season. Sometimes it is boorish behaviour in the stands by loudmouthed parents with no appreciation for the youth of the players or even the officials—the "bully parents" of organized hockey, the small minority who too often ruin it for the vast majority of parents who keep their emotions and rash judgments under control—and sometimes it is far more subtle, though equally irrational.

When Ken Dryden and I were researching material for *Home Game: Hockey and Life in Canada,* we were given a letter that had been sent to elite teams in the Greater Toronto Area. The letter contained a "scouting report" on a certain player, his lifetime statistics, his strengths and minimal, fixable weaknesses. The letter also contained information on the jersey numbers the player wore with the two different teams for which he played and contained a separate listing of all games and practices involving those two teams.

The "player" in question was all of eight years of age. The writer was his father, a doctor, using office letterhead.

A few years after that book appeared, I was privileged to spend some time with Gordon Juckes, the Grand Old Man of Canadian Hockey. It was shortly before his death, and he was reflecting at length on how the organization he had headed for so many years, the Canadian Amateur Hockey Association—now known as the Canadian Hockey Association—had grown over those years to a vast national organization that oversees the hockey played today by some 600,000 young Canadians. He talked with pride of the many excellent programs the national organization has produced over the years, the strides in coaching and officiating and the improvements in protection and insurance and organization. The CHA is the largest, by far, hockey organization in the world and can claim that over the years it has also been the most successful, not only producing the likes of Bobby Orr and Guy Lafleur and Wayne Gretzky, but also giving millions of Canadians, now women as well as men, a recreation for life, a passion forever.

Gordon Juckes would never maintain that this also meant that everything the organization had done had been for the best. He had his regrets, and one of them was a lingering doubt about the campaign to encourage families to bring their children to the hockey rinks of the nation rather than to send them.

He did not see then that a day would come when the biggest problem in the national game was not what was happening on the ice, but what could happen, all too often, off the ice.

The jury that sat and decided in Cambridge, Mass., was asked to bring in a verdict on a specific incident that had taken place on a specific date. Everyone understood, however, that a part of that verdict would apply to bad minor hockey behaviour on both sides of the border, in the past, in the present and unfortunately in the future.

Thomas Junta may have been given six to ten years in prison, but hockey also received a sentence. And more than a slap on the wrist—a good, hard slap across the face. As they say in the game itself, a wake-up call.

It is important to put this in perspective. In a dozen years of coaching through a variety of levels, I would have to say that almost all the minor-hockey parents I encountered were well-behaved and kept their emotions in check. I do recall boorish fathers screaming down from the stands, one father offering "bribes" of money to seven-year-olds, one mother who sat with a stopwatch to ascertain if her novice-level child was getting his fair share of ice time and one manager who was on the verge of hitting a twelve-year-old who had bodychecked his son when I reached out and pulled the furious man away—but still, when I consider the hundreds of games and thousands of individuals involved, I count myself a firm believer in minor hockey, with the joys far outweighing the problems. And yet we must not pretend there are no problems, that while the "Hockey Rage" case can be called isolated insofar as a death occurred and one parent has gone to prison for killing another, bad parental behaviour and irrational rage is not isolated at all—to any country, or any level.

What is truly surprising is that there have not been far more Thomas Junta stories over the years. In the weeks and months that followed, however, the incidents continued unabated. In Buckingham, just below Ottawa on the Quebec side of the Ottawa River, a father attacked and began pounding his twelve-year-old son's coach mere days after Junta's sentencing. The team had won the game handily, but the coach had reduced the man's son to tears by what he called "constructive criticism" on one of the goals scored against the team. The father took offence, barged into the dressing room and began swinging while other players scrambled to get out of the way. The father was properly charged; no one would argue that; but surely there are also some questions to be raised about a coach who would reduce a twelve-year-old player to tears at the end of a victory. Perhaps both adults need to think about what it is they are taking far, far too seriously here: a child's game. Not a child's career, and not a coach's career, either.

In Port Moody, British Columbia, one parent, a father, slapped another parent, a mother, at a game in which their respective children got into a small altercation with each other—while sitting on the bench of the same team. In a suburb of Denver, Colorado, parents in the stands came to a near riot while watching a Midget game; among those adults charged with disorderly conduct was a policeman. In Charlottetown, Prince Edward Island, a local minor hockey organization announced, a month after Junta's sentencing, that from now on parents will be asked to sign a pledge before each season not to attack or harass anyone at the rink—or else their child will lose the privilege of playing.

This is what happens when the local rink becomes less a place where the games of children are played than where the fantasies of their parents are played out.

There is nothing wrong with fantasies, of course, so long as one accepts the dictionary definition—"a product of the imagination"—and the grim reality of minor and professional hockey. Take the finest young player in town, and statistically we can prove he isn't going to make it.

Yet rinks are filled with parents who refuse to accept that reality.

At the "Open Ice" Hockey Summit, Canadian Hockey Association president Bob Nicholson said that the "biggest issue" facing hockey development in this country was not skills or ice time, but "parents—no doubt about it."

"That," added Wayne Gretzky, who came to open the session, "is the hardest problem. It's no different today than when I was nine, ten, eleven years old. Fifteen kids on a team, you have thirty parents—twenty-eight of the parents are outstanding, but you get one or two in every group that really make it difficult for everyone."

The most revealing comments, however, were made by Dave King, who has coached in the NHL, coached the Canadian national team and coached many years in Europe and Japan. What King wanted parents to understand was the reality of the average hockey experience.

King cited a study done on a group of Ontario young-sters born in the year 1975 in Ontario, meaning at the time they spoke they would have been twenty-three and twenty-four years of age and, possibly, established professional players by that point.

The study began with 30,000 players. By the time they reached Bantam age, thirteen and fourteen, 22,000 were still in the game, which is an impressive number. Of that group, 232 were drafted by junior clubs, and of that 232 only 105 ever played as much as a single game of junior hockey. Of that 105, ninety finished their junior careers and twenty-three went on to college hockey. Some forty-eight of all those remaining players were drafted into the NHL in 1993, the summer that age group turned eighteen, and two others were eventually signed as free agents. Of those drafted, thirty-eight ended up with contracts and twenty-two of the original 30,000 played at least one NHL game. As King spoke, in August 1999, eleven of the 30,000 were in the National Hockey League.

The percentage of youngsters who actually "made it," then, was .0036 percent.

Roughly 1 in 3,000.

Those, I would suggest, are numbers that should go up on the scoreboard of every hockey rink in the country.

Just before the puck is dropped.

Epilogue

We are headed for the Hockey Hall of Fame. We are driving down, two hours away from the Hall on the road and three-quarters of a century from each other in the car. My eleven-year-old son is in the back seat with his friends, Stan and Trevor, and my eighty-seven-year-old father is in the passenger seat beside me. He has decided to come at the last minute; we all hope he will be able to go at the last minute, as well, popping off in the middle of a book or a baseball game or a Stanley Cup playoff match, doing something he's still able to enjoy as he heads, unbelievably, towards his nineties.

My father has not been to Toronto in nearly fifteen years, not since that December day when his life as an Algonquin Park lumberman came to a close. The truck that hauled away the wood chips hit an icy patch in the mill yard and slid down a short hill. He had been walking towards the cookery for lunch, and the swinging rear end of the truck caught him by surprise, knocking him down, and the big double tires pushed him through the snow and ice until, finally, the truck came to a stop. By then, however, it had already shattered his pelvis and busted his hip. But getting hit by the truck, he says, was still a lot easier than getting to the hospital. The men at the mill panicked, throwing him into the back of a half-ton and, in twenty-below temperatures, bouncing this injured seventy-three-year-old out through rough roads to the nearest hospital in Barry's Bay, more than thirty miles east. They did it because they didn't think he'd make it. No surprise there; his children have been expecting him to die since the 1950s.

Sometimes when I am on a long drive such as this and

have nothing to do but try to make sense of life, I end up laughing at both it and him. He's been a heavy smoker—no filters—since age twelve, and the doctors in Toronto, where they sent him by ambulance from Barry's Bay, were more interested in his lungs than in his broken bones. One, who looked down his throat with a special light, said it looked just like the shaft to a coal mine. Another foolishly suggested he cut back. We are speaking of a lifetime of roll-your-own smoking, draft beer and fried foods, yet his mind is as clear as the four-lane highway this early Thursday morning. His cough, on the other hand, sounds like a dragging muffler.

We are headed for the Hockey Hall of Fame, three MacGregors who share a love of each other's company and a love of a game we have all played and two still do. My son, Gord, counts among his greatest accomplishments seeing Teemu Selanne play and getting a stick from the young European star with the Winnipeg Jets. Selanne was in Ottawa to play against the Ottawa Senators. My father, Duncan—he prefers Dunc—saw Frank Nighbor play for the Ottawa Senators more than seventy years ago and still considers Nighbor the greatest centre ever to play the game. Their memories reach from the Pembroke Peach to the Flying Finn, a distance so great that, for fifty-eight years of that span, Frank Nighbor's Ottawa Senators did not even exist. But the game is the same: hockey. And the love as intense.

It is my lot to bridge the gap between the Pembroke Peach and the Flying Finn. I was there, though I don't really remember, when our first home had no running water, no electricity, an ice house. My mother, Helen, with three in diapers to care for at one point, had to haul water nearly a quarter of a mile up a steep hill. It would make a great and instructive tale for the four children Ellen and I have, if only they would listen. But, of course, they do not, no more than I would once listen to my mother's stories of growing up in the heart of Algonquin Park, where her father was a ranger and where, one day, she met a young lumber scaler from across Lake of Two Rivers. I was there when their first home had so little and I am here when our city home has two bathrooms, an overextended shower, a microwave, a dishwasher and a VCR. My father believes that, compared to him, we are fabulously rich; my son believes, compared to some of his friends, that we are still living in a shack in the bush, with hollow-eyed children praying a partridge will fly into the kitchen window so there will be something to eat tonight. He doesn't understand yet that life, like sport, is to be looked back on with affection and exaggeration.

I remember vividly my first sports experiences. Dunc took my older brother, Jim, and me to a Dodgers game by grabbing the flashlight and walking us out the pathway to the highway. There, he fired up the old Pontiac and sat, a cigarette dangling, smoke in his eyes, as he walked the radio dial through the static and eventually pulled in a faint signal that had somehow bounced all the way from New York City to Algonquin Park.

My brother and I sat, our windows rolled up against the mosquitoes—our father's window down, but the mosquitoes and blackflies keeping shy of the smudge pot stuck in his lips—and the plastic seats would suck on our backs as we shifted with anticipation and summer heat. Mel Allen and the Yankees. Barber and the Dodgers. Dunc and Jim arguing over who was the greatest player of the day, Mantle or Mays.

Sometimes, in this strange ballpark in the middle of the bush, he would take the flash and head off to the tiny creek that ran along the road, returning a few minutes later with a couple of cold green bottles. Sitting, listening to the ball game, he would crack the caps off with his knife blade, the slightly skunky smell of beer cutting through the smoke and citronella. I was well into my twenties before I realized beer didn't grow wild in swamps.

It is important to tell this part of the story, for it matters that our games were initially played in the imagination. Jim and I and our sister, Ann, did not get to see a live sporting event until the mid-1950s, when one of the Toronto lumber buyers came to the mill and gave Dunc tickets to a Maple Leafs game. We drove down this very same highway to Toronto, my parents petrified that they would miss their turnoffs, stayed with family friends in Port Credit and—leaving our mother and baby brother, Tom, with the friends—went in to an experience that I am still reminded of every time I enter the Gardens. None of us had ever seen lights so bright. My brother and sister and I combined would not have seen so many people in our entire lives. When Jim and I went to the washroom after the second period, we found even the urinals intimidating.

I was there the first time my father saw a mountain. It caught me quite off guard even though I was driving and it was apparent from the road map that we had entered the Adirondack Range of upper New York State. He was eighty-three then, and I had decided to drive him down to Cooperstown to see the Baseball Hall of Fame. A man who had followed the game all his life in newspapers and, later, on the radio—he never saw a game on television until the chip truck put him out of the bush—deserved to see Cooperstown once. A man who, in the fall of 1928, had travelled to Hull, Quebec, to see Babe Ruth play an exhibition match during a rare barnstorm into Canada had a need to go to Cooperstown. A man who had a million beautiful names in his head—Home Run Baker and Rogers Hornsby and Twinkletoes Selkirk, a *Canadian*—and who could recite "Casey at the Bat" perfectly without a single pause had a right to go. But to get there from here, he had to cross a very old, very small mountain range.

"Is that a mountain?" he asked as we moved along Highway 3 near Childwold.

I looked to the left, then checked against the open map. "Yes. Mt Matumbia."

"Tch-tch-tch-tch-tch."

This has always been the sound he makes when something is either very special or very off-putting. This time he was expressing amazement. A man who was so well read—my older brother and I once found him sound asleep in a logging camp, a loaded .22 leaning against the wall, *Plutarch's Lives* lying open on his rasping chest—that he could locate any mountain range you could name, had never seen one.

We had a wonderful time at Cooperstown. He stood staring at the Babe's bat and Lou Gehrig's glove and Ty Cobb's spikes and Walter Johnston's photograph and Dizzy Dean's baseball and had a long afternoon of joyous *Tch-tch-tch-tch-tch*-ing. He must have quoted Dizzy a dozen times that day: "It ain't bragging if you done it." And when the day was over he fell stone asleep in the little motel room we had rented down by the shore of Otsego Lake.

Sometime during the night his heavy breathing stopped, and I lay awake for the longest time waiting for a sound, any sound but the soft lapping of the lake water under the dock. Finally I got up and went over to his bed and leaned down as close as I could—exactly as I have done a dozen times with each of our four babies—and eventually I poked him so he started, rolled over and began again breathing like that dragging muffler. It ain't bragging, but I done it.

Now we are off to the Hockey Hall of Fame in Toronto. It is new and the kids have heard about it and seen it on television, and they have been begging me to go. I thought my father might like to come along as well, but he had said he wouldn't come; he always said he wouldn't come. His unpredictability has been both his charm and a source of irritation. He will not change. The only certainty with him is that he has always insisted on knowing the scores the following day, and that knowing who played what last night and who won and who played well has somehow become more important with retirement. If it is what gets him going in the morning, then who am I to say the standings are not important?

Sometimes seventy-five years don't seem enough to separate the old man in the front seat from the boy in the back. Both love sports, but while the attachment may be equal, the object of the attachment has dramatically changed. The boy in the back wears clothes that seem manufactured by the games he plays. Vancouver Canucks cap, Mighty Ducks of Anaheim T-shirt, Toronto Maple Leafs windbreaker. And this but today's change of clothes. As the man in the front seat says, "*Tch-tch-tch-tch-tch.*"

My father grew up in the small Ottawa Valley town of Eganville. His father was also a lumberman, but my grandfather took ill in the bush when my father, the second youngest of seven children, was only four years old, and he died, leaving behind a widow with all those children to raise on her own. I have no idea how tough it was; I know that my father's brother, John, died in childhood, and that his sister, Marjorie, died of blood poisoning only days before she was to have been married, but knowing something happened is not the same as having it happen. An older brother and sister helped raise the family and, surprisingly, most ended up with excellent educations—a lawyer, an engineer, a teacher. My father, though, wanted nothing but the bush and quit school early.

He once explained his discomfort with tools as caused by having no father to hand down such knowledge to him. He could survive nights lost in the bush but could never change a carburetor, never even install a light switch. His father, as far as he was able to know, had no interest in sports. But then, there really were very few sports at that time. The modern Olympics were sixteen years old when his father died; baseball was an American novelty; the Stanley Cup was decided by two games, total goals.

My father came to sports entirely on his own. No one took him to the games, but no one had to. Saturdays were for play, and play was hockey in winter and baseball in summer. He was a fair baseball pitcher—sidearm delivery— at a time when baseball mattered a great deal to the small lumber towns in the Ottawa Valley. He had a gift for hockey, a good stickhandling centre who was, by his own accord, "a ruffian". He played on the outside rink with all the other Eganville youngsters, many of them not even wearing pads, and he was always a popular selection for the town teams, though he claims his skills peaked around age fourteen. I have a wonderful old newspaper photograph of the 1927–28 Eganville Senior Hockey Team, D. MacGregor standing third from the right with his hair slicked and split down the middle. I have searched for myself and my own son in that face, but find only my father, with hair.

When he talks sports from those days it is usually to tell wonderful stories. He remembers a match on the Bonnechere River, Eganville against nearby Renfrew, when the referee blew his whistle in the middle of play. Everything came to a puzzling stop, and the referee skated to the empty far side of the ice where he could stand with his back to the wind—and to the game. Then he calmly unbuttoned his pants and relieved himself before hurrying back for the faceoff. He tells about the first baseball game he played, August 30, 1929, when he arrived in the village of Whitney and the men he would be working with talked him into playing for them in a grudge match against Madawaska, the next village along the line. At his first at bat he hit a line drive that skipped once and went in through the open front doors of the Catholic church. Madawaska rules called for a ground-rule double, but the umpire that day, a good Catholic who had been taking a long draw on a mickey of whisky between each inning, ruled it God's will and declared the hit a home run.

He has always had these stories. Hundreds of them, thousands of them, about hockey and baseball and fishing, hunting, the bush. He could sing and play the harmonica— I am tone deaf, but his grandson is quite musical—and even though he was so much older than everyone else's parents, there was something about him that always made him seem much younger. My friends loved to talk sports with him. In time, as his friends all died and I lived in other centres, my friends became his friends. His most constant visitor in his late eighties has been my own lifelong friend, Eric Ruby, who went to kindergarten with me and was a team-mate on more hockey, baseball and lacrosse teams than we can remember. They sit once a week and talk sports and tell stories and get along so famously it is as if they had adopted each other.

My father loved sports from the first. They took place in the imagination, the game accounts and player stories available to him only through the printed word just as he later made them available to his sons through the car radio, games forever taking place in the head rather than on a field or a diamond or an ice surface. He read the *Ottawa Journal* at home every evening and, each day, one of his chores was to hurry down to the drugstore where a neighbour, Mr McFadyen, had an *Evening Citizen* reserved. Between the drugstore and Mr McFadyen's house, he could get through the entire sports section. He read the newspapers and the *Saturday Evening Post*, and after he had read a sports feature by the great Damon Runyon, he talked the library into bringing in a book of Runyon's short stories. His whole notion of sports and New York he gained through the printed word, and the notions never left him. He ended up with a charming inability to pronounce words, once saying he'd love nothing better for Christmas than a book on the "maa-fay-ya", his children eventually figuring out he was talking about the Mafia. I inherited this affliction from him: my head filled with words I let slide through the keyboard but never the mouth.

It is no surprise that he prefers his sports from those times. He read back then of great feats and marvellous quotes; today, though he reads as much, if not more, it is more often of greed and drugs and threats and contracts and strikes and lockouts. There are few good quotes any more, perhaps because there are no Damon Runyons or Ring Lardners around to polish up the words, perhaps because the rule-of-tongue around sports dressing-rooms in the final quarter of this century has become cliché or nothing, more and more nothing. My father is not a stupid man, not at all, but since his original use for sports was escape, he still prefers that world he once ran to where the truth about Ruth was unknown, where the mythical mattered more than the ethical, where fantasy was what you bought into when you paid for your ticket or picked up the newspaper.

It is perfectly understandable that one of the greatest joys of his life was meeting Gordie Howe. It happened, by accident, thirty-five years after he had once pointed Howe out to his children as they sat high in Maple Leaf Gardens and told them, "Don't ever forget, you're seeing the greatest hockey player who ever lived." We never did forget that moment. And when he sat and talked to this great hero so many years later—about, of all things, being poor and loving it in Saskatchewan and the Ottawa Valley—he came away convinced that Gordie Howe in the flesh was even finer than Gordie Howe in a Red Wings sweater. It was as if all the faith he had handed over to sports heroes so many years ago had, in fact, held up under the scrutiny of today. In his opinion, it had to: Gordie Howe was a good Canadian country boy; they shared the same values even if one had scaled all the available mountains and one had almost gone through a long life without even seeing one.

They come at it from two different sides, this grandfather in the front seat and this grandson in the back. The grandfather saw his first games in his head, the words suggesting images he knew from his own rough play down on the Bonnechere River. If Sprague Cleghorn's goal was described, my father would see it perfectly, magnificently, and in many ways nothing else would ever compare. He remembers the first radio coming to his town in the early 1920s, long before the first telephone arrived. "You had to wear headphones, you know. The crackle would all but knock you off your chair. But people would keep them on just because of how well you could hear human voices. No one had ever imagined such a thing. They discovered radio by accident, you know. They heard voices coming across the telegraph wire. They could hear faint, faint voices at the other end. Weren't supposed to be there at all. The first commercial use of radio was to broadcast a Jack Dempsey fight. And it's been all downhill since then."

He has no idea what access his grandson has to games. Young Gord lives in a city, Ottawa, where he can see NHL hockey live. He can see a game a night on television if he wants, two in a row on Saturday nights. He collects players cards and has hundreds stashed in boxes in his bedroom, convinced—absolutely wrongly, I try to tell him—that their value now rivals that of an NHL franchise. He plays hockey a couple of times a week in the winter and practises about once a week. He has two nets in the basement where he and his friends take turns putting on the "Felix Potvin" official street hockey mask and firing tennis balls at each other. He has a SuperNintendo game permanently hooked up to our television, and he and his friends have their choice of two games, one endorsed by Wayne Gretzky, the other by the NHL Players Association. By working their thumbs just so over buttons on a small piece of plastic, they can score on a slapshot from centre ice, the crowd cheering, and they can, unfortunately, call up replays for a father who may have been out of the room and foolishly missed the greatest goal ever scored by Control Pad on a VGA screen.

"*Tch-tch-tch-tch-tch.*"

I have coached this boy and many of his friends now for a half dozen years. For nearly fifteen years I have been involved in minor hockey in some capacity, usually coaching. I was required to take a course at one point, after which I was given two crests to identify myself as a "Level II" coach and a certificate suitable for framing. I neither put the certificate up nor sewed on the crests: the sole criterion for graduation was attendance. I went the first time in order to teach youngsters, including my daughter, Christine, how to play a very simple game. They taught us break-out patterns. At another course I was required to take, they handed out diagrams of drills that looked like a child's drawing of spaghetti. The children I would be passing this on to were five and six years of age.

This decade of coaching at the absolute lowest possible levels, always house league, has, at times, been disturbing. I have seen a father offer a child money for scoring. I have seen fathers attacking referees, screaming at each other, screaming at their own children and other children. I have seen a father so desperate to win that he was willing to use illegal players in a house-level tournament for ten-year-olds.

Those, unfortunately, are the images that too easily stick, and I am obliged to remind myself that coaching minor hockey and being involved with first a friend's son, then my second daughter and then my son in minor hockey have provided many of the best times and warmest memories of what will soon feel like our too-brief time together in the same home. Bad parents are such an extraordinary minority that hockey parents are a bit like heavy traffic, no one taking notice of the vast majority of cars that share the road and show courtesy, everyone fixating on the dramatic and unfortunately tragic. Sitting up in the stands, we also forget that most around us are well behaved and as embarrassed as we are by the boorish behaviour of some other parents.

Like so many fathers involved in minor hockey, however, I am a phoney. It is not that I wish to yell and scream and curse at other players and referees and—well, let's be frank—those hundreds of team-mates who fail to see that my own child is waiting for a pass, open for a shot, on the verge of a breakaway; it is that I must concentrate on being calm and reasonable and absolutely, categorically, indisputably fair when the parental instinct is to increase your own child's ice time, put the child with the best possible playmakers and, even at novice levels, with the biggest and toughest who can do the dirty work along the boards and pass all glory to the one child who shines brightest.

Brightest in the mind and eye of every parent. It is not rational, it is instinct, and we fight it off as best we can. One of the most difficult things at the house-league level— but probably only possible at the house-league level—is the ability to give equal ice time to every player. Those I have been fortunate enough to coach with over the past decade have felt the same as I have about this, and we have approached this with determination and success. If it means the weakest player is on for the final shift in a close game, so be it. If it means, as it once did, that a mother will still complain about fair ice times, so be it; we know we have done our best. And I am grateful at times not to have been a successful coach at higher levels when these coaches tell me stories of parents sitting in the stands with stopwatches, of parents writing letters to the hockey associations, of parents even serving legal notice over matters so trivial it makes one wonder if it is all worth it.

Hockey, they like to say, builds character. Hockey, Ken Dryden likes to say, *reveals* character just as much. I'm with him. Watching your own child on the ice surface in a country where one game matters above all else is a torturous, rapturous experience. Even when I coach I am so acutely aware of my own youngster heading out onto the ice that I must split in two: one, the calm, rational coach encouraging the other kids, pointing out a minor mistake, handing over a water bottle, making a line change because a defence wants to go up or a forward back. But God forbid one of these tiny charges should ask me to tighten his or her skates at this time. I cannot. I cannot look down and away from what the other half of me is doing, and that is watching the game like an isolated camera fixed on my own child. Why is he not going for the puck? Why does he not pass? Why do they not pass to him? Why did his winger shoot when he had a play? (Greed, obviously.) Why is he coming off when the puck is still in his end?

I look out when my own are on the ice and I do not see a hockey game, I see life itself—which is exactly what the calm, rational hockey coach is supposed to be battling. I see my daughter in goal and almost explode with anxiety every time the puck gets pushed her way (and I do mean *pushed*. Shots will not come for a couple of years). I see my son on a breakaway and I find myself praying: *"Dear Lord, just let the puck go in the net and I will go to church every Sunday, every day; I will take out Novas in every newspaper from here to Victoria; I will travel to Africa and build missions; I will…"* And then, when he misses the net, I say nothing. I am again the coach, not the parent, and when his line comes off I say the right thing and give him a quick squeeze between the neck and shoulder, and if he wants to talk about how there was an ice chip that made him lose the puck or how I didn't get his skates sharpened and so he kept slipping, I accept it as part of the silly dance of the excuse that goes on between parent and child until each learns to accept their own limitations and, perhaps as important, the limitations of their shared dreams.

He has tried out for travelling teams, but more, it seems, because friends and team-mates are going out than because he either wants to or thinks he can do it. He says, constantly, "I hate being tested," which is merely a better way of saying what we all fear about failure. There are, however, few failures quite so public as a travelling team tryout, the ice filled with fifty or sixty youngsters, the stands filled with nearly twice that many parents, the tension roughly equal to the dying minutes of a tied seventh game in the Stanley Cup final. For the most part, the child on the ice sees himself as far better than he is, the parent in the stands sees the child as far worse than he is, and they do not understand that, because of blood lines, they have the two poorest perspectives in the building. Someone else will decide for them, and since there are sixty on the ice and only fifteen on a team, the decision will hurt far more than it will cheer.

The dynamics of a tryout are fascinating. The parents in the stands feel compelled to carry on conversations with other parents they have known, usually from past hockey experiences. They talk but never make eye contact, their voices on each other but their eyes only for their own child. They are forever searching, forever wondering: why is he not first in line? why doesn't she try harder? why does he always get to go one-on-one with the fastest, with the biggest, with the best? Why, why, why?

At the end of the tryouts, they take them in, one by one, to a room where the coaches are waiting with their clipboards. The parents wait along the corridors like they are expecting bad X-rays. The kids go in, some come out in tears. One of the coaches comes out for a coffee and talks about how he is afraid to cut a certain player for fear of what the child's father will do: last year, when the child got cut, the father put him against the wall and throttled him. One of the waiting fathers says he will not even ask when his child comes out. "I'll wait for the car," he says. In private.

My own comes out, alive.

"How'd it go?" I ask.

"I don't know," he says.

"What do you mean, you don't know?"

"I might have made it."

"What did he say?"

"He told me I was pretty good. He said I still needed work on my cross-overs. He used the word 'unfortunately' an awful lot. 'Unfortunately, we have so many kids trying out.' 'Unfortunately, some of last year's kids are back.'"

I take him to the snack bar and buy him a pop and a chocolate bar. We both know where he will be playing this year. And, in a way, we are both relieved.

In a selfish way, I am also delighted, because it means we will be together again. I love coaching both my kids and others' kids. I love the feel of a dressing-room as it moves from the shy silences of October to the feisty, practical-joking, shouting zoo of March. I love it when a difficult youngster comes around, when a child who has played very little before suddenly finds his or her skates, a shot, an ability to stickhandle. I love it when they pile on the goaltender after a win—I even love yelling at them, "*Take it easy!*"— and how they comfort the goalie after a loss. I love the silly banquet at the end and how, at some point, a parent will stand up and, often awkwardly, thank everyone and say what a tremendous experience this all was for everyone. I love the sad, slipping-away feeling that comes when the season is indeed over, when the equipment goes up on a shelf, when the garden calls and hockey, for the time being, is only the playoffs, on television, and strangely distant from what is going on in real lives.

It is what he gets from hockey that matters, not what he takes. I want for him nothing less than what hockey has given me: my sport, my game. Something to treasure for a life. I regret the decade or so that I never played between university and suburban family life, and I hope that one day, like me, he will find friends and happiness in playing late-night games in empty arenas, the silly joys of childhood a temporary balm against the pressures of the week and the march of time. We call these games meaningless, but quite the opposite is true.

This past winter my son joined a team on which most of the kids had never before met, either at school or on past teams. The dressing-room was, as always, awkward at first and silent, but gradually the awkwardness gave way and the sound rose and, soon enough, there had been lasting friendships formed. My son began keeping his shinguard tape in a roll—his own little joke—and soon all the players were adding their used tape to the roll that grew larger and larger until it would barely fit in the end pocket of his hockey bag. When Andrew, one of the defencemen, found out he had to enter hospital for minor heart surgery, the team took out the ball, signed it, and presented it to him on his last game before the operation. Andrew took the tape ball like it was the Stanley Cup itself. A month later he was back in the line-up—but the tape ball would remain in an honoured shelf in his bedroom. I consider the tape ball one of my kid's best moments in minor hockey.

It surprises hockey fathers how quickly the seasons pass. I have friends in old-timer hockey who, usually in the summer, would bring out their lanky, often-clumsy sons of thirteen, fourteen and fifteen to play with "the men". Moments later, it seemed, they had become "the men"—the son of one off on an American scholarship, the son of another making the Philadelphia Flyers. Not long ago we had been humouring them; now, if they happen to come out again on a slow summer's night, they indulge us.

This shift of generations has happened in our own family, as well. About two decades ago we began an annual tradition in Huntsville, the Christmas Classic, in which anyone who happens to have come home for the holidays— and anyone who happens already to be home—is invited to play a road hockey game on Christmas Day. We play on a backroad, which we first shovel off. We have two Canadian Tire nets for which we all chipped in many years ago. A cousin who still plays supplies extra right-handed sticks, I supply extra lefts. There is no age limit—the oldest is nearing sixty, the youngest is usually around ten or eleven—and ever since our two older girls, Kerry and Christine, were the first to play several Christmases ago, there have been almost as many young women playing as young and ageing men.

My older brother still awards himself the Most Valuable Player award at the end of each match, but for some time now the dominant players have been his son Craig, and Craig's cousin, Jamie, and last Christmas, much to her own surprise, my daughter Jocelyn. There is no record of the scores, but an annual record by photograph: players growing, hairlines receding, shoulders widening, bellies sagging. The one constant our smiles and our appreciation of all being together for one more Christmas Classic. The sheer indescribable delight of fathers playing with their children—and perhaps, one day, mothers with their coming players.

My father hardly ever saw me play. Nor did anyone else's father. In Huntsville, the small town where I was fortunate enough to grow up, a wonderful local businessman, Don Lough, hired another man, Mye Sedore, and told him not to bother coming in to work. His "job" for the next twenty years or so would be to coach the hockey teams. Our coach was never another player's father. It was a sensible, if impractical, system.

A comparison of minor hockey in the 1950s and minor hockey in the 1990s is almost impossible to comprehend. Back then, it cost two dollars to sign up for the year. (My father says he paid ten cents for ice time.) Equipment was hand-me-down or used. Skates went over the stick, which went over one shoulder, and the duffel bag went over the other shoulder and you walked to the rink. There was no extra charge for extra ice time; there was really no extra ice time, apart from the beaver pond, the bay, the school rink and the street. It seems we spent more time in that decade just playing the game than there is time in this decade.

My father did not see me play because he could not. We played Wednesday nights and Saturday mornings in house league. He worked five-and-one-half days a week in the bush, coming out Saturday afternoon and heading back Sunday evening. When we played on the town teams, the games were either out of town or, usually, on Friday nights. My mother came far more often, but she, too, came rarely. It was, in fact, unusual to see a parent at a game. It was unheard-of for a parent to attend a practice, and I like to think Mye Sedore would have run them out of the arena had one dared to try.

One of my best friends in later years, Terry O'Malley, tells me it was much the same in the town in which he grew up, St Catharines. He began playing at age six, eventually made it to junior hockey and went on to captain the hockey team at Harvard University. In all those years, his own father saw him play once. But as the father himself of a good young hockey player in the 1970s and 1980s, Terry found that the game dominated both their lives.

"It takes approximately seven minutes for the Zamboni to flood a regulation sheet of ice," he says. "By my calculation, I spent about ninety-six hours, or four full twenty-four-hour days, watching that machine. So when the end comes, and I'm headed wherever, the organizers will be saying, 'O'Malley, let me see, O'Malley, that's right, you're the guy with the Zamboni time. You can get out of line and we'll see you back here on Thursday.'"

My brother Jim would relate to that. His son, Craig, played all the way from novice to junior, and Craig says his father never missed a single game. Nor a practice, even if they were at six in the morning. They had a ritual: Jim would get up, get dressed, and at the last possible minute he would wake Craig and hand him a chocolate bar Jim would have bought the night before. The chocolate bar for energy and, obviously, for bribery. "I love him for it," Craig says.

My own father probably saw me play more as an old-timer than as a child, and I have often thought that when he went to a game where there were players over thirty and often as old as sixty he must have wondered what it would have been like to keep going himself. But how? He was twenty years old the winter he played for the Eganville Senior Hockey team, and every winter after that he would spend deep in the Algonquin Park bush. Nowhere to play, and no one to play with. He could not even watch games, the granite hills and isolation putting the lumber camps well out of reach of any radio or, later, television signals. Hockey, for him, became once more a game of the imagination, to be read about and followed from a great distance.

That it should be a game of the imagination can be seen every time we travel back to Huntsville for a visit. He sits, reading, in his room with a distant view of the lake. The kids go up to sit and talk with him, the conversation between grandparent and grandchild always so much easier than that between parent and child, and he will ask them all about their lives. The oldest is interested in journalism, the second in diving, the third in people, and the fourth in hockey.

When the old man and the young boy talk about hockey, the seventy-six years between them shrinks to nothing. Howe remains Howe, Gretzky is Gretzky. When the grandson tells about his own game, the grandfather does not see stands filled with parents, has no sense of stopwatches, two cars, Zambonis, $130 skates, neck guards, aluminum shafts, Bingos for more ice time, a calendar on the refrigerator door, 6 a.m. practices, full face shield, official scoresheet, a coach, two assistants and a trainer certified in first aid. He sees the game the child describes: a puck, ice, a blade moving.

I do not know what they talk about up there. I know that, for years now, the grandfather has been teaching the grandson how to roll cigarettes and that, sometimes, when I go up there, the old man will be smoking one that the child rolled. It will be crooked and thin and tobacco will have fallen down his shirt. I know, too, that the child has tried tobacco up there, and I hope it is out of his system.

But he has picked up other habits. They talk hockey in winter and fishing in summer. Well into his eighties the old man was still trolling with steel line and bringing up the flashing white-bellied lake trout that are the essence of both his ego and his pride. The boy likes fishing just as much, and seems as adept. This summer, when the grandfather decided he should troll no more, he passed on his old trolling rod to the eleven-year-old. The boy took it out in the boat, put his own bait on—spit on the bait for good luck just as his grandfather has for the better part of a century—and barely had his line let out before a two-pound lake trout struck, and held.

Coming down Highway 11 and then the 400 gives a sense of "falling" towards Toronto. The rock and bush of Muskoka give way to rolling, sloping farmland; the speed and volume of the traffic pick up; the highway spreads to six, soon eight lanes; a long, sloping hill is crested and the final scream begins through the industrial area to the main junction. If those tickets to Maple Leaf Gardens had come forty years later, my parents would never have made it to Toronto.

"Just imagine," my father says, "if people from 150 years ago could wake up and see all this." He talks about Lord Simcoe and the first roads in Upper Canada. He goes from Lord Simcoe to the early revolutionary, William Lyon Mackenzie. "He was right, you know. The Family Compact did control everything—and it still does, as far as I'm concerned."

He goes from Mackenzie to the sports establishment, the cost of tickets, the way taxpayers have had to pay for the SkyDome but can't afford to go to games. The 1994 baseball strike is on and he is put off, to say the least. The greatest joy of his forced retirement was the opportunity to follow his sports on television as well as in the papers, and now his enjoyment had been taken away by greed. He talks about the first NHL game he ever saw—the Ottawa Senators versus the Hamilton Tigers—and he tells how the Hamilton team went on strike in 1925 for more money.

"They didn't get it, either," he says. "The team folded not long after." I am too busy negotiating the turn onto the Don Valley Parkway to check, but I think he is laughing.

The Parkway rolls and folds into the downtown, and his memory is moving faster than the traffic. He talks about the Ford Hotel, where he stayed when he came down to see his first Leafs game and where he and his cousin Donald stayed before Donald headed off to war and Dunc back into the bush. The Ford was torn down a generation ago. He talks about the time he and his good friend Eddie and some of the other millworkers were summonsed to a court hearing in Toronto over a failed attempt to form a union at the mill, and how none of them had ever before seen a streetcar. We pass by a payphone where a woman is hanging half-in, half-out, talking easily.

"Eddie had never seen one of those things before."

"A payphone?"

"Yeah, a payphone. He had no idea how it worked or what you did."

At the new Hockey Hall of Fame there is another technology gap. I have paid for us all to enter, but the boys will not wait. One of them, Stan, has been there before, and he knows his way to what matters. "This way," he says to the others, pointing left. "All the electronic stuff is over here." My father is already looking right: all the memory stuff is over there.

But I am not yet ready. I have already called ahead to see if wheelchairs are available, but I have not mentioned anything to him. Since the accident he has got around with a cane, well enough to walk down to the library and the local pub and to pick up the lottery tickets that will forever be his ship about to come in, but he does not care to walk or stand for long. A wheelchair makes sense, unlike, sometimes, my father.

"Well?" I say, pointing ever so subtly towards one of the Hall's wheelchairs. "Should I get us one? They're free."

He stares at it for a while.

"What would people think?" he finally asks.

What is it he is imagining? That someone here will see him in it and report back and, next time he hobbles down to the library or the pub, there will be car horns honking and people hanging halfway out of their windows to give him the raspberry and chide him for being such a big baby?

"No one here will even know you!" I say, the whispered exasperation of the grown child coming through.

But still he is not sure. We strike a compromise. I will get the chair and we will start off and, well, if he needs to sit at some point he can sit.

We start out, an old man hobbling ahead, a younger man pushing an empty wheelchair right behind him. No one will ever make the connection.

Soon, however, the wheelchair is forgotten. We enter a world in which your imagination does all the travelling. He comes to a display of original skates—Starr skates, a brand-new pair still in their original box, made in Dartmouth, Nova Scotia. "That's what I wore," he says. "You had to put them right onto your boot."

We pass the showcase on the career of the great little Montreal Canadiens player Aurel Joliat, and the mementoes send him spinning. "His father used to be the chief of police for Ottawa, did you know that?" Of course I did not. "You know what he did after he stopped playing?" No, I do not. "He worked as a clerk on the work trains. Used to bring men up into the park to build roads and air strips. He came into Whitney one day and everyone in town came down to see the great star. I went down, too. Everybody was there."

I can just see it. Poor Aurel, a green visor on his head, clips on his shirt, sleeve protectors for the lead pencil work, Aurel blinking as the traincar door slides open and an entire bush village is standing there waving and cheering. Aurel's memory; my father's memory; now mine.

He hobbles from showcase to showcase. The Rocket gets him talking about the Montreal Riot of 1955. He would have been at the Hay Lake mill then. He would have read about it in the *Journal* and the *Citizen* and he would remember every detail for forty years: who Richard hit to cause the suspension, what they threw at Clarence Campbell, what happened in the streets. Always one to talk with whomever happens by, he strikes up a conversation with a man who is actually older than he is. They count 176 years between them; there is not a member of this Hockey Hall of Fame whom they cannot remember.

He stops at the Bobby Orr exhibit—Orr's old Victoriaville stick with the single strip of tape around the blade—and he shakes his head in disbelief. By fluke of date of birth and proximity—Parry Sound being only fifty miles from Huntsville—my minor hockey and Orr's overlapped to the point where I have dined out most of my life on tales of playing against Orr. So long as no one ever asks how old we were, the tales sound magnificent, but they should know that, in squirt, Orr was the only kid on the ice who could hoist a puck and would sometimes do so, from the blueline, right over the head of little Guy Lassiter, our back-up goaltender. One of the few games my father made was a match against Parry Sound, with the remarkable Orr playing defence. He counts it among his best hockey memories. He finds it difficult to believe his son was on the ice at the same time. So, too, does the son now.

At the Household Finance "Family Room", he cannot believe what they have done with old 1950s furniture, dummies dressed in 1950s styles, and an old black-and-white television with a Leafs–Canadiens game on, the screen going periodically snowy with poor reception, the players sometimes overlapping images, ghosts of themselves. It reminds us both of Saturday nights when he would come in from the bush and, after supper, some of us would walk down Mary Street to where his cousin Sandy and Sandy's wife, Annie, lived and were fortunate enough to have a television not much different—reception included—from the one on display here. Sandy, who was working for another lumber operation, and my father would drink beer and talk about things like running feet and drawing logs and they would keep half an eye on the game. The kids who were lucky enough to be invited along would watch and listen with absolute fascination, even when the picture snowed out and Foster Hewitt's words—or perhaps his son Bill's—faded in and out through static like a voice from the battlefield. Armstrong and Stanley and Horton and Baun, Richard and Geoffrion and Moore and Plante, Howe and Abel and Lindsay and Sawchuk, Bucyk and Horvath and Schmidt and Lumley, Bathgate and…Sandy and Annie are both dead. We all have colour television and cable. But the games have never been as rich since.

He stops for a long while in front of the Howe exhibit. Gordie's Northland Pro sticks, his skates with blackened toes, his gloves with the number "9" painted in white at the base of the thumb. There is a photograph of Gordie Howe in a Hartford Whalers uniform, Gordie standing at centre with Marty on his left wing and Mark on his right. They are facing off against the Detroit Red Wings. The boys have caught up with us. The grandson wants to remind me of all the old hockey cards—surely a thousand Gordie Howe rookies included—that I once had and either destroyed or threw out. The grandfather wants to remind me, once again, of the time when we all sat in Maple Leaf Gardens and he pointed down at Howe and said, "Don't ever forget, you're seeing the greatest hockey player who ever lived." The grandson looks at me as if I'm hopeless that something so obvious had to be pointed out to me. Grandfather and grandson move together to the other side of the showcase, pointing things out to each other in a manner that presumes each will already know. And it seems they do.

We travel together as a group for a while, the names familiar to all, the meaning different—Bobby Hull is a youngster to the old man, the most exciting of all to the younger man, a lost rookie card to the youngest—but the game still hockey. They see the Stanley Cup together, the Hart Trophy, the Art Ross, the Lady Byng. The boys bore easily and want to return to the electronic displays, particularly the TSN booth where the three of them take turns broadcasting a televised game—their squeaky voices providing the play-by-play. The old man is tired.

"I guess maybe I'll sit in that thing," he says.

I say nothing. I put the wheelchair in position and help him settle down. He seems embarrassed by it, but too tired to protest. I suggest we take in the film. It will be quieter; he can sit and relax. I push him to the front of the theatre, between the rows, so he will be close enough to see well and yet not be in anyone's way.

The film takes place in what is called the Hartland Molson Theatre. Beer money—so my father has every right to be there. It is a large room, and when there are enough people gathered in it, they close the doors and turn down the lights and begin the film. It is, as you would expect, a film heavily dependent on nostalgia. There is old footage of kids playing shinny on farm sloughs. There are shots of kids putting old catalogues on for shin pads, just as my father once did. There is a shot of kids divvying up sticks as a way of choosing sides before playing, just as we once did down on the bay.

The soundtrack is syrupy and smooth, but soon begins to grate, almost as if there is dust on the needle. I sit watching, but can sense that people are looking around, trying to locate the source of this grating noise. I turn to check them and see that a man and his wife have located the trouble. He is pointing, smiling, and she is laughing one of those silent, open-mouth laughs.

The man is pointing to my father, whose head seems to have fallen off and onto his chest. He is snoring loudly, a dragging muffler. To everyone else in the room—now all aware of the sound, many of them smiling and laughing—he is an old man in a wheelchair, sound asleep in front of a movie screen, with young players flickering in grainy black and white behind him.

But not to me. When I look up, I see my father, on exhibit in the Hockey Hall of Fame. And I see what he is dreaming: Dunc, forever young, skating faster and faster through life.

WHERE THEY ARE NOW

Beginnings and Endings

Ed Jovanovski was drafted first overall by the Florida Panthers and was traded to the Vancouver Canucks on January 17, 1999, in the deal that brought Pavel Bure to the Florida Panthers. He finally blossomed in the 2000–2001 season with the Canucks and was selected to play for Team Canada in the 2002 Olympics, where he was a key player in Canada's first gold medal victory in hockey in fifty years. When he returned to Vancouver, his father, **Joe**, met him at the airport, weeping.

Radek Bonk was drafted third overall by the Ottawa Senators and remained there well into the 2001–2002 season. He developed into an excellent checking centre but by age twenty-six had never fulfilled the scoring promise indicated by his play as a seventeen-year-old in Las Vegas.

Tour of Memory

Wayne Gretzky retired from the game after the 1999 season. He held virtually every scoring record in the game, including goals (894), assists (1,963) and points (2,857), as well as a remarkable 122 goals and 260 assists in 208 play-off games. In retirement, he became part-owner of the Phoenix Coyotes and served as executive director of Team Canada in its Olympic victory at Salt Lake City. His father, **Walter Gretzky**, continued his astonishing recovery from that near-fatal aneurysm and, in the fall of 2001, published a bestselling book on his experience.

Mark Messier continued his NHL career after his great friend Gretzky retired, and in the 2001–2002 season captained the New York Rangers. He stood in third place behind Gretzky and Gordie Howe in the league's all-time scoring list. **Doug Messier** continued to act as his son's agent.

Paul Coffey retired from the game after the 2000–2001 season. His 1,531 career points in 21 season trail only Raymond Bourque. **Jack Coffey** remains retired in Toronto.

Marty McSorley was suspended for one year by the National Hockey League following a stick-swinging incident in early 2000 that led to the player being charged, and convicted, of assault with a weapon. He returned to play briefly in the International Hockey League. **Bill McSorley** passed away after suffering a heart attack in the fall of 1999.

The Promise

Brad Hornung joined the Chicago Blackhawks as a scout. He graduated with a degree in history in the spring of 1996 and received a standing ovation while being presented with the Campion College Award of Merit. **Larry Hornung** died of cancer in early 2001 at the age of 55.

The Gift

Gordie and **Colleen Howe** continued to prosper in retirement. **Mark Howe** retired in 1995 as a Detroit Red Wing, the team where his father had started out.

Salvation

Gino Odjick was traded to the New York Islanders by the Vancouver Canucks in 1998, then to the Philadelphia Flyers and, on December 7, 2000, came close to home again when the Flyers sent him to the Montreal Canadiens. **Joe Odjick** continued to live near Maniwaki, working at a wide variety of jobs.

La Future Vedette

Alexandre Daigle, the Number 1 draft pick of the June 1993 entry draft, was out of hockey by 2000 after unsuccessful stints in Ottawa, Philadelphia, Tampa Bay and the New York Rangers. In an interview he gave in early 2002, he claimed he had known he wanted to leave the game when he was 16 years of age, stayed only for the money, and was now happily living in Los Angeles, where he was pursuing a career in film production. His only regret, he said, was the bitter disappointment his abandonment of hockey had caused his father, **Jean-Yves Daigle**.

To each his own story

Ken Dryden remained president of the Toronto Maple Leafs. His son, **Michael**, was beginning a successful career in business. **Murray Dryden**, nearing 90 years of age, was still deeply involved in his Sleeping Children of the World program.

Bloodlines

Brett Hull signed with the Detroit Red Wings in the summer of 2001 and helped Team U.S.A. to a silver medal at the 2002 Winter Games. **Bobby Hull** continued to do public appearances in retirement.

Alexei Yashin was traded to the New York Islanders by the Ottawa Senators in the summer of 2001, after years of bitter contract disputes that, at one point, saw him miss the entire 1999–2000 season. **Valery** and **Tatiana Yashin** began to divide their time between Long Island and their home in Ottawa.

Pavel Bure was traded to the Florida Panthers by the Vancouver Canucks in January 1999. His brother, **Valeri**, joined him in 2001. In March 2002, Pavel was traded again, this time to the New York Rangers. Both sons remained estranged from their father, **Vladimir Bure**, who worked as a fitness consultant with the New Jersey Devils.

Epilogue

Gordon MacGregor "retired" after Midget hockey and went off to Trent University in Peterborough, Ontario. **Duncan MacGregor** died at 88 in 1995, the year this book was published. Four years later he was the subject of *A Life in the Bush,* a book that grew out of the final chapter of *The Home Team.*

Roy MacGregor continues to play old-timer hockey in Ottawa.